THE EVOLUTION OF LEISURE:

Historical and Philosophical Perspectives

THE EVOLUTION OF LEISURE

Historical and Philosophical Perspectives

THE EVOLUTION OF LEISURE:

Historical and Philosophical Perspectives

THOMAS L. GOODALE
George Mason University

GEOFFREY C. GODBEY
The Pennsylvania State University

Venture Publishing, Inc.

State College, PA 16801

Cover Design by Sandra Sikorski
Library of Congress Catalogue Number 88-50288
ISBN 0-910251-24-X

First Printing 1988
Second Printing 1995

Photo Credit
        Back cover: Photograph by Karl Cook
        Photo description: Mid-Atlantic UPA
                        Tournament—Haji and Dano

DEDICATION

To the memory of
Harlan "Gold" Metcalf,
for trying to teach us to sing.

ACKNOWLEDGMENTS

We have dedicated this book to "Gold" Metcalf, who tutored us during our years as undergraduates at what is now the State University of New York-College at Cortland.

Beyond that, it is difficult for two authors to thank via acknowledgments the many people who have contributed directly and indirectly to this volume. There would have to be three lists; for those like "Gold" who aided both of us, and separate lists for each of us. In addition, although we would know where to begin—with our respective parents and families—we would not know where to end, for we would have to include Mozart, Matisse and Mikhail Baryshnikov, and the woman who runs the little bakery on Main Street and makes the best muffins in town. How can we separate our work, much less a particular part of it, from our lives?

In "letting go" of a manuscript (for one never finishes), we are reminded of all those who have somehow made life richer, and also reminded that it is not a mere nicety to tell them so. And so we shall.

T.L.G.
G.C.G.

TABLE OF CONTENTS

Play and Technology; The Need for
Segmented Behavior; The Benefits of
Constraints: REFERENCES.

For permission to reprint copyrighted materials, we thank the following authors and publishers:

Alfred A. Knopf, Inc. for material from Alexis de Tocqueville's *Democracy in America*. (Tr. Henry Reeve), copyright 1899;

Columbia University Press for material from *The Harried Leisure Class* by Staffan Linder, copyright 1970;

Doubleday, a division of Bantam, Doubleday, Dell Publishing Group, Inc., copyright 1922 for "archys mission" from the book *archys life of mihitabel* by Don Marquis, reprinted by permission of the publisher;

George Braziller, Inc., New York, for material from *The Structure of Evil* by Ernest Becker, copyright 1968, by Ernest Becker, all rights reserved;

Lionel Tiger for material from *Optimism: The Biology of Hope,* New York, Simon and Schuster, copyright 1979;

Macmillan Publishing Company for material from *Science and the Modern World* by Alfred North Whitehead, copyright 1925, The Macmillan Company, for material from *The Aims of Education and Other Essays* by Alfred North Whitehead, copyright 1929 by The Macmillan Company; and for material from *Democracy and Education* by John Dewey, copyright 1916, The Macmillan Company;

Max Kaplan, for material from *Leisure In America: A Social Inquiry*, New York, John Wiley & Sons, copyright 1960;

Pantheon Books, a Division of Random House, Inc., for material from Josef Pieper, *Leisure: The Basis of Culture* (Tr. Alexander Dru), copyright 1963;

Random House, Inc., for material from the 1937 copyright Modern Library Edition of Adam Smith, *The Wealth of Nations: Inquiry Into The Nature and Causes of The Wealth of Nations;*

Sebastian de Grazia, for material from *Of Time Work and Leisure,* New York, The Twentieth Century Fund, copyright 1962;

INTRODUCTION

Human progress has a number of measures; all of them as imperfect as the subjects presumed to be progressing. To a great extent, from the era of industrialization on, measures of human progress have largely ignored the question of human purpose.

Thus, progress has been measured by material well being: freedom from disease, war, and accident; longevity; the extent to which we find paid employment; money left over after "necessary" expenditures; and so forth. All of these measures are of great importance but they represent the attainment only of means. The end remains unspecified. They do not measure the extent to which one discovers his or her life's purpose or exercises his or her will. Nor do they measure the extent of transcendence into the glorious, dizzying, terrible realm where one's life begins to truly reveal who one is through the process of doing what one chooses—leisure.

Few people have had a life of leisure; fewer still, perhaps, have wanted one. Nonetheless, in the evolution of leisure we see the ultimate measure of human progress, which is the highest level of need. Ultimately, it will assert itself. Leisure will assent itself because it is where human change, however unwittingly, is leading us.

Leisure always carries with it the responsibility for inventing an ideal. It is, therefore, of fundamental importance for those who have the potential for leisure to understand what leisure ideals those who lived before them invented and the extent to which those ideals were realized.

Because leisure is an idea and an ideal, which are both very old and very elite, leisure is, in many ways, foreign to us. This is more than a pity since it may well be the most important idea and ideal yet produced in the Western World.

This book traces the evolution of leisure from its ancient, occidental beginnings in the city-state of Athens through the modern era. Since our primary interest in writing was to examine how our concepts of leisure have evolved, this could be done only within the context of historical and philosophical change. The chapters, therefore, proceed more or less in chronological order.

While what appears here in no way constitutes a personal philosophy, our points of view enter frequently. Leisure, historically, has been the arena in which one developed a point of view from which to take in the world. So it is perhaps fitting that we have developed and expressed a few such personal points of view. Like human history itself, the chapters of this book begin slowly and then speed up. In some places, however, we felt it necessary to identify historical events or trends in more detail than others on the assumption that they were either less familiar to the reader and/or that they had a major impact on our concepts of leisure. The early chapters of this book were first drafted by Goodale and the later ones by Godbey. While we critiqued each other's work, Goodale was the final editor. To a remarkable extent, the authors discovered many common points of view (a situation which each could attribute only to the other's intelligence).

Writing such a book was a labor of love and an act of pretense. It took longer than we thought it would, more information than we had, more wisdom than we possessed. Like leisure itself, writing this book has been its own reward. It is our fond hope that reading it will be too.

T.L.G.

G.C.G.

If we say the twentieth is leisure's century, and if we want it to be that, we should know what is involved. Yet once you know what leisure is, you still may not want it. Leisure requires a sacrifice. This conclusion will doubtless disappoint many persons. . . . It's a pity there is no neat way around this. . . .

Now it may be simple free time you seek. . . . Time is a major element, since today's leisure is measured in units of time—hours, days, weeks. Work is included because today's time is considered free when not at grips with work. Work is the antonym of free time. But not of leisure. Leisure and free time live in two different worlds. We have got in the habit of thinking them the same. Anybody can have free time. Not everybody can have leisure. Free time is a realizable idea of democracy. Leisure is not fully realizable, and an ideal not alone an idea. Free time refers to a special way of calculating a special kind of time. Leisure refers to a state of being, a condition of man, which few desire and fewer achieve. . . .

If someone were to ask, Why do you take such trouble to distinguish leisure from free time and lesser concepts? I should answer, leisure cannot exist where people don't know what it is. There may still be some, perhaps quite a few, who would like at least to know what leisure may be.

(Sebastian de Grazia, 1962: 8-9)

I. LEISURE, PHILOSOPHY AND I

Whatever we think leisure is, even if only free time, we think it is a good thing. What leisure is, and why we think it a good thing, is the subject of this book, a subject which, by the nature of these questions, must be approached through philosophy. But what good is philosophy? This question, no doubt, is a more difficult one for most. Often the question is rhetorical. The poser of the question, rather than seeking an answer, already has one. And the answer is that philosophy is not much good.

THE UTILITY OF PHILOSOPHY

Rephrased, the question is: "Of what use is philosophy to me?" This is the crux of the matter. The questioner has equated good with useful. Too, it seems that "good" and "useful" are understood in a limited sense; limited to what is personal, direct, and immediate; limited, perhaps, to only those things which help put roofs over our heads, clothes on our backs, and bread on our tables. In that limited sense, philosophy is probably not very useful (Fuller, 1923: 12).

In that limited sense, leisure may not be very useful either. Neither is history, art, poetry, drama, dreams, sunsets, humor, friendship or banana splits. Still, we know that man does not live by bread alone. "To look for utility everywhere," Aristotle said, "ill becomes free and exalted souls" (In Stocks, 1936: 179). Leisure, and any philosophy of leisure, is about free and exalted souls.

The question, What good is philosophy? reflects our widespread uncertainty and anxiety about our future well-being and so is legitimate, even if often rhetorical. One of the uses of philosophy may be to help us understand ourselves and our circumstances and thereby reduce or at least better cope with our uncertainty and anxiety. An anxious person is not free. As Bertrand Russell suggested, philosophy can teach us "how to live without certainty and yet without being paralyzed by hesitation" (1946: 14). Another use of philosophy is to help us understand how limited a sense we have of what is good and useful. More importantly, however, philosophy may help us understand that the question itself, particularly if used rhetorically, is an expression of the questioner's philosophy. However loosely formulated it may be, and however unaware we may be of it, each of us has a philosophy. From that there is no escape. Neither can one escape the philosophy of others, whether parents and peers, prophets and priests, or presidents and prime ministers. Understanding that there is no escape and understanding the philosophy of others as well as one's own may be, in a broad sense, useful after all.

Philosophy may be best understood not as a subject but an activity by which one seeks an understanding of every fact, fiction and feeling and all relationships among them. Within philosophy, viewed as a discipline or field of study, there are a number of traditional branches: aesthetics examining beauty; epistomology dealing with knowledge; ethics dealing with the proper conduct of life, and so on. More recently we have come to speak of the philosophy of something, thus philosophy of law, government, science, education, or leisure. So it is an activity more so than a subject in itself. The activity is reflection: reflection upon information, ideas and experiences. Note that we can also think of the activity as contemplation or meditation, and speak of these as philosophical acts. Note too that the philosophical act is integrative, seeking to integrate and make congruent information, ideas, and experiences. We might pose that as a definition but there are many other, and better, ones.

The word philosophy derives from the ancient Greek language. Its original meaning, the search for the wisdom of life, is derived from the literal meaning, love of wisdom. Will Durant defined philosophy in a way which emphasizes the integrative, congruence building nature of philosophy. He stated, "Philosophy is harmonized knowledge making a harmonious life; it is the self-discipline which lifts us to serenity and freedom" (1981: xii). Finally, Josef Pieper has offered a definition of an educated person which seems also an appropriate way to define philosophy. An educated person has (and philosophy is) "a point of view from which to take in the world." Education (and philosophy) concerns the whole man, man "capable of grasping the totality of things" (Pieper, 1952: 36). From philosophers such as David Hume to fictional characters like Mr. Dooley, the literature is rich with references to the importance of philosophy in providing stability and steerage for our voyage through life. In this sense, too, this very broad and deep sense, philosophy is useful.

THE PERVASIVENESS OF PHILOSOPHY

The last thing a deep sea fish becomes aware of, the saying goes, is salt water. Philosophy, for us, is like that. It is as much a part of our internal environment as water; as much a part of our external environment as air. And like air and water, we can breathe and drink it but it is difficult for us to grasp and contain.

Almost anything that can take an "ism" suffix refers to philosophy: socialism, capitalism, liberalism, conservatism, hedonism, asceticism, rationalism, empiricism, romanticism, utilitarianism, puritanism, and so on. Our understanding of leisure and our leisure behavior is influenced by these "isms." In the case of hedonism or puritanism, for example, the influence is quite direct. It is somewhat less direct for capitalism or liberalism and still less direct for rationalism and empiricism. Even for the latter, as evident in Josef Pieper's philosophy, the influence may be subtle and abstract but pervasive nonetheless.

For each of us and for our culture, philosophy and circumstances interact. That interaction can be described as mutual causality; philosophy influencing circumstances influencing philosophy in constant and complex interaction. There are numerous examples in history which provide clear examples of the interaction of philosophy and circumstances, some of which had and continue to have a quite direct bearing on our understanding of leisure. Aristotle's philosophy of leisure was shaped in part by an economic system based on slavery and a political system based on an aristocracy of citizens. Calvin's philosophy, from which the Protestant ethic is a direct outgrowth, was shaped by an already entrenched capitalism and emerging middle class as well the growing protest against the doctrines and practices of Catholicism.

Care should be taken, however, in viewing philosophy as useful if by that we mean, as we often do, convenient or self-serving; as mere rationalization of the conditions of one's culture or of one's own way of life.

> Reason, as every schoolgirl now informs us, may be
> only the technique of rationalizing desire; for the most
> part we do not do things because we have reasons for
> them, but we find reasons for them because we want

to do them. It is the simplest thing in the world to construct
a philosophy out of our wishes and our interests. We must
be on guard against being communists because we are poor,
or conservatives when our ship is in. (Durant, 1981: 30)

That does not mean that Aristotle's philosophy of leisure or Calvin's
philosophy of salvation and work were merely convenient rationalizations. It
is enough for us to understand and be comfortable with our own rationalizations without speculating on those of others. Besides, it is our uneasiness with
our own rationalizations that makes us suspicious of those of others. More
important, however, is the fact that a philosophic understanding must be
developed out of knowledge, ideas and experiences which are widely shared.

If guided only by our own interests and desires, we become not
philosophical but peevish, our peeves including others whose interests and
desires are different from our own. Much of our language suggests such
peevishness: those who enjoy athletics become "jocks;" those who enjoy
social occasions become "party types" and those who do not, "party poopers;"
those who enjoy literature or poetry become "bookworms," and so on. No
philosophy of leisure can possibly grow out of that.

In addition, we must recognize that our philosophy, even if not self-
serving, is usually self-fulfilling. If we believe it is a dog-eat-dog world or a
rat race, we behave in ways that tend to make it so. If we view relationships
as transactions, we tend to make them so, and ask, "what's in it for me?" If
social interactions are viewed in terms of Berne's (1964) *Games People Play,*
we become players; quite cynical ones. Conversely, if we see ourselves not as
individuals but as participants in family, community, and polity, those units
become stronger. If we play for enjoyment, no one loses. Happiness is
contagious. It is also a product of philosophy. In particular, it is a product of
leisure, at least to Aristotle, and of a philosophy of leisure.

LEISURE—A PRELIMINARY VIEW

Although there are some exceptions, leisure is commonly defined as
free time; that is, time free from work and other obligations. That seems to be
a rather simple and straightforward definition. In fact, however, when we
examine the terms we use to define leisure, we find the definition is not clear
or straightforward at all. Such an analysis can lead to a quagmire in which we
do not wish to become bogged down, so we use leisure in a general sense
assuming that what is being referred to is free time.

It is a useful definition from the standpoint of social science. It is a good definition to the extent that the pragmatic and useful are the principal determinants of good. It reflects the philosophies, though perhaps in distorted form, of pragmatism and utilitarianism. Even more, it reflects the philosophy of empiricism, by which the good, or at least the true, can be determined only by controlled observation and measurement. With the calendar and the clock, time is quantified and measurable. But there is a problem here. Our concepts become limited to what can be quantified and measured. Leisure is equated with time, and time equated with periods during which things do, or do not, take place. Perhaps we do not measure time so much as we measure the distance traveled by the hands on the clock: Saturday and Sunday are simply four revolutions of the little hand.

We will examine concepts of time in more detail in a later chapter. Here we will only add the note that since all things take place in time, we do not learn much by using time in a definition, particularly a definition of leisure.

Since "leisure time" is often used as substitute for "free time," something needs to be said about the concept "free." This, surely, is also an extremely difficult concept, just as are the other key words in our definition. If leisure is time free from work and obligations, we need to be clear about the meaning of work and of obligation. Are we clear about those words? Not really. Even if we were, there are other difficulties with a definition which equates leisure with time free from. . . .

Freedom From

As Serena Arnold (1985: 6) pointed out, definitions usually do not give us the meaning of a word but rather synonyms with which to replace it. At best, free time is a synonym, so it does not tell us what leisure means. Secondly, the definition "free time" does not tell us what free time is but rather what it is not: free time is time not devoted to work or other obligations.

That aspect of the definition is problematic in other ways. It clearly assigns superior status to work, particularly, along with other obligations. Free time, then, is clearly of secondary importance: it is almost the leftover of daily life. It is residual time. In addition, it is clear that free time has to be earned: one cannot simply have free time. Those who are unemployed do not have free time, or if they do, they are not supposed to enjoy it. The more sophisticated among the unemployed are not unemployed but "between jobs." They, presumably, can enjoy the time "between" since they did have and will have a job. Free time is compensation: if one works overtime without pay, one is usually awarded "compensatory time," that is, time free from work.

Another difficulty with the notion that leisure is time free from something is that the time becomes an end in itself. Consequently, what is done with that time is unimportant. And particularly when we perceive that time as earned compensation, then it is nobody's (damn) business how we spend our time any more so than how we spend our money. That also, of course, expresses a distorted notion of independence and individualism.

Still another difficulty with a free time definition is that in yet another way our lives become atomized; parts divided and divided again until they are no longer divisible. The original meaning of atom, which can be traced to pre-Socratic philosophers such as Democritus, was "indivisible." "Individual" is a derivative of that: individuals are, in a sense, the atoms of communities and cultures. To break them down again is to break them down not only figuratively but also literally. But daily lives are broken down into roles and functions, and defining leisure as free time adds to the disintegration of life. Just as we dislocate art or history from a place in daily life by consigning them to galleries and museums (Lasch, 1984), we dislocate leisure by consigning it to particular periods during days, weeks and years.

Freedom To

In summarizing Aristotle's concept of leisure, and in his own elaboration, de Grazia (1962: 14) defined leisure as, "freedom from the necessity of being occupied." The time element has been eliminated but we have still not reached beyond freedom from. . . . Charles Brightbill (1960: 4), starting from the notion of free time, defined leisure as discretionary time. The time element has crept back in, but an important idea, the qualification that the time is discretionary, has been added. Leisure, then, becomes time with which we can choose what to do, so the focus has shifted from "freedom from" to "freedom to." The shift is inevitable because it is inevitable that we choose (even if we choose to avoid choosing) and inevitable that we do something (even if that is to do nothing). The choices we make and the things we do become central elements in our notion of freedom.

There are few words in our language that are more laden with positive value than words like free and freedom. But freedom is no more an end in itself than free time. It is valuable because of what it frees us to do. Similarly, when we speak of using our discretion, we mean using our judgement, in fact, using our good or best judgement. How silly it would seem if we thought of being free to use our worst judgement, or free to behave in ways destructive or detrimental, not only to others but to ourselves as well.

The notion that it is nobody's business how we spend our time and money is quite wrong. One cannot divorce freedom from responsibility any more than one can live in a vacuum.

Freedom can be defined in many ways, as is true of most concepts. One of the simplest definitions is the absence of impediments. But that definition of freedom is limited to "freedom from." A better definition of freedom is the ability to do what we want to do. If we do not want to do anything, there is no point in being free. So there is no such thing as goalless or purposeless leisure, just as there is no such thing as complete or absolute freedom.

Increasing Freedom

If we define freedom as the ability to do what we want to do, then it is clear that we can increase our freedom in one of two ways, or some combination of both. The first way, and the one we focus upon almost to the exclusion of the other, is to increase our ability. That can be done in many ways, of course. We have an enormous and complex legislative and judicial system which attempts to assure our freedom—thus our ability to do what we want to do. That includes, necessarily, laws protecting us from exploitation of and imposition upon each other. From the Bill of Rights to the local dog leash laws, freedom is the central issue.

More often, however, we think of increasing our ability to do what we want to do by increasing the resources we have at our disposal. Typically three resources come to mind: money, time, and skill. One need not elaborate the ways in which money can increase our ability to do what we want to do. Lack of time, as dozens of surveys assure us, is perceived to be the major limitation to engaging in various recreational pursuits. What seems lacking, for most of us, is not so much time but the ability to choose. What is required is the ability to establish priorities, make choices, and accept the fact that there is only so much one can do. It was indeed a wise Indian who, when someone complained to him about not having enough time, replied, "well—I guess you have all there is." As to skills, surely the ability to choose is the most important one. In addition, depending upon what one wants to do, social, intellectual and physical skills are requisite to engagement in activity and to the kinds and amounts of competence we seek for satisfaction. So there is much we can do to increase our abilities and thus our freedom to do what we want to do.

But that is only one side of our equation. It is surely apparent, hopefully to all, that no matter how much money, time and skill one has, one simply cannot do everything. Perhaps there are those for whom no amount of resources will ever be enough. They will never be free. They are to be pitied rather than envied. One can only be free when what one wants to do matches the resources one has available to do it. At some point, each of us must, if we want to be free, adjust our wants to our resources. We know that, but in a sense we have not learned that.

Contrary to popular misconceptions, for example, is the fact that primitive hunters and gatherers were much more free than we are. Studies of a number of aboriginal peoples demonstrate that they worked less than four hours a day and in some groups and locales only two. They had a great deal of free time and in that way were much more free than are we. And that is simply because their wants were limited. As Sahlins noted (1972: 14), "We are inclined to think of hunters and gatherers as poor because they don't have anything; perhaps better to think of them for that reason as free." They had everything they wanted, it seems.

Eric Fromm, in one of his many seminal books, made an important, related point about freedom. In *Escape from Freedom* (1941), he argued that we are largely free from external restraints and that our enslavement is mainly internal. Whether it is the freedom from which we escape, or the responsibility from which freedom is inseparable, we do seem to seek escape. Fromm was concerned about the mindless submission to authority and referred to the fascism of the axis powers in Europe during World War II. But he also referred to the relentless conformity of western man as a form of escape. One could fill a library with those who share Fromm's views about conformity and internal impoverishment. How much of our work, business, and harried pursuit of happiness is, in fact, an escape from freedom?

From this discussion, it seems clear that one's philosophy of leisure is the critical key to freedom and happiness. We are not, it seems, the possessors of free souls and certainly not exalted ones. No doubt one must be free from something in order to be free to (do) something. But "freedom from" focuses on external restraints, and external restraints are no longer the primary ones for most of us. In particular that definition focuses upon economic restraints and obligations which are partly economic but primarily social in nature. We might pause to reflect upon why we think of work and other obligations as a restraint rather than an endless source of purpose and meaning and joy.

It is for this reason, finally, that equating leisure with free time and limiting our notion of freedom to "freedom from" is not satisfactory. Again no philosophy of leisure can grow out of it. Inner impoverishment reflects the lack of a philosophy of leisure to help stabilize and steer our voyage. Leisure conceptualized as a periodic quantity of a certain kind of time has entered our dictionaries and conversations but it has not, and perhaps cannot, enter our experience. A different conceptualization and a different philosophy is required, one which lends harmony rather than dissonance to our lives.

LEISURE—A PHILOSOPHIC VIEW

> Leisure is living in relative freedom from the external
> compulsive forces of one's culture and physical environment
> so as to be able to act from internally compelling love in
> ways which are personally pleasing, intuitively worthwhile,
> and provide a basis for faith. (Godbey, 1985: 9)

Such a departure from the most commonly used definition requires, perhaps, some explanation. There is no reference to time. In addition, there is no reference to one's "state of mind," a phrase that is sometimes used to define leisure. Like time, a state of mind cannot be avoided, so defining leisure as a state of mind does not tell us anything. Sometimes the definition is elaborated: leisure is a state of mind in which the feeling of compulsion is minimal. This definition, too, is limited to a state of mind free from compulsion. Clearly, compulsion is used in a limited sense, referring only to external forces. Worse, however, is the implication that all compulsion is negative. But that, too, is not a part of our experience.

In noting that leisure is living we avoid the time and state of mind notions. Relative freedom recognizes that freedom is necessarily and appropriately limited: we are not and should not be free to do anything. Our freedom stems from not wanting to do many things. The definition utilizes the freedom from notion and states what it is from which we need to be (relatively) free. The definition does not stop there, however.

Freedom from external compulsive forces of one's culture and environment is a comprehensive, and mainly self-explanatory phrase. We need snow for skiing and water for swimming, and we need food, clothing and shelter. How much we need depends on our environment, but beyond what is minimally adequate it is our culture which compels us to acquire and consume as much as we do. Cultural influences are subtle and complex and for the most part we do not feel culturally compelled. Being unaware of such forces is not a mark of freedom; it is only a mark of lack of awareness. Sometimes we do feel such compulsions, however, and at those times we are aware of not being free. Often we feel the culture compelling us to conform and when we react and rebel in an effort to regain our freedom, or at least our independence and individuality, it is still the culture which is compelling us. So much, then for "freedom from," a necessary part of our definition of leisure but only a part. The focus now shifts to "freedom to."

We need to be relatively free from those external compulsive forces so as to be able to act, i.e., "freedom to." And the motivation for those acts is to be internally compelling love. Intrinsic motivation is something which we usually speak of as requisite to choices and actions which we consider play or recreation. By that we mean not being motivated by some external force or pursuing some external reward. This definition includes intrinsic motivation, but goes beyond it.

Almost all the decisions we make are composed of two considerations, or more precisely, two kinds of forces. We can label these forces simply as pushes and pulls. When we decide to do something as a way of avoiding something else, it is mainly push forces at work. One can go out on a date to avoid staying home. One can also decide to stay home to avoid a date. In a sense one is not being compelled but rather repelled; one is not drawn toward something (pulled) but pushed from the alternatives. This definition limits leisure to those things to which we are drawn or pulled. It is further limited to those things not extrinsically or externally motivated but to which we are drawn by internally compelling love.

Clearly love is not limited to feelings about people. One can love every sort of animate and inanimate thing: one can love an era, a locale, a subject, an activity and a principle. When we love, we are compelled to do things; we do those things because we have to. And when we act out of internally compelled love, the ways we act are personally pleasing, intuitively worthwhile, and provide a basis for faith.

In most explanations of play and recreation and of intrinsic motivation, reference is made to the pleasure that is derived therefrom. That much of the definition is widely shared and understood. Acting in ways which are intuitively worthwhile is a phrase which recognizes and makes explicit matters which may or may not be implied in other conceptualizations of leisure. It recognizes the role of intuition, a role once rejected by rational, empirical science but one increasingly acknowledged and accepted, even among those most insistent on "hard" data. Perhaps there are some things we will never know in the sense of demonstrable facts. In that sense of knowing, we cannot possibly know everything anyway. There are many things that we sense, and much of what we sense turns out to be true. In various degrees, we are all sensitive and sensible. We can speak, then, of common sense not as some dull perception but sense common to us all. Part of that sense is a sense of what is worthwhile. We do not live in a moral and ethical vacuum: do not and cannot. Our intuition tells us that. So does a mountain of evidence.

The intuitively worthwhile, however, does not mean the constant application of some moral calculus. There is, of course, a bottom line, but the intuitively worthwhile includes all of those things which we do not have to rationalize or justify, not even to ourselves. Sometimes an activity may become intuitively worthwhile only after we have undertaken it several times. Its meanings and pleasures may have to he learned, just as tastes are acquired and appreciations gained. Those activities which we find intuitively worthwhile provide us with a basis for faith: faith in the worthwhileness of the activity; faith in ourselves as the doers of activity; faith in our skills and other resources; faith, where others are involved, in those others. Faith includes belief and confidence and, like belief and confidence, it tends to spill over from action to action and activity to activity. Eventually, it becomes a very comprehensive thing. Faith in one's self, faith in others; faith in the moment, faith in the present and future; faith in the cauliflower, faith in the cosmos. You cannot take the cauliflower out of the cosmos.

We have defined leisure, then, not as a commodity of time or as a state of mind but as a way of living. The definition says what leisure is rather than what it is not. With words and phrases like compelling love, intuitively worthwhile and faith, it makes clear that leisure is positive as both attraction and response. Too, it is highly personal, and since it seeks to capture our experience as well as our knowledge and ideas of it, it is harmonious and integrative. It is also, clearly, an ideal.

THE UNMAKING OF LEISURE

Having gone to those lengths to define leisure, it is still necessary to ask your indulgence. The literature about recreation and leisure and the messages in the media and daily conversation are replete with references in which leisure is equated with free (unobligated, uncompelled, discretionary) time. For that reason, and to avoid bothersome repetition, sometimes we will use the word leisure in the sense of free time. Where the context does not make clear the sense in which the term is being used, we will try to add unobtrusive clarification.

Most of the chapters which will follow address leisure as a contemporary phenomenon and experience. As noted above, that typically refers to the consumption of a commodity of time. Commodification and consumption reflect the philosophy, or perhaps the lack of it, which characterizes our era. Think of all the references to saving time or to spending, using, buying, or borrowing it. "Time," said Ben Franklin, "is money."

Leisure did not begin that way. It began as an ideal and as a way of living. No one has thought more about leisure, and many believe no one has thought better about leisure, than the ancient Greeks. It is necessary, then, to begin with the ancient Greek philosophers, particularly Aristotle, and it is necessary to place the leisure ideal in the context of the ideals of the Greek culture. The mutual causality of philosophy and the conditions of living have already been noted.

The leisure ideal was soon overwhelmed by a complicated sequence of historical forces. It is only in our own time that we once again have the opportunity to pursue the ideal. During the interim, a period of nearly 2,400 years, our 20th century understanding of leisure and all the things related to it were formed. There is neither inclination nor space to examine the intellectual history of leisure. On the other hand, one cannot grasp the present without some understanding of the past. We need to know something about the many "isms" which have influenced our concepts and thus our philosophies.

Consequently, some of the major forces which have influenced our thinking about leisure have been lightly traced: specifically, religion, science, political economics and industrialization. These tracings are necessarily cursory and discursive in nature. Leisure is not always addressed directly, in part because the thinking about leisure cannot be divorced from its context; in part because the influences may be subtle and tracing them would be too time consuming and perhaps even condescending. In addition, however lightly we trace the history of leisure as idea and ideal, history, like philosophy, has a liberating influence. Those who ask, What good is philosophy? are also sure to ask, What good is history? To the explanations already noted we would add, like Bronowski and Mazlish (1960), only this:

> We have experienced the study of history as a liberation—a liberation from accepted ideas, and a perspective into their evolution which brings them sharply into focus. History liberates because it refines our understanding of men, ideas and of events. (p. xviii)

REFERENCES

Arnold, Serena. 1985. "The Dilemma of Meaning." In Thomas Goodale and Peter Witt, *Recreation and Leisure: Issues in an Era of Change* (2nd ed.). State College, Pennsylvania: Venture Publishing.

Berne, Eric. 1964. *Games People Play.* New York: Grove Press.

Brightbill, Charles. 1960. *The Challenge of Leisure.* Englewood Cliffs, New Jersey: Prentice Hall.

Bronowski, J. and Mazlish, Bruce. 1960. *The Western Intellectual Tradition.* New York, Harper Brothers.

de Grazia, Sebastian. 1962. *Of Time, Work and Leisure.* New York: The Twentieth Century Fund.

Durant, Will. 1981. *The Pleasures of Philosophy.* New York: Simon and Schuster.

Fromm, Eric. 1941. *Escape from Freedom.* New York: Holt, Rinehart, and Winston.

Fuller, B. A. 1923. *History of Greek Philosophy.* New York: Henry Holt and Company.

Godbey, Geoffrey. 1985. *Leisure in Your Life.* (2nd ed.). State College, Pennsylvania: Venture Publishing.

Lasch, Christopher. 1984. "The Degradation of Work and the Apotheosis of Art." *Harper's.* (February).

Pieper, Josef. 1952. *Leisure: The Basis of Culture* (Tr. Alexander Dru). New York: Mentor Brooks.

Russell, Bertrand. 1946. *A History of Western Philosophy.* London: George Allen and Unwin.

Sahlins, Marshall. 1972. *Stone Age Economics.* New York: Aldine Publishers.

Stocks, J. L. 1936. "Leisure." *Classical Quarterly, xxx:* 3,4. (July-October).

The wise man will cultivate thought, and will free himself from passion, superstition, and fear, and will seek in contemplation and understanding the modest happiness available to human life. Happiness does not come from external goods; a man must become accustomed to finding within himself the sources of his enjoyment. Culture is better than riches. . . . No power and no treasure can outweigh the extension of our knowledge. Happiness is fitful, and sensual pleasure affords only a brief satisfaction; one comes to a more lasting content by acquiring peace and serenity of soul, good cheer, moderation, and a certain order and symmetry of life. . . . Strength of body is nobility only in beasts of burden, strength of character is nobility in man. . . . Good actions should be done not out of compulsion but from conviction; not from hope of reward but for their own sake.

(Democritus, in Durant, W., 1943: 354)

II. THE ROOTS OF THE LEISURE IDEAL

While Aristotle believed philosophy began with the Egyptians, most scholars argue that philosophy began with Thales, a Greek from the City of Miletus, the first of the Milesian philosophers active throughout the sixth century B.C. Before Thales, whatever might have been considered philosophy appeared in the form of religion and government.

A CHORUS OF ETHICAL SYSTEMS

The code of Hammurabi, however secular in nature, was a gift from heaven. In the 2,000 years or so between Hammurabi's reign and the birth of Christ, the wedding of divine authority and social justice in the codes was repeated in other religious and political systems as in the governments of the great Jewish Kings, Saul, David and Solomon, about 1,000 B.C. The earliest prophets preached such virtues as gentleness, friendliness, mutual aid and, above all, simplicity.

Elsewhere, religious systems were being developed and elaborated. In Persia, Zoroaster (or Zarathustra) preached about reason, free will, and the importance of thoughts, words and deeds corresponding with divine purposes. Bliss or misery depended on the choices one made.

Within the same century, Buddhism was established further East, in India, and in China both Lao Tse (Tze or Tzu) and Confucius were active. While there are major differences between Eastern and Western religions and philosophies, the directions for living expressed in the aphorisms of Confucius or the Tao of Lao Tse are quite similar to the teachings of Judaism and Christianity. Too, the Noble Path of the Buddhists, stressing self-control, freedom from vanities, and conduct which is honest, kindly and peaceful is preached as much in contemporary North America as it was in ancient India, and is endorsed by those of every faith.

In a brief period around the sixth century B.C., then, major religious systems were developing in the eastern Mediterranean, Persia, India and China. With variations, they all sought to elevate man from his degraded and hopeless situation, to offer hope and dignity and, through piety and good actions, the prospect of fellowship with the divine. There was much agreement on the way of life most likely to lead to the kingdom of heaven. The good life was, in the long run, the happiest and most advantageous, but that had nothing to do with what individuals find pleasurable and profitable at the moment.

Greek Religion, Philosophy and Ethics

That sounds very much like the Greek philosophers of the fifth and fourth centuries B.C. Lacking a coherent religious system, the ethical systems established by Greek philosophers substituted for religious doctrine. In certain religious cults or mysteries, sin, punishment, purification, retribution and the like were included in the dogma and practices. Other cults offered the possibility of escape from Hades and of salvation in Heaven. But these movements constituted a religion for comparatively few.

Most of us are familiar with some of the many gods in Greek mythology: Apollo and Zeus, Psyche and Eros, Prometheus, Pandora, and dozens more. But unlike the gods of other religions, these gods had human characteristics, behavioral as well as physical: deceit, thievery, incest and murder together with loyalty, compassion, generosity, self-sacrifice, and wisdom.

The Greeks thought of their gods not as characters to worship or to fear, but as wise older brothers and sisters. These gods were the aristocracy of the universe, each responsible for a certain part, just as local aristocracies ran their own city-states. Greek religion differed from most others in another respect. It was not introspective: ancient Greeks were not given to self-doubt or questioning or analysis. Religion was outside of them: they were simply part of nature and part of the universe. Their language did not include words to convey self or individual (Fuller, 1923: 26-8). The city-state was a main object of worship for most Greeks, and they saw themselves first as Athenians or Spartans or Corinthians. Finally, there was no priestly class in ancient Greece. That may help explain the reverence for Homer and attributing so

much to him. The ancient Greeks worshipped their poets, politicians, philosophers, and body politic—the city-state.

Philosophy and science began in this context, and thrived in it.
Traditional views of the world and customary ways of life were breaking
down, as happened before in Babylon and would happen again in pre-
Renaissance Europe. Reason was needed to bring order to a physical and
social world in which it was lacking. Thales is often regarded as the first
philosopher as he was the first to reason, systematically, by deduction. With
Thales and several others, philosophy, for a century or more, focused mainly
on the natural world. Thales knew some math and was aware of the cyclical
behavior of the planets. He correctly predicted an eclipse in 585 B.C., which
helps us place him in time. Philosophers of the early period were also public
men as they engaged actively in the affairs of their respective cities. Over
time, philosophers withdrew from the affairs of city-state. Over the same
period, emphasis within philosophy shifted from nature to man. It is said that
Socrates created the soul, though perhaps his predecessors deserve credit for
that. But he contributed much to a secular religion, with the soul a key
element.

In addition to the influences already noted, Socrates, and thus those
who followed him, were influenced by two other circumstances. First,
Socrates was a youth during the age of Pericles, approximately 460-430 B.C.;
the period of the golden age of Greece: his middle and later years coincided
with the Peloponnesian Wars which lasted 30 years, with Sparta eventually
defeating Athens. Plato was an Athenian but his political philosophy, as seen
in the *Republic,* was Spartan. These early philosophers thought little of
democracy, preferring aristocracy instead, but one based not on bleed or
money but merit.

The second influence worthy of note was that of the sophists, whose
sharp witted argumentation aided the rapid deterioration of the established
order and orthodoxy. "Sophist" originally meant professor and we get from it
words like sophisticated and sophomore and also sophism and sophistry. The
Sophists traveled and taught oratorical and debating skills along with logic.
Those were skills required to succeed in the public life of the city-state;
success usually defined as wealth and power. The sophists provided practical
education for which students paid, often handsomely. Necessarily then,
students were drawn from the aristocracy and were taught how to guard and
further their own welfare. Russell compared the function of the sophists to
today's corporate lawyers (1946: 91). Socrates did not care for them, or at
least the absence of any moral principle or ideal in their teaching. Yet they
made an important contribution: they generated the first three of the seven
liberal arts (the trivium of rhetoric, dialectic and grammar to which was later
added the quadrivium of music, astronomy, geometry and arithmetic).

Their line of argument often led to skepticism, but they were clever. For example Protogorus, perhaps the best known of the sophists, is said to have taught a student on the condition that the student would have to pay his tuition only if the student won his first court case. Protogorus then sued him for recovery of the tuition fee!

Both the philosophers who concentrated on the natural world and the sophists teaching rhetoric, grammar and dialectic attempted by thinking and reasoning to bring understanding and order to the physical and social world. Soon, understanding and order in the internal world would become the focus as philosophers attempted to understand the workings of the intellect and the soul. The logic of the soul is the original Greek meaning of psychology (psyche-logike). Inscribed on the walls at the temple to Apollo at Delphi were the words, "Know Thyself."

ELEMENTS OF THE LEISURE IDEAL

"The life of leisure," as de Grazia noted (1962: 21), "was the only life fit for a Greek." But leisure was a very complex idea or, more accurately, ideal. Time is a necessary element for the elaboration and elevation of a culture. But time is not enough. Intellectual ferment, brought on by the necessity of mythological or metaphysical explanations of phenomena, is another element. Man was full of wonder about the world and the world was wonderful. A third element, more characteristic of ancient Greece than perhaps any other culture, was pursuit of an ideal. Leisure, as understood and used by early Greek philosophers, can only be understood in light of the ideals of Greek culture.

Culture

Their word for culture was *paideia.* The word *paidos* meant boy or child and a variant of that word, *pedo* forms the root of our word pedagogy, the art and science of teaching. In addition to culture, then, *paideia* also referred to the content and process of education. To the ancient Greeks, education was the ultimate justification of human life and human communities. As Jaeger argued (1939: xiii-xvii), education is just as instinctive as reproduction: education assures the continuation of culture just as reproduction assures continuation of the species. The Greeks set out to produce, via education, a higher order of man. *Paideia*, then, also referred to self-improvement and was considered the force which protected the good man and made him secure. Finally, *paideia* was used to indicate the fulfillment of divine promise. Education referred to the deliberate molding of character in accord with an ideal. And the Greek word for leisure, *schole*, was the origin of the English word, school.

Excellence and Virtue

The ideal of Greek culture was expressed by the word *arete*, a word frequently translated as virtue. Originally the word was used to convey heroic valor and evolved to mean nobility in thought and deed. Sometimes *arete* is translated as excellence; excellence in all things but particularly excellence of the soul. Virtue, then, is equated with excellence of the soul and thus the fulfillment of the divine purpose.

The great emphasis on education and learning is important not only for the preservation and transmission of culture but also for virtue and excellence of the soul. Unlike many religions, the Greeks did not consider man to be evil. In fact, they thought of man as simply a part of nature in which everything had its place. Natural justice as they viewed it (and as the origin of our notion of natural law) was that everything had its proper place, role and function. Justice was lacking when something exceeded its proper bounds and thus created disorder, whether in the universe or the community of man. At the temple at Delphi, along with the inscription "Know Thyself," was the inscription, "Nothing in Excess."

Man sinned when he exceeded the bounds of his natural place. But that was not caused by his evil nature, according to Greek philosophers. Man sinned because he was ignorant, and that can be avoided by a proper education. With knowledge comes virtue.

Civil Society

Two other matters are important to understanding the ideal of Greek culture and the leisure ideal within it. As was briefly alluded to earlier, the Greeks believed that the natural life of man was collective; it was life in the community. Their ideal was the perfection of civil life and political life, that is, the perfection of governance of life in the city-state. The proper life is that of a good citizen. Care was taken for the full development of individual character because that resulted in the character of the community. They fostered individual development not as an end in itself but as the essential means to collective social and political development of the city-state.

Free Will

The second matter essential to understanding the ideal of culture and of leisure was the belief that the soul included free will. That is to say, we are free to make choices. The symbol of the followers of Pythagorus was Y, indicating a choice of paths to follow. The ideal of *paideia* was founded on the belief that men can make choices. And the whole purpose of knowledge was to enable a person to make the right ones.

THE LEISURE IDEAL IN CONTEXT

Of the Greek philosophers, Aristotle is by far the best known. His voluminous writings on widely ranging topics are an important part of our inheritance. We could justly regard him as the father of leisure, but he could just as appropriately be called the father of several other disciplines or branches of knowledge. Our debt to him is great. But his debt to others was also great, and part of his great service was to organize and systematize much of what was thought and known at his time (384-322 B.C.). The excerpts from the writings of Democritus, with which the chapter begins, illustrates a philosophy held in common by Aristotle's mentors and contemporaries.

The Sophists

We have only a general acquaintance with the Sophists because they wrote little. Socrates wrote nothing and we are indebted mainly to Plato for most of what we know of Socratic thought. Only fragments remain of the writings of a number of other philosophers who preceded Aristotle. But it is clear from those fragments that have been preserved that Aristotle's thinking was widely shared. Heraclitus, who lived about two centuries before Aristotle, believed that men were capable both of knowing themselves and acting with moderation, which was the highest virtue. And he held that the satisfaction of bodily pleasures was not the stuff of which true happiness was made. "If happiness lay in bodily pleasures," he said, "we could call oxen happy when they find vetch to eat" (In Wilbur and Allen 1979: 75). Democritus, a contemporary of Socrates, was equally emphatic about that. "Men find happiness neither by means of the body nor through possessions but through uprightness and wisdom." In another fragment from his writings he stated: "Happiness is a tranquil cheerfulness attained through moderation of activity and enjoyment, limitation of desire, and avoidance of competition for the worldly possessions" (pp. 206-7).

Socrates and Plato

The most famous of Aristotle's predecessors were the two Athenians, Socrates and Plato. Aristotle, although not an Athenian, studied many years at Plato's Academy in Athens and later opened his own school, the Lyceum, in Athens. Because the city-state was the unit of government in ancient Greece, many references to Greek science, philosophy and culture might be more properly attributed to Athens.

Socrates claimed to have no knowledge, a reflection of humility and perhaps also the skepticism of the Sophists. But he was interested in the soul, as was Heraclitus before him, and he believed in one God. Out of this evolved the ethical system passed on to Plato and Aristotle. From the *Dialogues* written by Plato we can learn something of Socrates's ethical system. Virtue, he believed, was based on knowledge, again stemming from the belief that errors of conduct were the result of ignorance. Components of virtue (or the four cardinal virtues) were courage, justice, temperance (or prudence) and goodness (or godliness). Those who are independent of external things and who have tamed their impulses and desires can be said to be free and able to attain spiritual qualities. They are closest to God because God needs nothing (Jaeger, 1943: 56). This, to the Athenian philosophers, was perfect happiness.

The *Dialogues* focus on *arete;* virtue and excellence, and the knowledge required for them. That was the knowledge of true standards and values, the knowledge which instructs our will and leads to right choices. The good is pleasurable, but not all pleasures are good. Knowledge is required to help in choosing the right pleasures, which are not necessarily those closest at hand. The good life, then, is the life of right choice and right conduct.

In addition to the dialogues which preserved Socratic thinking, Plato shifted to the political question of how to prepare the best leaders and achieve the best state. This he does in the *Republic,* the first utopia, in which he sets out an educational program to produce philosopher-kings. To Plato, the ideal education was one which would make men desire to be perfect citizens who knew how to govern but also how to be governed. Most of us would disagree with much in the *Republic,* finding much of it distasteful. Infanticide was practiced, putting to death infants not up to standard. Religion was introduced to justify a rigid class structure and the practice of mating the best men and women to produce the best children. But the importance of the *Republic* was not the solution proposed but the questions raised. What is the best education? What characterizes the best leader? How should leaders be chosen?

What is the nature of the best government? What is the relation of the individual to the government and to the state?

Plato made ethics a political subject, a public or community subject rather than one limited to individual life and conduct. His interest was in resolving conflicts between individuals' wishes and desires and public or social good. Like Socrates before him and Aristotle after, ethics and politics were of particular importance. And like the others, he stressed the virtues of moderation, prudence, justice, freedom from material and bodily wants and the like. Plato's philosopher-kings had neither wives nor property, freeing them for government and the life of the mind. He believed we should be governed not by the majority but by the best, and sought a system of education and government to assure that.

Aristotle

One of his students, Aristotle, along with his other achievements, further developed the thinking of Plato and many others, particularly in *Ethics to Nichomachus* (or Nichomachean Ethics) and *Politics* where he addressed pleasure, happiness, leisure, virtue, and the good life.

To Aristotle, ethics and politics were inextricably related: in fact, he thought ethics to be a part of politics since individual life was important for its relation to collective life. Politics was, to him, the science of collective happiness as ethics was the science of individual happiness. Happiness itself was important to Aristotle because he found it an end in itself. The purpose of satisfying desires was happiness: the purpose of wealth, fame, power and the like was also happiness. So the central question, to Aristotle, was how to attain happiness.

The route to happiness was virtue or excellence of the soul; the practice of right conduct which to Aristotle meant nothing in excess. He described character traits as being either the appropriate amount of some quality, too much of it, or too little. The right amount was virtue: too much or too little were vices. Thus between the vices of greed and sloth was the virtue of ambition; between rashness and cowardice, courage; between quarrelsomeness and flattery, friendship, and so on through about a dozen sets of traits. Thus we have from Aristotle the notion of the "golden mean:" moderation in all things: everything in just proportion, in keeping with the concept of natural justice.

Elsewhere in *Nichomachean Ethics* he links virtue to pleasure and happiness. Virtue is pleasant because it is honorable and good. Virtue is, in itself, the source of true pleasure. A good man is one who practices virtue throughout a lifetime. Thus his happiness is continuous (In Gilles, 1886: 10). Here we get a clear indication that Aristotle is talking about leisure in a way very different than our notion of free time. A day or a brief period of time does not bring happiness in a true sense. Freedom from the necessity of being occupied meant, for Aristotle, a lifetime, not brief periods away from work or any other necessary occupation. We may, he said, use those brief periods for recreative pastimes. Those periods are necessary for rest and recuperation so that we can return to work. But amusements and pastimes are not a source of true pleasure or happiness (p. 360). They are not at all related to leisure.

It must be remembered that the culture of Athens and the other city-states of Greece was built on the backs of slaves. Work in the sense of providing food, shelter, clothing and other necessities was done by slaves. Citizens, including Aristotle, were exempt. That was essential to support a class of people who could pursue the ideals of Greek culture and who could perform their duties as citizens: governing and overseeing armies and public works and engaging in scientific and philosophic speculation. It is something of a vicious cycle, perhaps, that workers could not be admitted to citizenship because they did not have time to acquire the knowledge and experience, engage in speculation and contemplation, and exercise those virtuous energies essential to good citizenship. When Aristotole argued that leisure was better than work and is the objective we seek by working, he may have had in mind that it is better to be a citizen than a slave. Remember, leisure was not a brief period but a lifetime.

Two other points must be made regarding Aristotle's philosophy. He was very clear in distinguishing between voluntary and involuntary actions. Involuntary acts could result from the absence of self-control, the equivalent of a sin, or from coercion by others, which might include fear of punishment by God or the guardians of the church or the legal order. Virtue must be deliberately chosen. However good the conduct, if it is forced upon you, it is acquiescence and there is no virtue in it. So the notion of free choice, so fundamental to our notion of leisure, is essential to Aristotle because it makes virtue possible, and that makes happiness possible.

Finally, contemplation he regarded as the best activity, in fact, a divine activity. Like most of his predecessors and contemporaries, Aristotle believed that man was distinguished by his ability to think and reason. Because of that, and because God needs nothing, it was assumed that God spent his time in contemplation, thinking thoughts noble and divine. In contemplation we come as close as possible to practicing what is most godlike or divine within our own nature.

To the early philosophers, then, leisure was not simply the freedom from the necessity of being occupied nor was it time during which we could choose what to do. Leisure was an essential element in the realization of the ideals of the culture: knowledge leading to virtuous choices and conduct which, in turn, leads to true pleasure and happiness. Excellence of the soul, fellowship with the divine; these are the ideals within which the philosophy of leisure was born. The good life, in all of the religious and ethical systems mentioned sofar, was far removed from all of the images portrayed by modern advertisers. And just as we deplore materialism while living amidst material comforts, perhaps the Greeks preached nothing in excess because they were so prone to it.

Historians and philosophers point out that Aristotle's thought was shaped by his assumption that the existing social order was natural and therefore right. The aristocratic leanings of philosophers of this period (and, incidentally, most other periods) has already been noted. Were Aristotle's notions about work and leisure, slavery and citizenship little more than an elaborate rationalization?

> All the philosophers had to do was to give precision to those higher activities for which the man of leisure was to be set free, and to transmute the social prejudice against manual labor as unworthy of a gentlemen into a reasoned demand for the exclusion of mechanics, tradesmen, etc., from citizenship. (Stocks, 1936: 182)

We are much more egalitarian than were the Greek philosophers and we reject leisure if that refers to the privileges of an elite class supported by slavery. Too, we are appropriately skeptical of philosophies that are self-serving. But Aristotle's *Ethics* and *Politics* have instructed every century for 2,000 years and although the leisure ideal seems beyond our grasp, we have all the resources required to pursue it. Material well-being, rather than being a means to the leisure ideal, has become the ideal. But it has not made us happy. A philosophy that may be self-serving might also be very sound. Aristotle's philosophy has withstood the test of time and experience, even including our own.

Leisure and Pleasure

Before leaving this period of Greek philosophy in the centuries before Christ, it may be useful to briefly summarize some of the different attitudes toward leisure, all the result of philosophies and belief systems which were reflected in ways of life. We still use these terms in describing people's attitudes to knowledge, worldly pleasures and life's conditions and events. They describe some of the many viewpoints from which to take in the world. The meanings we associate with some of them have changed over the centuries but here the original sense is retained as much as possible. The five attitudes are: Cynicism; Skepticism; Stoicism; Epicureanism; Hedonism.

Cynicism. The Cynics believed that the only knowledge of which we could be certain was the knowledge of the senses. Physical pleasure and the avoidance of pain, they believed, was the driving force behind human behavior. But, with the exception of sexual pleasure, which they thought of as simply a natural act and which was provided by prostitutes as they shunned marriage, they disdained other pleasures, particularly those satisfied by material goods. They did not want to be possessed by their possessions, often dressing in rags and sleeping wherever they could find a place. To them, virtually all social arrangements and institutions did nothing but cause grief and destroy man's natural state. In some ways theirs was a back to nature movement; not fleeing the cities but living in an almost primitive way. One of the best known of this school lived in a bathing basin and was called Diogenes, which means dog. He is best remembered for asking King Alexander (the Great), who said he would grant him any favor, to move because he was blocking the sun. The story goes that the King said, "If I were not Alexander, I would be Diogenes." Diogenes, apparently, did not return the compliment (Durant, 1943: 507). That is a concise summary of Cynic thought and way of life.

Skepticism. The Skeptics were a group of philosophers who taught at the Academy after Plato's death. The Skeptics doubted everything, including the knowledge of the senses as well as all the doctrines and philosophies of the period. Life to them was not necessarily good nor death bad. Nothing was certain, including the assertion that nothing was certain. We are indebted to them for clarifying the concept of probability and for challenging astrology, magic, divination, and other mystical and mythological practices which were beginning to establish a foothold in the Greek mind. Since to them, truth was unattainable, the wise man should simply try to live a peaceful life. And since the doctrines and habits of whatever time or place could not be shown to be good or bad, right or wrong, they merely accepted whatever was conventional.

Stoicism. Skepticism as a separate school was eventually absorbed by Stoicism. So prevalent was the Stoic line of thought that most philosophers during the four or five centuries before Christ could probably be called Stoics. Even today, "stoic" is often used to mean philosophical. It is not surprising that Stoicism falls in the middle of the five philosophical attitudes. It is a compromise, a middle-ground.

Zeno, the leading figure of Stoic philosophy, studied with the Cynics but rejected much of their doctrine and way of life. His followers believed that man had free will but that the universe was determined. Thus as to the good and bad fortunes which befell man, their attitude was very much, "what will be, will be." The best life, then, was a life in which one chose to accord oneself with, and accede to, the laws of nature. They did not seek pleasure or enjoyment as such things were temporary and often more bother than worth. They lived simply, disdaining other than a few modest possessions and they avoided the strife and turmoil of economic and political affairs. They accepted good fortune without joy and they bore hardships and misfortune without complaint or distress. A ten-year-old's letter to grandfather which says: "I am on a soccer team. We win some and lose some," gives notice of a Stoic in the making.

Epicureanism. Perhaps the stoic philosophers were Epicurean at heart. Of the writings of Epicurus little remains and we are indebted to the Roman poet Lucretius for preserving Epicurean philosophy. Of particular importance to this philosophy, reflecting the belief that the soul was not subject to cosmic time, was the belief that one does not have to live in fear of God. Death was final and the Gods did not concern themselves with human life. Above all, Epicurus sought to free man from fear. Bodily as well as other pleasures, then, can be enjoyed without fear of judgment except by those people with whom one shares social and political life. Virtue is prudence in choosing pleasures. Justice is acting so as not to impose upon and cause resentment among others. Virtue and pleasure were quite compatible so long as one was prudent and responsible.

The Epicureans believed, however, that there were two kinds of pleasures with one kind of pleasure clearly superior to the other. The superior pleasures were ongoing; in general these were the intellectual pleasures of contemplation, appreciation, and developing understanding. The inferior pleasures could be roughly equated with those which were cyclical and recurring in response to natural appetites. It is pleasant to relieve one's self of an itch, but it is better not to have the itch. Epicurus himself lived a simple life, often subsisting for long periods on nothing more than bread and water. He believed that pursuit of wealth, honor or power was completely vain because the path to it was made terrible by the quest. So kindly and gentle was he that his followers thought him a saint. Even if he was, he would have fought to free man from irrational fears, including fear of the gods' interventions in this life, which is the only one we have.

Hedonism. Hedonism was never a school of philosophy as were the other "isms" noted here, but now and then one or a few individuals would espouse the Hedonistic philosophy. Cyrus of Persia was one of the first, followed in some degree by the poets of Ionia. They were like the Cynics in believing pleasure to be the primary motivator of people. They included the bodily, sensual pleasures but also fame, power, wealth, and other sources of pleasure. In some cases, Hedonism was espoused and practiced in ways unchecked by ethical standards. Perhaps that was intended to mock and scandalize some of the supposedly respectable people. Perhaps Hedonism as a philosophy is little more than a rationalization for self-indulgence. It appears to have few adherents. But since it is not a philosophy to boast about, the appearance may be deceiving.

In any case, different philosophies and beliefs shape different behavior and ways of life. Circumstances shape philosophy and are shaped by them in turn. Probably most people, if asked their philosophy of life, would be dumbstruck for not having thought it through. Probably all of us, though in different measures, are part cynic, skeptic, stoic, epicuric, and hedonic. It is important to be happy and the enjoyment of various pleasures can contribute. But it is also important to attain whatever wisdom we can. Ignorance may be bliss, but it is more likely suicide. It is also the principal source of enslavement, as wisdom is the principal source of freedom.

LEGACY

The Greeks sought to overcome ignorance and set out in pursuit of virtue and excellence based on knowledge of what is true and good. Leisure was part of that; in fact, leisure was bound inseparably with knowledge and virtue, pleasure and happiness. The good life was made of that.

Greek philosophy, especially Stoicism, paved the way for Christianity. Though overrun by Sparta and Rome, the Athenians prevailed after all, even if we were to hear little of them, or of philosophy, science, rationality or empiricism for nearly 1,500 years.

Our inheritance from ancient Greek philosophers cannot be overstated. Their contributions in science, philosophy, education, government, art, drama, poetry—there is hardly a field that is not strongly influenced by the ancient Greeks even after twenty-three centuries. So much of what we attribute to other times, places and people began in Greece some centuries before Christ: the Hedonistic calculus and the pleasure principle; the Protestant Ethic expressed in Hesiod's *Works and Days;* the war of everyone against everyone in Lucretius; the escape from freedom in Cynicism and cults; the social contract in epicureanism; intrinsic and extrinsic motivation of free or coerced choices; educational systems recognizing nature, learning and practice; government systems balancing individual and collective interests; judicial systems sorting out what should be equal and what proportionate; rationalism and empiricism. Above all, the search for the good life and ways to attain it is particularly of Greek origin. And the good life was one in which ideals such as wisdom, virtue, and leisure were pursued.

Greek words permeate our English language: grammar; rhetoric; dialogue; logic; pedagogy. Like them we have the gymnasium and stadium, lyceum and academy. A symposium, to us, is a gathering of learned people to share ideas. To them, it was also a drinking party. The Greek *schole* became not only school but also *skole,* a drinking song. Ancient philosophers were full of life.

REFERENCES

de Grazia, Sebastian. 1962. *Of Time, Work and Leisure.* New York: The Twentieth Century Fund.

Durant, Will. 1943. *The Life of Greece, The Story of Civilization, Part II.* New York: Simon and Schuster.

Fuller, B. A. 1923. *History of Greek Philosophy.* New York: Henry Holt and Company.

Gilles, John (Tr.). 1886. *Aristotle's Ethics.* London: Routledge.

Jaeger, Werner. 1939. *Archaic Greece—The Mind of Athens: Paideia—The Ideals of Greek Culture, Volume I.* New York: Oxford University Press.

Jaeger, Werner. 1943. *In Search of the Divine Center: Paideia—The Ideals of Greek Culture, Volume II.* New York: Oxford University Press.

Russell, Bertrand. 1946. *A History of Western Philosophy.* London: George, Allen and Unwin.

Stocks, J. L. 1936. "Leisure." *Classical Quarterly, xxx:* 3,4. (July-October).

Wilbur, James and Allen, Harold (Eds.). 1979. *The Worlds of the Early Greek Philosophers.* Buffalo: Prometheus Books.

archy s mission

well boss i am
going to quit living
a life of leisure
i have been an idler
and a waster and a
mere poet too long
my conscience has waked up
wish yours would do the same
i am going to have
a moral purpose in my life
hereafter and a cause
i am going to reclaim
cockroaches and teach them
proper ways of living
i am going to see if i cannot
reform insects in general
i have constituted
myself a missionary
extraordinary
and minister
plenipotentiary
and entomological
to bring idealism to
the little struggling brothers
the conditions in the insect
world today would shock
american reformers
if they knew about them
the lives they lead
are scarcely fit to print
i cannot go into
details but the contented
laxness in which i find
them is frightful
a family newspaper is no place
for these revelations
but i am trying to have
printed in paris

for limited circulation
amongst truly earnest
souls a volume which will
be entitled
the truth about the insects
i assure you there is nothing
even in the old testament
as terrible
i shall be the cotton mather
of the boll weevil
archy

(Don Marquis, 1966: 74-75)

III. WORK—DO NOT DESPAIR

Christianity sunk its roots not so much in Athens as in Rome. The Athenians, it seems, were more intellectually skeptical and curious than complacent, and more likely to find pleasure compatible with morality than were the Romans. Stoicism, as much a religion as a philosophy, dominated Rome in the centuries just before and just after the time of Jesus. Zeno, the founder of Stoicism, prepared the way for Christianity by preaching of one God who resides within us. Thus, there is a brotherhood of man irrespective of nationality or socioeconomic class. That readily converts to the fellowship of Christianity but also to the Roman idea of a single empire. The stoic acceptance of good and bad fortune is conducive to accepting God's will as well as the good and evil cohabiting in Rome. Seneca thought Rome a supreme achievement, but the satirist Juvenal found it a disaster (Hamilton, 1957: 138). Different philosophies—different perceptions.

ROME—A PRELUDE

The Romans faced the practical problem of overseeing an empire; a more difficult task than managing a city-state. Wars, taxes, barbarians and other perils made Christianity attractive, with its sacred rather than secular laws, and the promise of Heaven in the hereafter. Further, the empire's need for order, given such an enormous enterprise, took precedence over the individual's need for freedom. Besides, man's inclination toward evil had to be held in check.

To the Athenians, a gentleman could be left free and trusted not to get too obnoxious to others over his wine. The Romans thought he could not be, but that he could and should be kept in order. The Athenians would argue for freedom because the good life was in conformity with man's innermost desires. Discipline and careful regulation were required, the Romans would argue, because the good life must be imposed upon human nature that desired evil (p. 107).

Throughout this period, the Romans agreed with the Athenians, at least in this respect, they did not think much of work. The earliest Greek poets, Homer and Hesiod, found no inherent value in work. Homer thought the Gods were displeased with man and condemned him to toil. Hesiod recognized the necessity for farmers to toil in the fields to extract from it their escape from hunger and subjection to others. Other than that, work was a curse: the Greek word for work, *ponos,* meant sorrow.

The philosophers agreed with the poets. The only solution, as most clearly expressed by Plato and Aristotle, was to have the vast majority, the slaves, provide the necessities and material goods for all so that a minority, the citizens, could engage in the arts and sciences, politics and government, philosophy and leisure. The Romans took a more moderate stance, but not much. Agriculture was acceptable; business, too, but mainly because it could lead to an early and honorable retirement, preferably in a peaceful rural environment.

As to wealth, the attitude was characteristically stoic. Wealth did not really matter. One could be happy and virtuous with or without money. Having some made it possible to exercise the virtue of helping others and supporting civic undertakings. Beyond that, money had no value.

CHRISTIANITY, WORK AND WEALTH

The teaching of Jesus was similar. He thought wealth and the work required to obtain it were problems but not evils of themselves. The problem was that work and wealth were distractions from the important matter of seeking and serving God. Worldly goods and efforts to obtain them resulted in cares and woes and the peril of squandering the opportunity to reach the kingdom of heaven. If you put your faith in the Lord, the necessities of every day life would be provided.

Yet to the early Christians, physical work was not separated from mental or spiritual work. Was not Jesus a craftsman, a carpenter? And Paul, in his missionary work, was quite clear; if you want to eat, then you must work. "From the sweat of thy brow. . . ," he insisted. As with Hesiod, this would at least free you from dependence on others. But in addition, this is the model Christians should follow. Still, in itself, money had no value. If anything, wealth indicated lack of Christian faith and service; it was clearly not the route to a favorable view in God's eyes.

At the present time, our view is quite different. The comedian Woody Allen pleaded for God to give him some sign of salvation, suggesting a large deposit in Allen's name in a Swiss bank account. Clearly, religious philosophy had done an about face. In this chapter, we will trace some of our heritage of religious doctrine, views of the nature of man, and how work and material wealth came to be signs of God's favor. Following chapters will review other influences leading in the same direction. By the time North America was settled, idle hands had become the Devil's workshop. The leisure ideal died of neglect and was buried with the sages of ancient Greece.

St. Augustine's Influence

The first of the monasteries in the western world was that founded by St. Augustine in North Africa. A century earlier, the Egyptians had founded monasteries and even earlier monks had taken to the desert, living as hermits rather than in communal monastic orders. Both in isolation and in communes, monks sought to dissociate themselves from worldly affairs so as to concentrate upon the divine and the spiritual life. Over the centuries, the association or dissociation of religion and everyday life would ebb and flow. The monasteries represented an early sign of lives segmented into discrete parts.

The early monks are perhaps the best examples of religious ascetics. As hermits and members of monastic orders, they practiced self-denial, sometimes carried to the extreme of emasculation, as a way of purification. In somewhat milder forms, the earliest settlers of North America practiced asceticism in an everyday life inseparable from religious life. Had they not, the rigors of settling a new continent might have been too much for them, with settlement delayed to a later time. To this day, asceticism and puritanism convey much the same meaning: the former for one's self, the latter for everybody.

As is clear from St. Augustine's *Confessions,* one of his contributions to classic literature, his conversion to Christianity was a difficult one. He was much preoccupied with his sins as a youth; severe in self-criticism for an act of petty theft. And he enjoyed sex. As a youth he had prayed to God, "Give me chastity and continency, only not yet." The idea of original sin was not original with him; several predecessors had spoken of it. But it was a central part of his doctrine. In addition, St. Augustine preached the doctrine of predestination; salvation or damnation according to God's will. Salvation was the proof of God's mercy; damnation the proof of God's justice. Despite whatever acts of faith, piety, sacrifice or good works, man cannot influence God's predetermination of his destination. Over 1,000 years later, the protest of Martin Luther and John Calvin led to a different interpretation of the path to salvation, and thus a new ethic—the Protestant (work) ethic.

St. Augustine's second contribution to classic literature, *The City of God,* was written to assure Christians that the sack of Rome was due not to its adoption of Christianity but to its unending corruption and incessant sinning, a simplistic view but one still espoused by some moralists. *The City of God* was the community of Christians, or perhaps the community of the church as distinct from and obviously superior to the secular, temporal community of man, especially Rome. For centuries, popes, cardinals, bishops and priests used that argument to support their claim that emperors and kings should be subservient to the church and pope. So St. Augustine planted the seeds of medieval thought and also the eventual protest within the church, backed by secular authority, which became, eleven centuries later, the Reformation. Meanwhile, work was being clothed in new meanings and values.

St. Benedict's Rules

At Monte Cassino, the first of many Benedictine monasteries that were to spread throughout Europe, the monks did not practice the severe, self-punishing forms of asceticism. St. Benedict regarded such mortification as too egotistical. The Benedictine monks had plenty of food and wine and sleep. They did, however, take vows of poverty and chastity, humility, obedience, and silence. They owned no property whatever. Exclusion from the outside world was sought and achieved, with the exception of being gracious hosts to visitors. The poor were especially well-treated; monks engaged in charitable work not for itself but as a way of becoming more like Christ and following his example.

In addition, all the monks were to engage in physical labor. According to the seasons and the work required to make the monastery self-sufficient, monks would typically spend four to six hours a day in the fields, kitchen or workshop. The early church fathers and the apostles had set the example. Monks were never idle, in fact, idleness was considered an enemy of the soul.

St. Augustine and others had suggested that. The Benedictines put everyone to work, and lived by the labor of their own willing hands. It was St. Benedict who said, "Work, do not despair."

This became the model of monasticism throughout Europe, a model that is followed even today. The monastic influence during that period in European history was far greater than we might think. There were many thousands of monasteries scattered throughout Europe; Lewis Mumford estimated as many as 40,000 under Benedictine rule (1963: 60). So, in addition to the dissociation of religion from everyday life, the monastic order became part of our heritage in other important respects.

In monasteries, human activity came to be governed by a machine which produces time. Few machines have done so much for us—and to us— as has the clock. Nothing pervades our lives more thoroughly than the measurement of time; natural rhythms are converted to mechanically dispensed units of seconds and minutes. Days and lives become divided into increasingly precise units and human activity becomes synchronized not by song but by an endless stream of tics and tocs. Our urban, industrial society can function without steam engines, but not without synchronized watches. Sometimes we protest against the tyranny of the clock. Rousseau was one of the first to throw away his "watch" (what an interesting term for a "time piece"). But we also protest if the mail and newspaper are not delivered on time. "Regular as a clock" has become a virtue of man, or at least of servants, but that includes just about all of us, with time our master.

In addition, one cannot overestimate the importance of the monasteries in the preservation of classic works and even of study, teaching and learning. Though limited by religious doctrine and geared primarily to the education of priests, much of our heritage would otherwise have been lost. For 1,000 years, monks gathered, copied and preserved our intellectual heritage. Popes and emperors, most notably Charlemagne, were anxious to assure the preservation and spread of knowledge in monastery, cathedral and palace schools.

Over time, adherence to St. Benedict's rules weakened, and thus also the discipline of monastic order. In consequence, periodic efforts at reform and the establishment of new monasteries and orders, according to original Benedictine practices, dotted the centuries and the countryside. Especially noteworthy was the founding, at the beginning of the 13th century, of the Dominicans and the Franciscans, the black friars and grey friars, respectively. These orders differed from others in that they did not retreat to monasteries but lived, worked and preached among the people. They lived by donations and by begging, thus being known as the mendicant orders and friars. But both orders lost their discipline and commitment to poverty and to service, and since they chose life among the people, they commonly served as inquisitors during the period of the papal inquisition. The inquisition was the manifestation of a terrifying religious intolerance, ending with heretics ruthlessly pursued and put to death.

But the Dominicans and Franciscans also included, and in fact helped educate, some of the best minds of the centuries which closed the Middle Ages and led to the Renaissance and Reformation. Some of the best known names in philosophy and theology were Dominicans like Albertus Magnus and St. Thomas Aquinas who taught at Paris, and Franciscans like St. Bonaventure and John Duns Scotus who also taught at Paris, and William of Occam and Francis Bacon who taught at Oxford.

Before leaving the centuries known variously as the Dark Ages, Middle Ages, the age of faith, or medieval period, space allows but a few brief additional comments. For several centuries, the encompassing mood was one of pessimism, doom and gloom. Life, to borrow Hobbes's phrase, was "solitary, poor, nasty, brutish, and short." It was widely believed that mankind was being punished for its sins and sinners, which was nearly everyone, had better repent because the end was near. There was little hope for a better life in this world, and there was little hope of a better life in the hereafter. It was not so much an age of faith as an age of resignation.

Even chivalry, if that can be called a bright spot, while it remains an ideal of courtesy, must be understood not only as legend and romance (which means fictitious and wonderful tale) but as warriors righteously defending the fief and the Christian faith. Chivalry really means "mounted soldier:" the crusades were religious wars. Pomp, ceremony, and knights in shining armor live in our imaginations still. Better that, perhaps, than the reality of centuries of slaughter.

Scholasticism

For a period of several hundred years, with one or two exceptions, there was very little philosophy. Not until two Arabic scholars, Avicenna in the 11th century and Averroes in the 12th, resurrected and translated several Greek writings, did scholarship begin to break out of the constraints of religious, particularly Augustinian, doctrine. The translations of the work of several Greek scientists and philosophers contributed to intellectual ferment. Several others, including Franciscan and Dominican scholars, broke with traditional theology, including the Dominican Roger Bacon, the forerunner of empiricism and modern science. Bacon was active during the 1200s, sharing several decades with St. Thomas Aquinas.

St. Thomas is recognized as the best spokesman of what is known as scholasticism or scholastic philosophy. Remember that schools were attached to monasteries and cathedrals. As a result, what was referred to as philosophy was inseparably mixed with theology. Scholastic philosophy, then, as best exemplified by St. Thomas's multivolume *Summa Theologica*, was an attempt through logic and reason to reconcile Christian doctrine with the philosophies of Aristotle and others, including those who had rejected parts of traditional theology. Finally, however, St. Thomas took the scriptures as unassailable truths so reason was governed by faith. He used logic to demonstrate and substantiate the scriptures. For these and other reasons, St. Thomas supported the inquisition, believing heretics and heresies as serious dangers to the established order. But his defense of the inquisition was too late and of too little avail. Knowledge could no longer be circumscribed in monastery and cathedral schools.

When the university began is uncertain, though most date it to the later part of the 1100s. Some place it a bit earlier in the century, at the time that Abelard, a man interested in logic and the theory of knowledge, established his own school, though still within the cloisters of Notre Dame. But he fell out of favor with the church and was removed to a monastery because of his insistence that reason rather than faith should be the arbiter of truth.

ORIGINS OF THE MODERN UNIVERSITY

During the later part of the 12th century, schools at Bologna, Solerno, and Toledo were active. But Paris, at which the traditional liberal arts were emphasized, is usually regarded as the birthplace of the modern university. A number of schools sprung up along the banks of the Seine. The "Latin Quarter" is so named because of the schools established there. Latin was the language of instruction and students, drawn from throughout Europe and from a variety of language groups, conversed in Latin. One of the streets in the area, translated into English, is the "street of straw," since for many students that was all the bedding—and furniture—they had (Coulton, 1961: 33). Many, quite literally, had to sing for their supper. Among the earliest written work of students, along with the words to bawdy and irreverent songs, were letters to parents requesting money.

Paris received recognition first from secular authority and then the church. Its charter was for a "Universitas Societas Magistrorum et Scholarium"—a universal society of masters and scholars. The meaning of "universities," as also of "collegium," was really a corporation or guild. Guild is perhaps the closest parallel, and universities grew and prospered much as did other guilds throughout this and later periods, and as did unions in the modern period. The best definition of the university, even today, is that it is a community of masters and scholars (Haskins, 1957).

As with guilds, undergraduates were apprentices, graduate students were student-masters, and those who completed their studies became masters. Then, as now, they were licensed to teach. Students, organized as a guild, had the power, very much like that of collective bargaining in modern unions, to negotiate with their teachers and their landlords: the teachers were placed under bonds to teach certain subjects on a certain schedule; negotiations were made with landlords for the rental of lodging and lecture halls. "Town and gown" battles were more frequent and violent than now. Coulton suggested that more blood may have been spilled on the streets around Oxford University than in any other place (1961: 21).

Colleges within universities began as residences for university students. Gradually they grew and expanded into units which hired their own teachers and provided their own courses of instruction. Then, as now, there were rivalries between colleges and between universities. Sometimes they were friendly. Since the very beginning, people at Oxford said that the worst fate that could befall an Oxford student would be to have to complete his studies at Cambridge. Several centuries later, when President John F. Kennedy was presented with an honorary doctorate by Yale University, he remarked that he had "the best of two worlds: a Harvard education and a Yale degree."

We dwell on this topic for a number of reasons. Most university students, and even professors, know precious little of the rich history and tradition of universities. Too many mistake it for buildings and classrooms, libraries and laboratories and a thousand extracurricular activities. Those are important. But the university is first and foremost a community comprised of masters and scholars, and should be so regarded. Secondly, the university we know today is organized and conducted in essentially the same way, and with the same purposes, as it was 800 years ago. Of contemporary institutions, it is second only to the Catholic Church in longevity, and so far it has not been subjected to the kind of defection the church experienced with the Protestant Reformation.

More importantly, however, is the link between learning and the leisure ideal held out by the early Greek philosophers. Recall that the Greek word for "leisure" becomes "school" in English. Recall, too, that in the phrase "liberal arts," the word "liberal" refers to liberation from ignorance and from the errors for which we may have a penchant but from which we may also learn. Knowledge has always been related to freedom, and freedom has always been related to leisure. If leisure involves freedom to choose, then knowledge is required to choose wisely. Over the portals of universities everywhere are the words, "You shall know the truth, and it shall set you free."

THE RENAISSANCE

The word is French and best understood by hyphenating: re-naissance means re-birth. It is an appropriate term given the gloom and doom and resignation of the earlier centuries. The most glorious result of this re-birth was seen in the arts; literature, sculpture, architecture and especially painting, beginning in Italy and spreading northward throughout Europe during the 15th and 16th centuries.

The Renaissance was the result of so much turmoil and so many converging forces that, since volumes are required to recount them, paragraphs will have to suffice. The spread of knowledge and the emergence of the university was of particular importance as it broke through the bondage of religious dogma. Europe was flooded with heresies and heretical sects. The church was corrupt and immoral; political infighting even resulted in the "papal schism," a period during which there were two popes, and for a brief time, even three. The efforts of the church to reign supreme over the secular authority of kings, queens and emperors were increasingly resisted and thwarted, and the secular authorities were often supported by a growing middle-class and a new aristocracy of wealth created by an economy shifting from an agriculturally based feudal system to commerce and trade. Capitalism had taken firm root, particularly in southern Europe, by the 1200s. To these major forces could be added the plagues, particularly in the 1300s, the fall of Constantinople and the eastern empire in 1453, and so much more.

What a testimony to human resilience and spirit was the Renaissance and its peak in the arts. Freed from the oppression of ignorance and superstition and with church, state, and private wealth limiting each other's powers, the "Renaissance man" was born. Artistic creativity and expression flourished, and with the unprecedented wealth, patrons of the arts were sufficiently numerous to turn palaces, churches and cities into galleries. Leonardo da Vinci and Michaelangelo were part of this period; art historians could name 100 more artists of near equal merit.

So much genius and talent in an area originally limited to a few cities in northern Italy can only be explained by conditions of that time and place. Freedom in a variety of forms, including the sponsorship of wealthy patrons, was surely the key. Spontaneity, exuberance, independence, passion, sensuousness and a number of related descriptors help characterize the age.

But so do expedience, vanity, jealousy and immorality. Discipline and order had broken down. Nicolo Machiavelli was also a product of that period. *The Prince* was written just as the Italian Renaissance was on the verge of collapse. It uncovered the dark side of power politics; the ends, without ties to values and morals, justified the means, and the ends were acquiring power and holding on to it. Might, to Machiavellians, makes right. Expedience was all. So the Renaissance became perhaps our clearest example, though history provides numerous others, of the necessity of a balance between freedom and order, individual interests and social and political stability, rights and obligations, power and responsibility. Leisure and license—both terms stem from the Latin *licere* which means "to be permitted." Freedom is a synonym. But license is also defined as the abuse of freedom, as in licentious.

THE REFORMATION AND THE PROTESTANT ETHIC

There had been many attempts to reform the church from within. None succeeded. In Germany, Martin Luther was becoming increasingly incensed with the corruption, and particularly the "harlotry" of the church in Rome.

All of the conditions which gave birth and sustenance to the Renaissance led to the Reformation as well, along with some additional ones. Trade and commerce continued to expand: particularly significant were the voyages of Columbus and Vasco da Gamma starting at the end of the 1400s. Even more important was the advent of printing in Europe. Paper had been available for some time, but printing in quantity awaited Gutenberg's press. In particular, the Bible had been translated into a number of languages and, with the invention of the printing press, became available to people throughout Europe without requiring knowledge of Latin and without requiring interpretation by popes and parish priests. People could confront the scriptures directly, as so many reformers had wished. Humanism, which led to the Renaissance and was further promoted by it, was also an important factor. Originally, humanism referred mainly to the study of the classic periods and literature; it gradually came to mean a human centered outlook on life. It focused on individual well-being in this life rather than salvation or damnation in the next.

Luther's Protest

The most immediate antecedent of Luther's protest (thus the word Protest-ant) was the church's efforts to raise money through various practices which Luther found questionable, if not blatantly corrupt. For a fee, marriages could be confirmed and divorces purchased. One could also buy positions as church officials, and that was a lucrative business both for the church and the office holder as millions of dollars were involved. The particular practice which Luther challenged on the eve of All Saints' Day (Halloween) in 1517 was the sale of indulgences. Indulgences were a monetary form of penance. Sinners, who since St. Augustine includes all of us, could wipe the slate clean with sufficient payment. One could even lighten the sentence of deceased friends and relatives in purgatory. Luther's 95 theses, which he wished to publicly debate with the pope's representatives, challenged the authority of the pope and church to sell indulgences. It was not his intent to break with the church.

Luther was a pious man, passionate, independent, and very popular. Well-organized in thought and clear in speech, he had a devoted following and could appeal to what people intuitively knew to be right and just. Like Epicurus nearly 2,000 years before him, Luther sought to free people from fear of a vengeful God or, perhaps more correctly, a vengeful church and pope. He had the support of secular authorities who thought even less of the pope and the sale of indulgences than did Luther. He was, then, strong enough to challenge the church. He died in 1546 of natural causes.

In 1520, he wrote the three great tracts of the Reformation: *The Liberty of a Christian Man*; *The Babylonian*; *Captivity of the Church*; and *The Christian Nobility of the German Nation*. The titles give us the flavor; the later tract was a call for Germany to unite against the church in Rome (Lindsay, 1906: 243).

With printing and devoted followers, these works were disseminated within days: printers could not keep up with the demand. The pope ordered the burning of Luther's works and Luther ordered the burning of the pope's edicts. Eventually, the pope excommunicated Luther and Luther excommunicated the pope. That had happened with others before, but not with so much flair—or such widespread publicity. The power of the press had been established.

Luther's theology was formed by scholasticism, much of which he rejected. Although a monk, he rejected monasticism, too, along with religious days, crusades and other practices because they were a waste of time and produced idleness, which was a sin. From Luther we also get one of the clearest statements of the idea of the "calling;" that is, performing dutifully that work which God calls you to do. In practical, secular terms, this meant keeping your place. But there was a consolation for Luther's idea of the calling. All callings were equally worthwhile in God's eyes; the maid in the kitchen as well as the priest in the pulpit.

In most respects Luther followed the lead of St. Augustine. Man was incapable of anything but sin. Salvation was possible by faith alone, but that was uncertain because of the doctrine of predestination by which God alone determined who were to be the few elect and the many damned. Divine grace was a gratuitous gift from God.

Capitalism After Calvin

Luther fostered the Protestant Reformation; Calvin fostered the Protestant Ethic. Capitalism, as Tawney (1926) and others argue, was well-entrenched in the centuries which preceded the era of Luther and Calvin. Weber (1958) in his classic work, addressed the relation between *The Protestant Ethic and the Spirit of Capitalism*. The Protestant Ethic did not create the spirit of capitalism; the spirit came before the ethic. But the ethic, as the word implies, made the spirit morally legitimate by aligning it with divine will and grace. That was a momentous change.

Until this point, money and material goods beyond what was required for a modestly adequate but not uncomfortable life were shunned by all religious and ethical systems. Agriculture was always acceptable, as was work with the back and hands. Later, the trades and crafts were accepted as they produced goods which were useful. Later still, merchandising and commercial trade became acceptable, but Luther, Calvin, and other reformers argued that only a fair price could be charged and a modest profit earned. In More's *Utopia,* everyone had to work, as St. Paul had argued, but no one need work more than six hours a day. That was enough to provide for everyone's needs and modest comforts. In another utopian work, Campanella's *City of the Sun,* four hours of daily work were all that was required. The use of capital, lending and borrowing money, was unacceptable, despite the large and powerful bankers of which many were Luther's German, and Calvin's Swiss, contemporaries.

One further note must be added to religious attitudes toward work. Since the early monastic period, hard, back-breaking, strenuous, physical work was useful in this respect: since man was basically evil and work hard and strenuous, working was a way of performing penance; recognizing and admitting sinfulness and trying to make amends. Even in a more secular sense, work was and sometimes still is thought of as useful and necessary discipline.

Rather than examining Weber's analysis of the relation between Protestantism and capitalism, we will look briefly at Calvin's arguments. The inevitability of sinning, salvation by faith alone, and predestination continue intact with Calvin. In fact Calvin's theology was often more harsh than St. Augustine's. As an example:

> Man sins willingly; by eager inclination of the heart; not by forced compulsion; by the prompting of his own lust; not by compulsion from without. Yet so depraved is his nature that he can be moved or impelled only to evil: man is subjected to the necessity of sinning. (Calvin, 1960: 295-96)

With sin inevitable, with salvation by faith alone and election by God's grace alone, there seemed no way out. But Calvin identified one. He cited the scriptures (1 Cor., 12: 5,6), "There are different kinds of service, but the same Lord. There are different kinds of working, but the same God works all of them in all men." He also cited St. Augustine. "See in me thy work, not mine" (1960: 786). That is the key. If you have the will to do good work, the energy to accomplish it, and you prosper because of it, that is given to you by God, Calvin argued:

> We must always remember that God 'accepts' believers by reason of works only because he is their source and graciously by way of adding to his liberality, designs also to show 'acceptance' toward the good works that he has himself bestowed. For whence come their works, save that the Lord, having chosen them as vessels unto honor is pleased to adorn them with true purity. (1960: 80)

> Those whom the Lord has destined by his mercy for the inheritance of eternal life he leads into possession of it, according to his ordinary dispensation, by means of good works. (1960: 787)

> Good works are pleasing to God and not unfruitful to their doers. But they receive by way of reward the most ample benefits of God, not because they so deserve but because God's kindness has of itself set this value upon them. (1960: 791)

To put it simply, prosperity was a sign of God's grace, and evidence of eventual salvation in the hereafter; success in this life and the next.

Like the many theologians before him, Calvin was concerned about the pursuit of wealth because of the likely distraction from the spiritual life. But neither he nor Martin Luther agreed with or practiced ascetic self-denial. One should not be self-indulgent but it was not wrong to use and enjoy the good things which God had provided. Similarly, Calvin accepted the notion of one's calling as "minding one's own business," that is, keeping to one's own place, again with the consolation of all work being equal in God's eyes. But Calvin was more theologian than social psychologist. Suppose one's own business was a failure? Perhaps one failed from being in the wrong calling. The right calling must be the one at which one was most successful, and that must be the one most "pleasing to God and not unfruitful to the doers." Unwillingness to work or lack of success in whatever calling were likely signs of damnation. Hard work, especially fruitful hard work, may not assure salvation, but there is surely some sign of hope. That notion was certain to be comforting to the emerging middle-class and the new aristocracy of wealth. Calvin, it is said, created the God fearing businessman. Perhaps social psychology cannot be divorced from theology.

A Secular Protestant Ethic

The Protestant Ethic has evolved to a secular form which is related more to the evolution of economic thought than to theology although it owes its birth to the Protestant theology of the reformation period. There is an assumption underlying both Calvin's notion of success in a calling and Adam Smith's notion of "an invisible hand," about which more is said in Chapter V. The assumption is that your calling, that is the work which God calls you to perform, benefits your fellow man and contributes to the welfare of your community. The scriptures state (1 Cor., 12: 6), "There are different kinds of working, but the same God works all of them in all men." They also state (1 Cor., 12: 7), "Now to each one the manifestation of the spirit is given for the common good." The Apostle Paul, in writing Corinthians during the first century A.D. or Calvin referring to it during the 16th century, could not have anticipated the industrialization or urbanization, or the secular philosophy of capitalism which transformed the world. We no longer see our work as a calling and the same God may not be working all things in all men. So the assumption of serving the common good may be too generous for modern man. The Protestant ethic is not yet dead. It has simply left its home in 16th-century Protestant theology to take up residence in 19th-century capitalism and "Social Darwinism." Ideas, in parental form, are sometimes devoured by their offspring.

OUR PURITAN ANCESTRY

The spread of Protestantism in central and southern Europe was partly checked by a reform movement within the Catholic church. The Jesuit order, founded by Ignatius Loyola, was instrumental in that and at a later time the Jesuits were instrumental in settling Canada and in exploring the interior of the North American continent. But in England, Protestantism was well established by the time of Queen Elizabeth's coronation and the period in England known as the Elizabethan Age. England had long since rejected the authority of the papacy in Rome and the church of England, the Anglican church, was formally established at the beginning of Elizabeth's reign.

Elizabeth and her successors sought a compromise between otherwise warring religious groups. The Puritans were dissidents who sought to purify the church along lines suggested by Luther and Calvin. The term Puritan describes that interest but was often used in a derisive way to describe the moral pretensions of the dissidents. That is the sense that we have in referring to puritanical views and attitudes.

Defectors—Church and Crown

Here, then, are two of the principal reasons for the defection of Puritans from the church and from England. They objected to a church hierarchy including bishops and priests and to religious services they found too ceremonial and lavishly ornate. Secondly, they wished to purify Elizabethan customs and morals which they considered vain, wanton, and wasteful in ostentatious display. There was, in part, also an element of class rivalry. The Puritans were drawn from the poor and middle classes and class consciousness was present in their protest against the pleasures enjoyed by the wealthy. The Puritan mind, Dulles noted:

> ... resented the amusements of the more wealthy, leisured classes, making a moral issue of their discontent. These two influences, spiritual reform and economic envy, can never be disentangled. (1965: 9)

By the early 1600s, these Protestant dissidents also became entangled in the political struggle between parliament and the king. Here again were elements of class rivalry as well as religious rivalry. That struggle led eventually to civil war, the beheading of a king, Cromwell's government, and the restoration of royalty to the throne.

Meanwhile, a wave of migration, particularly between 1630 and 1640, ensured the vitality of settlement in North America. Although Puritans were a minority, the majority not being church members, church membership was a requirement for participation in the government of the settlements until about 1700. By that time, religious influence had begun to decline and moralizing replaced the earlier piety.

The Two Sides of Puritanism

The piety, strict morality, and suspicion of pleasure which character-ized the Puritans are no longer considered virtues by most of us, though surely not all. Yet we may be too harsh on our Puritan ancestors, especially those of the early decades of settlement. They were not, for example, opposed to recreation but they were opposed to idleness and to wasting time. The emphasis was clearly on work and recreation was seen mainly as functioning to rest from and prepare for work. Had their attitude toward work been different, they may not have survived. But they had toys, dolls, games and sports, though opposing those activities which were often accompanied by gambling. They were not opposed to drinking; they drank a great deal of beer and cider and some spirits as well. They opposed drunkenness, just as we do. Their attitudes were very practical, if not, at least for several decades, essen-tial. They were familiar with drunks and debtors languishing and deteriorat-ing in London's prisons.

They were opposed to the theater as a waste of time. Too, they opposed it as an upper-class privilege, not to mention that they had often been ridiculed by England's actors and playwrights. They were opposed to art as merely sensuous display, a reaction to both an ostentatious church and Elizabethan court. They opposed instrumental music, including church accompaniment, for these reasons as well. They certainly did not oppose singing. They were not opposed to art or beauty. Simple, functional beauty and art they produced and appreciated as being closest to God's design. They had neither the time nor wealth for art in other forms.

They surpassed us in cooperative activities which were both produc-tive and festive. They were literate and well-schooled, especially in church doctrine but also in science, politics and other subjects. They were prolific readers and writers and the art of conversation was among them widespread and secure. They founded Harvard University (1636) and it did not take them long to do so.

Their opposition to premarital and promiscuous sex, and thus activities such as "mixt" dancing which might somehow lead to it, has become legendary. Doubtless their suspicion of pleasure was part of that. Perhaps even today there are some for whom sex should produce progeny but not pleasure. But again, there was a very practical side to their attitudes towards sex. To them, the family was almost as sacred as the scriptures and they would tolerate nothing that would disrupt it. In London, lawyers, landlords, magistrates and prostitutes conspired to capitalize on bad marriages (Levin, 1974: 150). Too, the Puritans were concerned to establish responsibility for and care of children, and they wished to protect young men from wrongful attribution of parentage, as well as young women from unwelcome solicitation. There is a practical side to sexual morality.

By no stretch of the imagination could Puritans be thought of as capitalists. In fact they thought it an abomination to capitalize on another person's needs by charging an unjust price. They regulated wages and had consummatory laws governing the type and amount of goods that could be consumed. Competitive striving to exceed others in material wealth was unknown to them. On the other hand, their attitude toward those who could not provide adequately for themselves was that they should master the practical virtues related to work. Those secular, material virtues, which to the Puritans were also spiritually rewarding, remain part of our heritage: thrift, frugality, diligence, self-reliance, industry, perseverance, sobriety, punctuality, and more. Puritans placed a high value on time. That these virtues were conducive to the demands of industrial capitalism is obvious. But they had as little to do with competitive materialism as they did laissez-faire attitudes toward government regulation of economic-activity.

To the Puritans, we owe much of our sense of human and personal responsibility. Their belief in that was almost unqualified. Although they believed in predestination, they were not fatalists. Rather, they believed that both their spiritual and material welfare were dependent on their own efforts. They were, in the main, indifferent to worldly wealth and pleasure, particularly the sensate as opposed to intellectual and spiritual pleasures. Perhaps they carried that sense of responsibility too far, but there seems less danger in that than in carrying it not far enough. And because of that sense of responsibility, they understood history as a series of human choices, for good or for evil. Given our comparatively abundant time and wealth, and the centrality to leisure of the freedom of choice, our own sense of responsibility is of paramount importance.

But one should not get caught up in the puritanical habit of strenuous self-analysis and constant rummaging about one's conscience. We should not ignore it, surely, but there seems to be enough neurosis, including pleasure neurosis, already extant in modern society. We should at least be careful to distinguish between moralizing to mask our envy and adhering to those virtues which in practical ways promote our own and other's welfare. H. L. Mencken once described a Puritan as someone hauntingly fearful that someone somewhere might be having a good time.

The voices of saviours, prophets and theologians, continue to echo over the centuries. Some still hear the voice of the Puritan theologian, Cotton Mather, invoking images of fire and damnation at the time of the Salem, Massachusetts, witch hunts of 1692. Perhaps, then, there are already enough reminders for all of us. Even the boll weevil, with "archy" (a fictional cockroach, free verse poet) playing the role of Cotton Mather, has been looked after.

REFERENCES

Calvin, John. 1960. *Institutes of the Christian Religion.* (Tr. Ford M. Battles). Library of the Christian Classics, Vol. XX and XXI (Ed. John McNeil). London: SCM Press.

Coulton, G. G. 1961. *Horizons of Thought: Medieval Panorama, Vol. II.* London: Fontana Library.

Dulles, Foster R. 1965. *A History of Recreation: America Learns to Play.* Englewood Cliffs, New Jersey: Prentice Hall.

Hamilton, Edith. 1957. *The Roman Way to Western Civilization.* New York: Mentor Books.

Haskins, Charles H. 1957. *The Rise of Universities.* Ithaca, New York: Cornell University Press.

Levin, David. 1974. "Essays to do Good for the Glory of God: Cotton Mather's Bonifacius." In Bercovitch, Sacvan, *The American Puritan Imagination.* New York: Cambridge University Press.

Lindsay, Thomas. 1906. *A History of the Reformation.* New York: Charles Scribner's Sons.

Marquis, Don. 1966. *archy's life of mehitabel.* New York: Dolphin Books.

Mumford, Lewis. 1963. "The Monastery and the Clock." In Lewis, Arthur O., Jr. (Ed.). *Of Men and Machines.* New York: E.P. Dutton and Company.

Saint Augustine. 1853. *Confessions: The Confessions of St. Augustine,* (Rev. and Tr. E.B. Pusey). Oxford: John Henry Parker.

Tawney, Robert. 1926. *Religion and the Rise of Capitalism.* New York: Harcourt Brace and Company.

Weber, Max. 1958. *The Protestant Ethic and the Spirit of Capitalism.* New York: Charles Scribner's Sons.

The seventeenth century had finally produced a scheme of scientific thought framed by mathematicians. The great characteristic of the mathematical mind is its capacity for dealing with abstractions; and for eliciting from them clear cut, demonstrative trains of reasoning, entirely satisfactory so long as it is those abstractions which you want to think about. The enormous success of the scientific abstractions, yielding on the one hand matter with its simple location in time and space, on the other hand mind, perceiving, suffering, reasoning, but not interfering, has foisted onto philosophy the task of accepting them as the most concrete rendering of fact.

Thereby, modern philosophy has been ruined. It has oscillated in a complex manner between three extremes. There are the dualists who accept matter and mind as on an equal basis, and the two varieties, those who put mind inside matter, and those who put matter inside mind. But this juggling of abstractions can never overcome the inherent confusion introduced by the ascription of misplaced concreteness to the scientific scheme of the seventeenth century.

(Alfred North Whitehead, 1926: 81-2)

IV. THE SCIENCE OF MAN

Man's struggle for freedom is one of the central themes of human history. During the 1,000 years or so from the birth of Christ to the rediscovery of ancient Greek science and philosophy, that struggle had progressed slowly. The pace increased dramatically during the next 500 years with the rise of the university, the Renaissance, beginning in northern Italy and spreading northward through Europe, and with the Protestant Reformation.

The constraining authority of religious dogma, the doctrines of an intolerant church and the subtle arguments of scholastic philosophy had been successfully challenged. The struggle for religious freedom was accompanied by the struggle for political freedom. Luther had challenged both the religious and political authority of the papacy in Rome and had championed German independence and nationalism. In England, a Church separate from the Roman Catholic Church was established and thousands of defectors, entangled in the struggle between Parliament and the King, broke from both the Church and the crown.

The world was not yet safe for ideas, however. There would still be witch hunts and heretics put to death. Censorship, still widely practiced in many nations, was practiced extensively in Europe, though there was more latitude than previously. In general, the spread of Protestantism in northern Europe made those countries somewhat more tolerant than such countries as France and Italy, where the counter-reformation led by Ignatius Loyola had checked the spread of Protestantism. But the struggle for both religious and political freedom had begun to produce some results.

THE BREAK FROM ROME AND RELIGION

One of the consequences of the religious and political turmoil of this era was that, for the western world at least, the center of individual, social and cultural development shifted from the Mediterranean region to northern and central Europe. The Mediterranean, as the name implies, was no longer, in these respects, the center of the earth, although it was and is the birthplace of western religion, philosophy and culture. Exploration, colonization, and the expansion of trade and commerce were led by Spain, Portugal, France, England and Holland and the industrial revolution struck first in England and then spread to the European continent and to North America.

Related to that shift was a shift in intellectual activity from one tied to the Catholic philosophy of St. Augustine and the scholastic philosophy of St. Thomas to one almost exclusively Protestant. In fact, even links to the Protestant theology of Luther and Calvin were weak and with the age of science, particularly the period from the mid-1500s to the early 1700s followed by the "enlightenment" period of philosophy, the religious influence on intellectual life was increasingly limited.

From its origins several centuries before Christ, philosophy had been inextricably tied to religion. The classic Greek philosophers were particularly concerned with systems of ethics in the governance of individual and collective life in the city-state. The Apostles and the early church fathers preached Christian philosophy, followed by Augustine and Thomas Aquinas and then the Protestant reformers. The interpenetration of philosophy and theology was about to be broken.

Since the Renaissance period, the full development of the individual had become the central historical and cultural imperative. For that development to be realized, individual freedom was necessary, especially the freedom of thought and expression. That freedom leads to creativity in every field. The artistic creativity of Renaissance Italy was an example, before the excesses of freedom led to collapse of the social order. But that intellectual freedom prepared the soil of Europe for the scientific revolution.

THE AGE OF SCIENCE

We have seen the ideas of modern science discussed by Roger Bacon prior to the Renaissance and the application of science in the inventiveness of

Leonardo da Vinci, the prototypic Renaissance man. But we usually think of the "scientific" revolution as beginning at a later date.

The Astronomers

Sometimes we speak of the Copernican revolution, which fixes the date at 1543, the year Copernicus died and the year in which his work on the orbits and revolutions of the planets was published. The idea that the Earth was not the center of the universe was certainly revolutionary, but Copernicus had no such intention. He was a Polish churchman and he dedicated his work to the Church. Perhaps for that reason his work was not condemned by the Church until after Galileo had elaborated upon the Copernican system. Perhaps Copernicus was politically astute in dedicating his work to the Church but more likely it was done with the piety and humility of a dedicated servant (Russell, 1946: 513).

While important discoveries were being made in a number of fields in the later 1500s and 1600s, the greatest names in science during that period explored astronomy and physics. Throughout the late 1500s, Tycho Brache carried out extensive, systematic observations of the positions of the planets. Kepler, Brache's assistant for many years, was able to formulate his laws based on the wealth of data so patiently accumulated. And though no great monetary wealth resulted, both Brache and Kepler reportedly earned some money as astrologers, as astrology was very popular in their time, perhaps as much so as in our own (Durant, 1961: 575-76). Science aside, superstitions were numerous enough to fill a large volume, evidenced by the fact that many thousands were yet to die in Europe and some in New England, before the witch-hunting ended.

To the galaxy of eminent scientists must be added that of Sir Issac Newton, who was born the year Galileo died. It was Newton who solved the riddle of gravitation and was celebrated in the oft quoted lines of Alexander Pope in his *Essay on Man:* "Nature and nature's laws lay hid in night, God said let Newton be, and all was light."

Empiricism and Rationalism

Along with the developments in physics, astronomy and many other fields was the development of science per se: the development of science as a way of knowing; the development of the philosophy and method of science. Francis Bacon, in exploring *The Wisdom of the Ancients,* turned not to

Socrates, Plato and Aristotle but to the pre-Socratic "natural" philosophers; to Thales who believed everything came from the sea; to Democritus who believed everything was made of atoms; to Pythagorus who believed everything could be explained by mathematic relations. In the *Novum Organum*, Bacon explained the "idols," his term for the causes of error in our thinking, and he appealed for the use of the inductive method; of knowing things in precise particulars from which we can then generalize. In the *New Atlantis* he described a utopian world based on and ruled by science.

Bacon's attitude toward the natural world was that it was God's endowment, just as the scriptures were God's word. He thought it foolish and arrogant to think we could understand that endowment—or the scriptures—without study. Unlike his predecessors, he believed nature could be commanded not by breaking her laws but obeying them, and he was the first person to use the phrase "knowledge is power" (Bronowski, 1978: 20).

Another early contributor to our notion and understanding of the philosophy and method of science was Rene Descartes. "Cartesian doubt" refers to his insistence that if we want to know anything we must start by doubt. If we start by certainty we end in doubt but if we start by doubt we will end with certainty. Descartes's *Discourse on Method* also explained the method of analysis; the method of reducing everything to its minute particulars and of grasping the particulars before proceeding.

Bacon is often cited as the father of empiricism. In science, empiricism refers to experimentation and controlled observation as the only valid basis for knowledge. We learn by using our senses to observe the physical or material world. Descartes, on the other hand, is regarded as the father of rationalism. Rationalism is based on the argument that knowledge can be ascertained by the power of reason. It holds that there are *a priori* grounds or concepts which we know prior to and independent of experience. While empiricists and rationalists have argued over the centuries (with empiricists getting the upper hand), science requires both reason and experience. But the central point is that both reject previous authority and faith as sources of knowledge. In addition, empiricism and rationalism are as much philosophies as ways of knowing. This scientific philosophy supplanted the earlier philosophies rooted in religious precepts.

Related Developments

Three other developments deserve brief mention. Descartes's *cogito ergo sum* (I think, therefore I am) led toward the subjective and idealistic rather than the objective and realistic base of science as Bacon and others would have it. But Descartes was also among many who advanced mathematics during this same period. Physics, astronomy and other sciences could not have made such strides had there not been equal strides in mathematics. Newton and Leibniz made important contributions, as did Pascal, Napier and others.

The latter part of the 1600s also included the beginning of statistics and "political arithmetik" by Sir William Petty and others. Increased trade and increasing population and thus work in demographics, currency exchanges and other types of probabilistic forecasting became increasingly scientific and quantitative.

A second essential development was the invention of increasingly accurate measuring devices. One measuring device, the calendar, was found to be "off" by 10 days, and the Julian calendar was adopted in 1582. The telescope, microscope, thermometer and barometer were all invented within a few decades starting in the late 1500s. The clock was dramatically improved, first with the pendulum and later with the balance wheel and spring. By the late 1700s clocks were accurate to within one minute every 600 days.

A third important development, although of a different nature, was the beginning of scientific organizations. The Royal Society of London for the Promotion of Natural Knowledge and the Academie Royale des Sciences based in Paris were both founded in the 1660s. Of particular interest was the London group's practice of publishing scientific papers, in part as a means of giving its secretary, Thomas Hooke, some remuneration. But the greater importance was that the results of work was made public, for the scrutiny and criticism of those interested in the matter. The standard of truth became manifestly public and an earmark of science since that time.

THE SCIENCE OF MAN

Along with the astronomers, mathematicians, and scientists in medicine, chemistry, and other fields, and along with Bacon and Descartes came scores of philosophers: Hobbes, Locke, Spinoza, Hume, Voltaire, Rousseau and Kant are a few of the better known among them. As was found among the early Greek philosophers, "natural" philosophy (which we would equate with scientific speculation and observation) developed a century or so before the emergence of philosophy centered on man. That pattern was repeated in Europe: the central question shifting from what we know to how we know, and to what we now think of as epistemology and psychology. Philosophy ("philosopher" and "scientist" were still used interchangeably), as David Hume described it, was to become an "empirical science of man," utilizing the methods of natural science and dispensing with its own methods which were to be exposed as shams and illusions (Berlin, 1956: 163).

Locke's Liberalism

John Locke's *Essay on Human Understanding,* was an example of the empirical science of man but our legacy from Locke stems mostly from his thinking about government and the philosophy of liberalism. Locke's predecessor, Thomas Hobbes, was concerned about the political chaos and breakdown of social order in Europe and had proposed a system of government in which the sovereign, once chosen, had unlimited power and reigned supreme. As with Hobbes, Locke believed that government should be based on a social contract but the people should be sovereign in case the government does not uphold its obligation under the contract to maintain the rights and security of its citizens. Locke clearly expressed the philosophy of liberalism which characterized thought in England and Holland during the late 1600s. That included religious toleration; the importance of commerce and industry; respect for property if produced by individual effort; a preference for the emerging middle class over the aristocracy; the right of people to choose their own government; suspicion of government and thus checks and balances; the idea that people are born equal, that social conditions create inequality, and thus placing great stress on education. In addition, liberalism was and is highly individualistic because of its stress on liberty from imposition by both church and state.

Locke's philosophy and approach to government clearly influenced the founding fathers of the United States and it is almost second nature to most Americans. That philosophy, along with the empiricism of Locke as well as Sir Isaac Newton, impressed Voltaire and he carried that spirit and attitude back to France. Locke has been criticized for the emphasis he placed on property and for his interest in limiting government power. These became supports for capitalism and laissez-faire government. But it should be remembered that, historically, all property had been held in very few hands and that the long arm and heavy hand of unchecked government had done little for the welfare of all but a few. Locke sought reform of these time-worn abuses.

More will be said in the following chapter about economic developments. For the moment, we will return to Hume's "empirical science of man." All of Hume's writings were condemned by the Church. That was not unusual. Much of the writing in science and philosophy challenged religious precepts and was condemned. Many works were published anonymously because of church censorship, and Holland was a haven for many philosophers seeking to escape persecution in their homelands. Hume had argued that neither reason nor experience could account for moral judgements, contrary to the theological philosophy of many centuries, nor could the existence of God be proven. But Hume also argued that the proof offered by science was also suspect and that one should be skeptical of the rationalism and empiricism of science as well. In particular, he argued that science could not establish causality; that the cause of anything could not be determined because one thing did not have to, necessarily, follow the other.

Kant's Critical Philosophy

This left both religion and science in disarray and Immanuel Kant tried to put them back together. As Durant observed, Kant attempted to "save religion from Voltaire and science from Hume" (1967: 531). Kant is generally regarded as one of the most important philosophers since Aristotle. He is also one of the most incomprehensible writers of a philosophy which had by this time become extremely abstract and rationalistic. But one aspect of Kant's thinking is of particular importance to the philosophy of leisure. Josef Pieper in *Leisure: The Basis of Culture* (1963) pointed in particular to the "critical philosophy" of Kant.

Kant, as did Hume, rejected the idea that the existence of God could be established by reason and logic. In fact, Kant argued that God could be deduced from our conscience and moral sense rather than the reverse. But that was not the source of Pieper's particular criticism. What Kant had argued is that experience was not the result of passive acceptance of impressions taken in by our senses. Rather, it was the product of the mind actively working on the impressions of our senses. Our senses take in mere raw data. Thus, our concepts are not a gift but an achievement: our knowledge is acquired, not given. The mind is not a passive recipient but an active agent with inherent modes and laws of operation which transform sense impressions into ideas and concepts. That is Kant's central thesis and it is that to which Pieper took issue.

Science as Avocation

Before turning to Pieper's philosophy of leisure, however, an additional comment should be made about this period of science and philosophy. First, while Bacon and the empiricists who followed him were practical men who believed that science could and would lead to improving man's lot, the discoveries of Galileo and Kepler or the mathematics of Pascal and Descartes were of no immediate practical use. Just as leisure is the mother of philosophy, it is also the mother of discovery and invention. Second, while many of the scientists and philosophers had "independent" means of support, others had vocations and their "work" in science and philosophy was actually their avocation; that is, their "free-time" pursuit. Francis Bacon was in the employ of the King of England, eventually rising to the position of Lord Chancellor; Copernicus was a priest of the church in Poland. Spinoza was a lens grinder in his adopted homeland, Holland.

Their attitude toward leisure is difficult to surmise. It seems clear that they were Epicurean regarding worldly pleasures. Bacon regarded the indifference and apathy of Stoicism and asceticism as premature death. Voltaire, who had a knack for making money and who accumulated a tidy fortune, detested idleness and equated it with nonexistence. Pierre Bayle, who preceded Voltaire as father of the enlightenment in France, probably represented their attitude toward the use of "free time:"

> Public amusements, games, country jaunts . . . and other
> recreations . . . were none of my business. I waste no time
> on them . . . I find sweetness and repose in the studies in
> which I have engaged myself, and which are my delight.
> (Durant & Durant, 1963: 609)

It seems, then, that they thought highly of the freedom to engage in their essentially intellectual activities and were opposed to idleness and indifferent to amusements and other recreations. But it must be recognized that they were privileged in ways unknown and unavailable to the masses, washed or not.

PIEPER'S CONCEIT OF LEISURE

Leisure: The Basis of Culture was the response of a 20th-century Catholic philosopher to the critical philosophy of Immanuel Kant. But more than that, it was a response to a philosophy which had become an empirical science of man and had lost, as a result, its historic link with religion and theology. That point is made especially clear in T. S. Eliot's introduction to Pieper's book (1963: 12-13). Elsewhere Eliot (1948) noted that the religious point of view is inescapable since one either believes or disbelieves. In particular, he argued that culture is impossible without religion and that western culture is a culture precisely because of its common religious heritage. On this basis, Pieper linked leisure to culture through divine worship, festival and celebration.

Before examining Pieper's particular response to 18th-century philosophy, especially Kant's, *Critique of Pure Reason* and *Critique of Practical Reason,* his understanding of the key concepts, leisure and culture, must be stated. In his preface, Pieper wrote:

> Culture depends for its very existence on leisure, and
> leisure, in its turn, is not possible unless it has a durable
> and living link with the cultus, with divine worship.
> It (cult) really means fulfilling the ritual of public sacrifice
> . . . the cultus is the primary source of man's freedom,
> independence and immunity within society. . . .

> Culture . . . is the quintessence of all the natural goods of the
> world and of those gifts and qualities which, while belonging
> to man, lie beyond the immediate sphere of his needs and
> wants. All that is good in this sense, all man's gifts and
> faculties are not necessarily useful in a practical way; though
> there is no denying that they belong to a truly human life,
> not strictly necessary, even though he could not do without
> them. (1963: 17-18)

Interestingly, Pieper reminded us that, while we always use the word "cult" with reference to a religious or spiritual group, we seldom think of the religious or spiritual connotations of the word "culture." It is a case of most of us having "never thought of it that way."

Leisure, to Pieper, is a mental or spiritual attitude which is not the result of external factors, not the result of spare time and not idleness. Pieper argued that leisure has three characteristics. First, leisure is "an attitude of mind, a condition of the soul. . . . Leisure implies an attitude of nonactivity, of inward calm, of silence; it means not being busy but letting things happen." Second, leisure is a receptive, contemplative attitude and both the occasion and the capacity "for steeping oneself in the whole of creation." It is, "an attitude of contemplative celebration," and requires of man affirmation of God's work and his own. Third, since leisure is a celebration, "it is the direct opposite of effort (and) opposed to the exclusive idea of work (as) social function" (pp. 41–43).

In passing it should be noted that a companion essay, "The Philosophical Act," is usually joined with "Leisure the Basis of Culture." Pieper defined the philosophical act in much the same way as he defined leisure. That act, he said, "is an attitude which presupposes silence, a contemplative attention to things, in which man begins to see how worthy of veneration they really are" (p. 18). Thus leisure and philosophical activity had, to Pieper, the same essence.

Pieper and Kant

Leisure, as Pieper viewed it, is impossible with the philosophy of Kant and the empiricism and rationalism of the 18th-century philosophers. Recall that Kant argued that knowledge is exclusively the result of the mind actively working to organize sensory data. Knowledge is acquired or achieved: it is not given but comes from mental effort. The consequence, as Pieper argued, is that all activity becomes work. If you want to know something, you have to work. Moreover, knowledge is the exclusive result of our own effort. Nothing is intuited or inspired; nothing comes to us as a gift.

Pieper objects, then, to the notion that all knowledge is exclusively the product of mental work and effort. That is also the basis for Whitehead's concern that the "fallacy of misplaced concreteness" has ruined philosophy by limiting knowledge to demonstrable fact. Whitehead suggested and Pieper insisted that there is another way of knowing. The best description of these two ways of knowing was provided by Walter Kerr (1962: 216–17).

> To be perfectly plain about the matter, we are here positing that the intellect is capable of grasping the knowledge it seeks in at least two different, mutually exclusive but happily complementary, ways. It can come to possess knowledge by a discursive method, by thought, by logical deduction from defined abstract principles. This method is laborious and constitutes 'work,' the exhausting work of 'proving things out.' When things are so proved out, they are ready to be used; because the knowledge can be demonstrated, on paper or in the laboratory, it can be profitably employed in the strict disciplines of all our further work. The method is itself work, and it is the cornerstone of whatever other work we do.

The intellect can also come to possess knowledge by a simple, submissive, eye-to-eye contemplation of the object to be known. It possesses the knowledge by gently and quietly possessing the object—not in the fragmented state in which the object's concrete clothing is forcibly divorced from its informing principle but in its whole or 'natural' state, with its informing principle resting comfortably, invisibly, and quite unmolested deep within the nest of the tangible. Because this knowledge is singular and must be eternally private, it cannot be proved out, it cannot be used in our work. Intuitive knowledge is knowledge without a future; it has only a present. The object known is not known for the sake of some other gain; it is known in itself, as itself, for itself alone. The act of knowing is not in this case grasping; it is gratuitous. Its end is not profit; it is love.

Leisure is characterized not by effort but effortlessness, not by activity but receptivity, not acquisition but acquiescence in being, not by grabbing hold but letting go, not by profit, but love. Thus, the claims of work on man and by man preclude leisure. In addition, effort, that is work or labor, becomes a criterion of worth; the more difficult the better. This is one of the conclusions that can be drawn from Kant's philosophy but, although Pieper did not mention it, is also one of the conclusions that can be drawn from a theology in which man was naturally inclined toward the evil and sinful and must, therefore, work to overcome that nature. Effort, difficulty or hard work becomes the measure of what is morally good.

That notion pervades our thinking more than we may realize. We have many common expressions that convey that message. Some people may believe that the best things in life are free but more likely believe that you get what you pay for—by money or effort. How arrogant we would think someone who attributed his or her success to a God given gift rather than to hard work. In this world, we believe, no one—presumably including God—is going to give you anything; you have to work for it. As Pieper writes: "man mistrusts everything that is effortless, he can only enjoy, with a good conscience, what he has acquired with toil and trouble; he refuses to have anything as a gift" (p. 14).

Leisure—A Gift

Our notion of free time is almost exclusively that of "time off" which we have earned by working. Seldom do we equate the word free with something that is given to us as a gift. Holidays recognize free time earned by work: holy days recognize what we receive as a gift. Since primitive times, holy days have been set aside to worship or placate the Gods or to celebrate good fortune in feasts or festive celebration. Our Thanksgiving is an expression of thanks for the harvest. Even such secular holidays as the birthdays of Washington, Lincoln, or King were, presumably, set aside to give thanks for their lives. Even Halloween, the eve of All Saint's Day, marks the day of a Druid festival in which ghosts and witches were part of the religious rites.

The Sabbath tradition, which has its origin in Judaism several centuries before Christ, was a cessation of work motivated by gratitude and thanksgiving. Karl Barth has offered an interesting interpretation of the Sabbath. He pointed out that man was created, according to the Old Testament, on the sixth day of creation. Thus, God's seventh day was man's first day. The Sabbath, therefore, is a gift of grace and is prior to rather than a reward for work. Thus, we start with freedom and festive celebration and then proceed to work, service and the serious business of this world. The Sabbath is tied to leisure as a celebration of the gift of grace (In Lee, 1964: 188-89).

The idea that leisure and even free time is a gift is a novel—if not strange—idea for us. But it is hardly a new idea. The early Greek philosophers were aware of it and clearly incorporated it in their thinking about leisure, contemplation and happiness. Our own definition of leisure, although not so steeped in theology as with Pieper and other philosophers, incorporates terms like love, faith and intuition. In so doing, we recognize philosophic traditions and schools other than, but not excluding, the empiricism and rationalism characteristic of an empirical science of man. Nonetheless, we owe a tremendous debt to the pioneers of modern science and modern philosophy and should acknowledge it.

OUR DEBT TO MODERNITY

Though censorship and persecution still had to be endured, freedom of thought and expression took giant strides forward during this period. Throughout the 1600s and 1700s, agnosticism and atheism were fashionable, even in some church circles. Deism, a religious philosophy stressing a personal relationship with God, came to characterize enlightenment thought as much as it characterizes our own. The civil war in England and later the American and French Revolutions brought freedom from the despotic powers of monarchy.

Along with that freedom came a new recognition of natural law and natural rights. Not since the ancient Greek philosophers had these natural laws and rights received much attention. Hugo Grotius, a Dutch jurist specializing in international law, viewed them as the immutable rights of the smaller and weaker nations and we quickly adopted them for individuals, particularly in their relations with secular authorities. These natural, God given rights became the inalienable rights of life, liberty and the pursuit of happiness. With these rights came our belief in equality. Locke and others believed men, in a natural state, were equal, though they differed as to how and to what degree that was to be maintained. Between liberty and equality, a balance, a very delicate one, must be struck. Notions of liberty, equality and natural rights form the core of our political philosophies and government policies and services.

Of particular importance, too, was the great faith placed in man, even the common man, and in progress and in the future. As Becker noted, the 18th-century philosophers

> . . . knew instinctively that man in general is natively good,
> easily enlightened, disposed to follow reason and common
> sense, generous, humane and tolerant, more easily led by
> persuasion than compelled by force; above all a good citizen
> and a man of virtue, being well aware that, since the rights
> claimed by himself are only the natural and imprescriptable
> rights of all men, it is necessary for him voluntarily to assume
> the obligations and to submit to the restraints imposed by a
> just government for the commonwealth. (1932: 103)

Further, they were convinced that their century was better than the past and could see no reason why following centuries would not be even better.

> Thus the philosophers called in posterity to exorcise the
> double illusion of the Christian paradise and the golden
> age of antiquity. For the love of God they substituted love
> of humanity; for the vicarious atonement the perfectibility

of man through his own efforts; and for the hope of
immortality in another world the hope of living in the memory of
future generations. (p. 130)

Scientists and philosophers of the age believed, as do we, that by
applying our intelligence we can continuously improve the human condition
and thus man himself. This is so much a part of our thinking that it is hard to
imagine how anyone could think otherwise, even though our enthusiasm has
been dampened in the face of dangers and crises not known to them and not
yet effectively addressed by us. We share more of their view than their
optimism.

At his trial before the church's inquisitors, Galileo expressed the
modern attitude of science and philosophy. He said to them: "I do not believe
that the God who has endowed us with sense, reason and intellect has intended
us to forgo their use" (Durant & Durant, 1961: 607). With that, the wisdom of
ancient, medieval and scholastic philosophy, so stultifying to the advance of
natural science, was set aside. The idea, philosophy, and methods of science
were firmly in place by the time Halley, a colleague of Newton, discovered
the comet which bears his name. Inductive thinking, empirical evidence,
controlled observation, the formulation of mathematical certainties and
statistical probabilities replaced previous authority and established the
standard of truth. With the tradition of publication and criticism, that standard
became public. The insistence on clear, efficient writing probably improved
the style of writing of all kinds. Chafe though we may at some of the mecha-
nistic, deterministic assumptions of science, we are the benefactors of the
profound changes it has made in every aspect of life.

There were, of course, a number of reactions to the rationalism of the
age. The romantic movement of Rousseau, and others, which helped fuel the
storming of the Bastille and the French Revolution, was of particular importance. He and his followers also had a significant influence on education,
particularly in the early years of childhood, and we have a rich genre of
literature which traces its ancestry to Rousseau. Other reactions led to
idealism and irrationalism and later to existentialism and phenomenology.
But the main trust of science and philosophy of this age led to the philosophies of utilitarianism and pragmatism, which we address in following
chapters.

A final result of the intellectual, political and religious ferment of this
age was the dissociation of many things that were previously associated, if not
integrated. The separation of the material from the spiritual has already been
noted as has the separation of church from state. The church and the state

were also separated from business. The puritans separated art from religion, state, and business and the practical things in life from the finer things (Muller, 1963: 294). Science was separated from faith and art. Values became divided into the values of science, or business, or government; with some overlap but also some variation and confusion. All this contributed to a society growing increasingly individualistic. The break with the authority of church, state, and wisdom of the ancients left the individual on his own. The stress on the natural rights of liberty and equality had the same effect. And with the divorce of civic activity from inner life, economics became dissociated from morals and ethics, thus fostering economic individualism as well (Bronowski & Mazlish 1960: 90).

SCIENCE, PHILOSOPHY AND LEISURE

The modern era, the origins of which can be traced to the age of science, confronts modern man with a number of difficulties. One such difficulty is the proliferation of knowledge, or at least the proliferation of information, recognizing T. S. Eliot's lament: "Where is the knowledge lost in information? Where is the wisdom lost in knowledge" (In Cousins, 1981: 126). He and countless others have expressed concern about the fragmentation of knowledge and disciplines and a science which has become, as Becker argued, "mired in data and devoted to triviality" (1968: xii). The opposite problem, of course, is that without the standards and methods of science, we lose our base for objective knowledge.

This is not a new problem. Hume, Rousseau, Diderot and other philosophers recognized the problem over two centuries ago and sought some superordinate, unifying concepts and principles by which to make sense of man's everyday life. That search continues and may well be unending. Meanwhile, it has become impossible for any of us to acquire an encyclopedic knowledge, so ignorance, paradoxically, has come to characterize the human condition. There is much that we must accept based not on our own empirical, scientific evidence but upon faith; faith particularly in authority, including the authority of science which itself rejects faith as a basis for knowledge.

What is especially clear from this is that we have to depend on each other, that life in society is thoroughly and increasingly interdependent. And this, also paradoxically, in a culture which has made individualism and independence the cup and platter of a secular grail.

A second problem with the proliferation of knowledge is that, in order to gain even a minimally adequate understanding of some body of knowledge we become increasingly specialized and in that respect narrow. That problem, too, has been addressed by many authors, the best known of which is probably C.P. Snow's essay, "The Two Cultures" (1959). Snow observed that our intellectual life was becoming increasingly divided between the sciences and humanities, each living in its own culture, each having difficulty communicating with and understanding the other, both caught up in misconceptions and stereotypes: one dealing with facts, things and "hard" data; the other dealing with values, people, and "soft" data. The additional problem is that, depending on what kind of work we do or seek to do, neither may be particularly useful and therefore both may be regarded as irrelevant.

These problems and paradoxes will remain until our philosophy becomes sufficiently developed and comprehensive to provide some superordinate unity—some point of view from which to take in the whole of life. Knowledge includes but is not limited to the facts of science. And science is not facts but an activity guided by values that are as important to social life as they are to science (Bronowski, 1965). They are not the only values—there are also religious values like love and charity—but they are fully compatible.

Just as resolution and unity is in the philosophic domain so it is in the domain of leisure. In the simplest sense, our work and other obligations may not often allow us much opportunity to reflect in a comprehensive way on the meanings and relationships of things. Freedom to do that is a prerequisite. Additionally, our work, even if our chosen and rewarding work, is often guided by (and sometimes impeded by) rules and regulations, policies and procedures. But in another sense, particularly as outlined by Pieper, philosophic activity is essentially the same as leisure. Further, our definition speaks of acting not in accordance to manuals of policies and procedures but according to internally compelling love and doing that which is intuitively worthwhile and which provides a basis of faith.

In our era, science and work may be too highly valued. That seems evident in our penchant to attach these words to so many of our enterprises. Karl Marx understood that when he referred to his economic philosophy as "scientific socialism," and that is somehow related to political science. Today we have leisure science, and also domestic science, secretarial science and so on. And we do school work, homework, community work and volunteer work.

That is not to denigrate science or work. Our enormous debt to both, historically and in our own lives, can only be repaid by full appreciation. Rather, the importance of leisure and philosophy has been undervalued. The right relationship between science and work on one hand and leisure and philosophy on the other requires not devaluing the former but revaluing the latter. It seems likely that that will yield a large increment in the appreciation of all things and perhaps also a small increment in humility. Perhaps we have claimed too much for ourselves, and in that sense have become more arrogant than those who claim to be "gifted." Clauses in insurance contracts often preclude recompense for losses due to acts of God. We do not, of course, buy insurance against gains. In any case, gain is attributed not to God but the exclusive product of our effort. It is hard for us to recognize, accept and appreciate gifts, not least of which is leisure.

REFERENCES

Becker, Carl. 1932. *The Heavenly City of the Eighteenth-Century Philosophers.* New Haven: Yale University Press.

Becker, Ernest. 1968. *The Structure of Evil.* New York: George Braziller Inc.

Berlin, Isaiah (Ed.). 1956. *The Age of Enlightenment.* New York: Mentor Books.

Bronowski, Jacob. 1978. *Magic, Science and Civilization.* New York: Columbia University Press.

Bronowski, Jacob. 1965. *Science and Human Values* (rev. ed.). New York: Harper and Row.

Bronowski, Jacob and Bruce Mazlish. 1960. *The Western Intellectual Tradition.* New York: Harper and Brothers.

Cousins, Norman. 1981. *Human Options.* New York: Berkeley Books.

Durant, Will and Ariel. 1961. *The Age of Reason Begins: The Story of Civilization, Part VII.* New York: Simon and Schuster.

Durant, Will and Ariel. 1963. *The Age of Louis XIV: The Story of Civilization, Part VIII.* New York: Simon and Schuster.

Durant, Will and Ariel. 1967. *Rousseau and Revolution: The Story of Civilization, Part X.* New York: Simon and Schuster.

Eliot, T. S. 1948. *Notes Toward the Definition of Culture.* London: Faber and Faber.

Kerr, Walter. 1962. *The Decline of Pleasure.* New York: Simon and Schuster.

Lee, Robert. 1964. *Religion and Leisure in America.* New York: Abingdon Press.

Muller, Herbert J. 1963. *The Uses of the Past.* New York: New American Library.

Pieper, Josef. 1963. *Leisure: The Basis of Culture.* New York: New American Library.

Russell, Bertrand. 1946. *A History of Western Philosophy.* London: George Allen and Unwin.

Snow, Charles P. 1959. *The Two Cultures and the Scientific Revolution.* New York: Cambridge University Press.

Whitehead, Alfred North. 1926. *Science and the Modern World.* New York: Macmillan Co.

I draw the conclusion that, assuming no important wars and no important increase in population the *economic problem* may be solved, or at least be within sight of solution, within a hundred years. This means that the economic problem is not—if we look to the future—*the permanent problem of the human race.*

Why, you may ask, is this so startling? It is startling because—if, instead of looking into the future, we look into the past—we find that the economic problem—the struggle for subsistence, always has been hitherto the primary, most pressing problem of the human race—not only of the human race but of the whole of the biological kingdom from the beginning of life in its most primitive forms.

Thus we have been expressly evolved by nature—with all our impulses and deepest instincts—for the purpose of solving the economic problem. If the economic problem is solved, mankind will be deprived of its traditional purpose.

Will this be a benefit? If one believes at all in the real values of life, the prospect opens up at least the possibility of benefit. Yet I think with dread of the readjustment of the habits and instincts of the ordinary man, bred into him for countless generations, which he may be asked to discard within a few decades.

To use the language of today—must we not expect a general 'nervous breakdown? . . .'

Thus for the first time since his creation man will be faced with his real, his permanent problem—how to use his freedom from pressing economic cares, how to occupy the leisure, which science and compound interest will have won for him, to live wisely and agreeably and well.

(John Maynard Keynes, 1963: 365-7)

V. HOMO ECONOMUS

As everyone knows, the year 1776 marked the beginning of the American Revolution when John Hancock and his colleagues drafted, signed and delivered the Declaration of Independence. In the same year, economics, in a formal sense, was born as that is also the year in which Adam Smith's *An Inquiry Into the Causes of the Wealth of Nations* was published. Throughout the previous 4,000 years or so of recorded history, there had been philosophers, artists, statesmen, politicians, theologians and scientists. There were traders and bookkeepers, borrowers and lenders, but no economists.

Throughout those many centuries, work and wealth had been distributed by force, necessity and tradition. Religious and ethical systems had provided some general guidelines, but the predominant attitude had been simply to accept the order of things. That was true of Aristotle 400 years before Christ and Thomas Aquinas 1,200 years after. In the main, brute force had governed the distribution of work and wealth, if anyone were to question it, and there was no economic system other than slavery and feudalism and the spoils of victory.

With the Renaissance and Reformation, the firm grip of tradition and religion was broken. Trade and commerce flourished with exploration, expansion and colonization in the Americas and elsewhere. Individualism, the natural rights of liberty and equality, and a Protestant Ethic equating success with prosperous employment: all this required some attempt to understand work and the production and distribution of wealth.

TOWARD A SCIENCE OF WEALTH

None of this could have come about, however, without also the age of science. We have seen natural philosophy in ancient Greece, followed by the man-centered philosophies of Socrates, Plato and Aristotle. Man-centered philosophy carried over to politics, but the politics only of the city-state and a social and economic order based upon slavery. The city-state was overrun by the Roman empire; slavery remained. With Bacon and Descartes, and particularly the astronomers, "natural" philosophy ushered in the age of science. For a century or so, philosophy was tied to math and physics, and in the following century or so philosophy was tied to psychology. By the late 1600s, the focus had shifted to politics and government, but this time slavery (although not exploitation) was in decline, feudalism was about to expire, and the authority of the ancients, monarchs and theologians had been successfully challenged.

More important, however, was the scientific attitude toward society. How was it to be understood except by discovering the mechanisms which drove it and the laws that governed its motion? The language as well as the attitude of physical science was thought to be applicable also to man and society. In psychology, for example, we speak of defense mechanisms and physical educators have laboratories for biomechanics. Accompanying the physical sciences was mathematics and the effort to establish mathematical relations and understandings. William Petty, in the 1600s, had begun the development of "political arithmetic," compiling statistics on trade, population, and other matters.

Prior to the development of a systematic exposition of the economy, a group in France had been dealing with questions about trade and balance of payments, including the accumulation of precious metals like gold and silver. They also explored, quantitatively, the flow of wealth between different parts of the economy. That they were called physiocrats, the name linked to physics and natural law, indicates the scientific bent. Later, August Comte, widely regarded as the father of sociology, referred to his work as "social physics." Still later, William Graham Sumner, often regarded as the father of American sociology, was to prefer the name social science to sociology. Marx sought to create scientific socialism, and economists since the earliest days have been searching along with natural scientists for laws which govern economic phenomena.

From 1776 to the present day, nothing has governed our thinking or our lives more than "the worldly philosophers," that is, economists (Heilbronner, 1980). In exploring the development of our worldly philosophy, it should not be necessary to point out how critical it is to our understanding of free time and to the distribution of the kind and amount of work we do, the goods and services we produce, and the amount and distribution of income and financial resources available to us. It also helps us to understand why leisure, as we have defined it, has been lost in the confusion of not only our concepts but also our lives.

THE FABLE OF THE BEES

In the early 1700s, Bernard Mandeville published a poem entitled "The Grumbling Hive," and subsequently added much prose to it and it reappeared as *The Fable of the Bees: or Private Vices, Publick Benefits*. He was, of course, referring to man, but in a way that was irreverent and cynical and wicked. What better reason to quote several lines?

>The root of evil, avarice,
>That damn'd ill-natur'd baneful vice,
>Was slave to prodigality,
>That noble sin; whilst luxury
>Employ'd a million of the poor,
>And odious pride a million more;
>Envy itself and vanity
>Were ministers of industry;
>Their darling folly, ficklness
>In diet, furniture, and dress,
>That strange ridic'lous vice, was made
>The very wheel that turn'd the trade.
>Their laws and cloaths were equally
>Objects of mutability;
>For what was well done for a time,
>In half a year became a crime;
>Yet whilst they altered thus their laws,
>Still finding and correcting flaws,
>They mended by inconstancy
>Faults which no prudence could foresee.
>Thus vice nursed ingenuity,
>Which join'd with time and industry,
>Had carry'd life's conveniences,
>Its real pleasures, comforts, ease,
>To such a height, the very poor

> Live better than the rich before;
> And nothing could be added more. (1924: 25-6)

There is one better reason for quoting these lines. What Mandeville had done was to identify what came to be understood as the mechanism which drove the economy. That mechanism, he said, was the desire for wealth (avarice), a taste for the lavish, luxurious, and extravagant (prodigality), and vanity, greed, pride and all those inclinations and habits which mark not virtue but vice. Self-interest, in brief, is the road to prosperity. Mandeville also said something else, as revealed in the last few lines quoted above. He said that as a result of self-interest, even the poor would live "better than the rich before." In the grumbling hive, then, are the basic tenets of capitalism, free enterprise and laissez faire, as well as its morality and ethical legitimacy. Voltaire and the French physiocrats, who spent little time moralizing, thought Mandeville, in however a scandalous fashion, had put his finger on something important. Adam Smith had read Mandeville, too.

THE INQUIRY OF ADAM SMITH

Economics, and capitalism as an economic system, received their identity via Smith's inquiry which is generally referred to in abbreviated form as *The Wealth of Nations*. Some of the central ideas in the book had been in the air since well before Mandeville's fable. As early as 1656, a man named Joseph Lee had suggested that, "by light of reason and nature, everyone will do what is advantageous for himself. . . . The advancement of private persons will be the advantage of the public" (In Russell, 1946: 602). That general idea we have traced to earlier times; to Calvin but in fact even to the Bible. The difference is that in Calvin and Corinthians, it is assumed that one's work contributes to the welfare of the whole; in Adam Smith that happens automatically and inevitably. Competition and the laws (note: laws) of supply and demand lead to prosperity and the common good.

The basic premises of economic order, as viewed by Smith and others, were that (a) self-interest is the prime motivation, (b) there is a natural order or law by which individual striving leads to social or common good, and (c) the best regulation is none, that is, laissez faire, a term borrowed from the French physiocrats which means, in essence, leave the economy alone and let it go its own way. Among the best known passages from *The Wealth of Nations* is Smith's explanation of the division of labor, using pin making as his example, and the advantages in productivity that result. There are two other passages that are well-known and which explain the basic premises noted above. First, self-interest:

> Man has almost constant occasion for the help of his brethren, and it is in vain for him to expect it from their benevolence only. He will be more likely to prevail if he can interest their self-love in his favor, and show them that it is for their own advantage to do for him what he requires of them. Whoever offers to others a bargain of any kind, proposes to do this. Give me that which I want and you shall have this which you want, is the meaning of every such offer, and it is in this manner that we obtain from one another the far greater part of those offices (i.e., goods and services) which we stand in need of. It is not from the benevolence of the butcher, the brewer or the baker that we expect our dinner, but from their own self-interest. (1937: 14)

Second, self-interest leading to the common good:

> As every individual, therefore, endeavors as much as he can to employ his capital in support of domestic industry, and so to direct that industry that its produce may be of the greatest value; every individual necessarily labors to render the annual revenue of the society as great as he can. He generally, indeed, neither intends to promote the public interest, nor knows how much he is promoting it. He intends only his own security . . . (and) his own gain, and he is in this, as in many other cases, led by an invisible hand to promote an end which was no part of his intention. . . . By pursuing his own interest he frequently promotes that of the society more effectively than when he really intends to promote it. (p. 423)

The "invisible hand" was, of course, divine providence, and that was not, to Smith, a mere rationalization of greed as later capitalists were to use it. It is quite unfair to attribute to Adam Smith much of what was to follow. His deep social concerns were often lost among those who took up his economic laws. Had he lived at a later time, he may well have been a socialist (Becker, 1968: 35).

The principle of laissez faire, for example, was not only a necessary adjunct to the working of natural law but also a significant reform since, throughout the past, almost all government regulation had worked to the benefit of the rich and powerful. Who made the laws if not the landed aristocracy, the early owners of industry and wealthy merchants? Too, private property was important to Smith as it was to Locke because for centuries, the church and the monarchs and aristocrats had consistently deprived the workers of the product of their own work. The masses had never had more than the most meager subsistence and often not even that. It was generally understood that the poor would never have any more than that for reasons we will note presently, but Smith wanted to assure subsistence, plus a little bit more. As Tawney noted, Smith and other thinkers of that period, "shot their arrows against the abuses of their day, not of ours" (1922: 19).

Throughout the *Wealth of Nations*, it is very clear that Smith was on the side of the laborers, farmers, artisans and the oppressed and was hostile toward big business and the aristocracy and gentry. At times he sounded more like Marx than Marx himself.

> The interests of the dealers, (he wrote) . . . in any particular branch of trade or manufacture, is always in some respects different from, and even opposite to, that of the public. . . . The proposal of any new law, or regulation of commerce, which comes from this order ought always to be listened to with great precaution. . . . It comes from an order of men . . . who have generally an interest to deceive, and even to oppress, the public and who . . . have, upon numerous occasions, both deceived and oppressed it. (In Durant & Durant, 1967: 771)

Smith also recognized the stultifying effects of a division of labor which reduced man to a mere mechanism monotonously repeating the simplest of tasks. David Hume, Smith's friend and colleague of the "Scottish enlightenment," had suggested that such monotony could cause mental disorder. Smith devoted several pages championing government provision of schools for the education of youth. He also favored the provision of public amusements. He should be remembered not only as the father of capitalism but also as a Professor of Moral Philosophy and author of *The Theory of Moral Sentiment* in which he argued that human behavior was based on sympathy; on our sentiment derived from the ability to share and understand the experiences of others.

THE PRINCIPLE OF UTILITY

The year 1776 was eventful in one further respect: it was the year in which Jeremy Bentham published his *Fragment on Government.* In it, he introduced what came to be called, particularly with the elaboration of James Mill and his son John Stuart Mill, utilitarianism. Like John Locke and others before them, Bentham and the two Mills were epicureans who believed that happiness resulted from pleasures if pursued and taken in moderation, with the most permanent pleasures found in intellectual pursuits. All of the utilitarians were concerned about making harmonious private pleasure seeking with public welfare. Whereas the prudent individual found happiness in private pursuits governed by God's moral laws, the prudent law maker was to govern in ways which assured the greatest amount of happiness for everyone. "It is the greatest happiness of the greatest number," Bentham said, "that is the measure of right and wrong" (In Russell, 1946: 147).

In addition, these were practical men who were concerned not so much with theories and ideas as they were experiences and consequences. Mill, particularly, did not accept the scientific philosophers distinctions between is and ought, fact and value. All should be subject to the test of experience. Mill's philosophy is often regarded as the philosophy of experience. Experience was the test of utility, and utility was measured by the contribution of behaviors and actions to the greatest happiness of the greatest number. Utility, then, was a principle of conduct.

Since John Stuart Mill was also a champion of individual freedom, his essay *On Liberty* being the most forceful argument we have for it, he was taken to be a proponent of laissez faire capitalism. He did accept the classic view (from Smith and his followers) regarding the production of wealth but he argued that the distribution of wealth depended solely on human institutions and could be changed if we so decided. During the later part of his career, he supported mild forms of socialism.

Utilitarianism influenced the government in England and the United States and it remains, intuitively and practically, a highly respected principle. But it is not without its problems. Perhaps it credits legislators with more foresight and good will than can reasonably be assumed. It also tends to ignore not simply the smallest number but any minority, a criticism which de Tocqueville stressed in his analysis of *Democracy in America.* Another problem with the greatest happiness principle is that, despite the insistence on the operation of this principle "in the long run," all of us are subject to what is called time discounting. The more distant the pleasure (or pain to be avoided) the less this principle governs present behavior. This is particularly true, especially in our own time, when we are uncertain about the future. It is easier to defer gratification if you are certain of gratification in the future. Otherwise, we will take what pleasures we can and let the future take care of itself. A final critique of the greatest happiness principle is that happiness is individual and not something institutions can promote in common. The common object is thus resolved into individual ambition and acquisition (Tawney, 1922: 32).

THE DISMAL SCIENCE

Throughout the 1700s, political and economic philosophy was decidedly optimistic. In the 1800s, it became decidedly pessimistic and Thomas Carlyle called economics "the dismal science"—a name which economics has yet to outlive. The problem was population, a problem which the Reverend Thomas Malthus, in reaction to the optimism of reformers of the time, described in *An Essay on the Principle Population*, published in 1798. Food, Malthus observed, is necessary for existence. His second observation was the passion between the sexes and he saw little hope for abstinence and virtue checking vice. The consequence could only be widespread misery. Population, if unchecked, increases in a geometric ratio. The means of subsistence, food particularly, increases in an arithmetic ratio. How can food and population be kept in balance?

> (By) a strong and constantly operating check on population from the difficulty of subsistence. This difficulty must fall somewhere; and must necessarily be severely felt by a large portion of mankind. (1926: 14)

> I see no way by which man can escape from the weight of this law which pervades all animated nature. No fancied equality, no agrarian regulations in their utmost extent, could remove the pressure of it even for a single century. And it appears, therefore, to be decisive against the possible existence of a society, all the members of which, should live in ease, happiness, and comparative leisure; and feel no anxiety about providing the means of subsistence for themselves. (1926: 16)

Unlike others who were aware of this problem, Malthus did not believe this could be prevented by controlling the birth rate. Consequently, the death rate, and particularly infant mortality due to the lack of subsistence, would necessarily be high and population growth would thus be held in check.

For this reason—actually this was seen as a law of nature—Malthus and many others were opposed to almost any attempts to alleviate the misery of the poor. He and others opposed the poor laws as they would simply cause inflation and, by raising both the hopes and conditions of the poor, increase the population and cause more inflation due to increased competition for the same amount of goods, including food. Thus more misery. David Ricardo, a friend of Malthus and second only to Adam Smith among classical economists, held the same views. Among the laws Ricardo elaborated was "the iron law of wages." Workers, Ricardo argued, would never receive more than the minimum required for subsistence. If they received more they would simply reproduce more, thus driving wages down due to the oversupply of labor. He, too, believed that compassion was not only wasted on the poor but in fact was detrimental: the poor would be worse off rather than better.

The poor laws in England were influenced by these "natural laws." One consequence was the establishment of work houses (or poor houses) with the sexes strictly separated for those unassailable Malthusian reasons. And since it was believed (as many believe today) that those in poor houses should not fare better than the poorest of those receiving no public beneficence, the fare of the poor house was oatmeal gruel, and young Oliver Twist asking for more. Similarly, the passage and later repeal of the Corn laws in England (corn was a generic term for grain, including wheat) had little to do with helping the poor. The law imposed a duty on imported grain, keeping the price high since most farmers paid the landowners with grain. The law was repealed because the industrialist had come to power, and lowering the price of grain would allow lowering the subsistence wage paid to workers. Similarly, during the famine in Ireland (1845-47), the head of the treasury refused to intervene by providing food. He felt that the laws described by Malthus and Ricardo were operating and that God was solving the problem. The "invisible hand" of God had become, as Galbraith described it, "the hand of a rather ruthless God who couldn't have had much liking for the Irish" (1973: 38).

SOCIALISM—UTOPIAN AND SCIENTIFIC

At the close of the 1700s and in the first few decades of the 1800s, a number of philosophers had become concerned with what they considered a destructive application of scientific laws to the workings of human society and they were increasingly concerned about the emerging evils of industrial capitalism. So emerged a group of utopian socialists, among whom Saint-Simon, Charles Fourier, Robert Owen and later Joseph Proudhon are best known. Their principal interest was to reassert the primacy of moral order and to reinfuse a moral order into a society which seemed to be in great need of one. August Comte, often regarded as the father of sociology and the father of "positivism," was a disciple of Saint-Simon. Positivism, to Comte, was the third and climatic stage of evolution in thought: positivism being characterized by empirical science whereas the earlier stages, the theological and the metaphysical stages, were characterized by faith and a priori reason respectively. Lost to history was Comte's intention to make all the sciences subservient to a unifying science of man and to use the sciences as a basis for a widely understood and shared moral order. He sought, in effect, a religion that would be substantial in this life (Aiken, 1956: 123).

One of the main influences of the utopian socialists was their influence on Karl Marx and his collaborator, Friedrich Engels. Their "scientific socialism" was a response to the utopians with whom they were sympathetic but whose thinking seemed only wishful and without foundation. Marx and Engels set out to provide one. They argued that the arrangements for producing material goods determined the social, political and spiritual currents of society. As with Comte, they viewed these arrangements as evolving from one stage to another, with capitalism a stage, following slavery and feudalism, but not the final stage. Socialism, they believed, was the next, inevitable, stage.

They accepted the argument that earlier arrangements, including capitalism, in which a small leisure class was supported by the labor of the masses was necessary; that it was essential for a few to be free to look beyond immediate needs so as to advance society economically, politically, socially and in other ways. But the productivity of industrial capitalism provided the means of ending the injustice and exploitation, thus providing to the masses the leisure required for fully human development (Sawell, 1985: 82). Leisure was the realm of freedom; they saw little prospect for meaningful work. And with the abolition of private property, man would no longer be enslaved by material things and thus would be free to shape his human personality and destiny.

Marx and Engels, aside from their revolutionary economics, were champions of the poor and they assailed the excesses of capitalism in the strongest terms. In the first volume of *Capital*, they devoted many pages to the exploitation of the proletariat, and spoke of the "moral degradation" and "intellectual desolation" which ensues from industrial capitalism. More than 20 years earlier, in 1844, Engels had published his study of *The Conditions of the Working Class in England*. To a modern reader, it is even more an indictment than it was at the time. Also in their early writings, they addressed the problem of alienation, the result of the division of labor, the class structure, and the production of capital by creating value beyond what workers were paid. Alienation from both their work and their product spilled over into alienation from their fellow man. Truly human work would be an affirmation of oneself and one's social relations. As it was, work was the imposed torment of external and arbitrary force.

However flawed their economics and discomforting their proposals, they cannot be faulted for their hopes and aspirations, including the prospect for leisure and with it the full development of man and society. As a young man, Marx wanted nothing more than to be a poet. Even as a poet, a not especially gifted one, he could not have been poorer. For virtually all of the last 50 years of his life (1818-1883), he lived on handouts, mostly from his friend, Engels. His work was much too important to him to spend time earning a living.

SOCIAL DARWINISM

We have seen the idea of social evolution in the historicism of Marx and Engels and the positivism of August Comte. These notions arose without particular reference to biological evolution, the roots of which can be traced back to the pre-Socratic, natural philosophers of the sixth century before Christ. The application of the principles of evolutionary biology, then, cannot be attributed to Charles Darwin. By the time he published *The Origin of the Species* and *The Descent of Man*, phrases like "survival of the fittest" and "struggle for existence" were already in use. Herbert Spencer had used them and he was not a biologist but a sociologist. Rather than "social Darwinism" we should probably speak of "social Spencerism." Darwin did, however, provide the detailed, biological science base for theories already announced and applied to the social order. The principle of natural selection completed a picture already outlined by Smith, Malthus and Ricardo.

> The early progenitors of man must also have tended, like
> all animals, to have increased beyond their means of
> subsistence; they must have, therefore, occasionally been
> exposed to a struggle for existence, and consequently to
> the rigid laws of natural selection. Beneficial variations
> of all kinds will thus, either occasionally or habitually,
> have been preserved, and injurious ones eliminated.
> (Darwin, 1874: 63)

Darwin, however, was content to be a biologist and he did nothing to encourage the extension of biological evolution to other spheres of life. In fact, he observed that too much may be attributed to natural selection, noting a role for habit and direct intervention on surrounding conditions. He devoted Chapters IV and V in *The Descent of Man* to man's moral sense and social tendencies and to the advantages these have in the evolution not just of society but of man himself.

By the middle of the 1800s, the confluence of many ideas and practices produced the social Darwinism of the late 1800s and early 1900s: laissez faire, the invisible hand, Malthusian misery, the iron law of wages, the inevitability of scientific laws, Calvinism, the puritanical attitude toward the "undeserving" poor, individual liberty, property rights, and now natural selection and survival of the fittest. All was governed by competition; that was the natural law which led to the development not only of society but man himself. The fact that these ideas had been wrenched out of context and often seriously distorted received little attention.

Spencer was opposed to virtually every government effort to ameliorate social and economic conditions. Naturally, he was the darling of the industrialists and other capitalists as well as conservatives of every stripe. He opposed poor laws, public education, laws governing sanitation and adulterating foods—even efforts to end medical quackery (Hofstadter, 1959: 41). William Graham Sumner, a sociologist at Yale, became Spencer's American disciple. He regarded the tendencies of a democratic political order to intervene in economic affairs as a peril to the otherwise inevitable progress of man and society via natural law. Sumner was a champion of the "forgotten man and woman," those who had not much but a little, as our greatest hope. But their interests were in conflict with the poor, the weak, and the other "petted" classes, upon whom any expenditure to assist was simply wasted effort. He shared Spencer's view that if the wealthy wanted to make charitable contributions, that was permissible—not because it would help the poor but because it would ennoble the rich.

The result was the ruthless capitalism of the middle and late 1800s led by men generously known as the "captains of industry and commerce" and less generously as the "robber barons." Listen to them. First, Andrew Carnegie:

> . . . while the law (competition based on biological prin-
> ciples) may sometimes be hard for the individual, it is best
> for the race, because it assures survival of the fittest in every
> department. (In Hofstadter, 1959: 45)

Next, John D. Rockefeller, after observing that the rose is so beauti-ful because the smaller buds around it are pinched off: "this is not an evil tendency in business. It is merely the working out of a law of nature and a law of God" (p. 46).

Is it any wonder, then, that the public recreation movement, the sand gardens of Boston and Halifax and the Settlement Houses of Chicago and Winnipeg had their beginnings at the close of the 19th century? And is it any wonder that the founders of the movement were considered radicals, commu-nists, and worse? In that sociopolitical environment, efforts to improve conditions of the poor and to actively intervene to promote human welfare were indeed radical (Duncan 1985). Sumner had railed against reformers and argued that you couldn't change the inexorable pace and direction of industrial capitalism. One of his essays, "The Absurd Effort to Make the World Over," attacked social reformers.

Spencer and Sumner have, mercifully, fallen out of fashion. The practice, if not also the theory of social Darwinism, simply turned out to be too repugnant to tolerate. Survival of the fittest in economics turned into raw and brutal power and exploitation. Yet there is evidence of vestigial remains of social Darwinism among politicians and capitalists, both at home and abroad. Another manifestation of survival of the fittest, war between nations, troubled Spencer and Sumner and it still troubles all of us. Let us hope that its ugliest form, the racial supremacy manifested in Nazi Germany, has perma-nently departed the human scene.

THE PROTESTANT ETHIC—AN UPDATE

It is easy to see how the Protestant ethic contributed to the develop-ment of capitalism, in practice as well as in spirit. Prosperity, since the time of Calvin, was a sign of God's grace: a likely blessedness in the hereafter and a certain one in the here and now. Over the past four centuries, the religious connotations of the ethic have all but disappeared. But the basic tenets of capitalism and social Darwinism gave it renewed life, albeit a secular life. Reports of its death, then, are premature. The emphasis is no longer salvation, it is freedom.

> Thus, anyone may choose his own trade or profession,
> or, if he does not like it he may change. He is free to work
> hard or not; he may make his own bargains and set his price
> upon his labor or his products. He is free to acquire property
> to any extent, or to part with it. By dint of greater effort or
> superior skill, or by intelligence, if he can make better wages,
> he is free to live, better, just as his neighbor is free to follow his
> example and learn to excel him in turn. If anyone has a genius
> for making and managing money, he is free to handle his
> tools. . . . If an individual enjoys his money, gained by energy
> and successful effort, his neighbors are urged to work the
> harder, that they and their children may have the same
> enjoyment. (In Whyte, 1951: 17)

The speaker was a Wall Street banker; the year, 1909; the place, Yale University. Twenty years later, bankers and investors were committing suicide as a result of the stock market crash. Perhaps some of his listeners were among them.

The Harried Leisure Class

That is the title of an insightful and delightful book by Staffan Linder (1970). It relates ways in which economic and social understandings and forces, as we have traced them thus far, combine to limit leisure if not preclude it entirely. It is contemporary—but it is not new. Americans, particularly it seems, have always been harried.

In the early 1830s, a young French aristocrat, Alexis de Tocqueville, visited the United States and reported his observations in *Democracy in America*. He observed that America and the American people were unique in many ways, the result of the ideas and forces from which its character was derived: separation from its ancestral home and history; equality; individual-ism; puritanism; commercialism and much more. Among the results he found were an almost exclusively practical, this-worldly orientation, the dominance of the majority in government and public opinion, and a sense of being completely on one's own; in short, restlessness. He found that, as a result, there was no leisure class and none of the meditation out of which come art, science, philosophy and culture beyond that of the practical and day-to-day. He found everyone materialistic and hectically active. "The whole life of an American," he said, "is passed like a game of chance, a revolutionary crisis, a battle" (de Tocqueville, 1899 Vol. I: 432).

On the subject of the harried leisure class, circa 1832, de Tocqueville's words are far better than any interpretation or paraphrase.

> The greater part of the men who constitute these nations are extremely eager in the pursuit of actual and physical gratification. As they are always dissatisfled with the position which they occupy, and are always free to leave it, they think of nothing but the means of changing their fortune or of increasing it. To minds thus predisposed, every new method which leads by a shorter road to wealth, every machine which spares labor, every instrument which diminishes the cost of production, every discovery which facilitates pleasures or augments them, seems to be the grandest effort of the human intellect. (Vol. II: 46)

> Not great lavish splendor—but little comforts and conveniences here and there: these are small objects, but the soul clings to them; it dwells upon them closely and day by day, till they at last shut out the rest of the world, and sometimes intervene between itself and heaven. . . . The reproach I address to the principle of equality, is not that it leads men away in the pursuit of hidden enjoyments, but that it absorbs them wholly in the quest of those which are allowed. By these means, a kind of virtuous materialism may ultimately be established in the world, which would not corrupt, but enervate the soul, and noiselessly unbend its springs to action. (Vol. II: 140-41)

Over the past three decades there have been hundreds, perhaps thousands, of commentaries which have described us in similar terms. It is interesting to note how little has changed. Perhaps it is also disconcerting. As de Tocqueville makes clear, Americans seem to have broad, though seldom explicit, areas of agreement—but no philosophy. Particularly, they have no philosophy of leisure. Leisure, for us, is like the jam for Alice in Wonderland to put on your bread. You shall have jam on your bread tomorrow, but tomorrow never comes. It is always today.

The New Slavery

It is well-known that over the past century or so, the average number of work hours per week has decreased substantially. It is also well-known that there has been very little decrease during the past few decades and in any case, as de Grazia well-noted, fewer work hours does not necessarily mean more free time. There are a number of explanations for these phenomena. Some of the dramatic reductions resulted from humanitarian concerns for exploited labor; some the result of labor union strength; some the result of social insurance and social welfare programs stimulated particularly by the depression of the 1930s. But there is another reason; the declining urgency for material goods (Galbraith, 1958: 344). The enormous productive capacity of North America made it possible for all of us to have everything we needed and much of what we wanted. The problems of poverty and unemployment are problems of distribution, not production. By the close of World War II, the economic problem had changed. The dismal science, the allocation of misery according to Malthus and Ricardo, the allocation of scarcity according to later economists, had suddenly become the allocation of a surfeit of goods. The economic problem was not to stimulate production; not with shelves and warehouses full and plants operating well below capacity. The economic problem, for the past several decades, has been to stimulate consumption. How rapidly our economy would collapse if we practiced those old Protestant Ethic virtues of frugality, simplicity and deferred gratification.

Enslavement no longer results from brute force or the pangs of hunger but from the more gentle art, and increasingly science, of persuasion. The legitimation of gratification and the incessant messages which tie happiness to consumer goods and services have come to be the primary shapers of choice and behavior. Shop, as one retailer put it, until you drop. Pay later, in easy, but unending, installments. Consumption is no friend of free time; it is almost the antithesis of leisure.

IS OPPORTUNITY KNOCKING?

Since the 1950s, a few economists, John Kenneth Galbraith among them, have been trying to show us that we are guided by ideas that are no longer relevant and by a variety of economic myths. Before that, of course, there have been utopias envisaged in which comfortable lives had been procured for all and work time reduced 50 percent or more below its present average of approximately 40 hours per week. More instructive, however, are the insights of John Maynard Keynes; insights with which the chapter began. Keynes revolutionized economic thought after World War I and was unquestionably the most influential economist of this century. In an essay written in 1930, "Economic Possibilities for Our Grandchildren," Keynes peered into the future. He saw a society whose needs could be satisfied with no more than 15 hours of work per week if we chose to devote our energies to noneconomic purposes. But he said that would be most difficult for us to do because our entire evolutionary past has shaped our instincts and habits to struggle for subsistence. The real, permanent problem for man was how to use freedom from economic cares and how to occupy leisure so as to live "wisely, agreeably and well." He wrote:

> I see us free, therefore, to return to some of the most sure
> and certain principles of religion and traditional virtue—
> that avarice is a vice, that the exaction of usury is a misde-
> meanor, that the love of money is detestable, that those walk
> most truly in the paths of virtue and sane wisdom who take
> least thought of the morrow. We shall once more value ends
> above means and prefer the good to the useful. We shall
> honor those who can teach us how to pluck the hour and the
> day virtuously and well, the delightful people who are
> capable of taking direct enjoyment in things, the lilies of the
> field who toil not, neither do they spin. (1963: 371-2)

Keynes's forecast would have this take place around the year 2030, perhaps a bit later. That it would take so long was the result not of the inability to produce but, in a sense, the ability to know when enough was enough, and the ability to identify those higher and more meaningful activities for which freedom from economic want has always been a dream. But, as Marx said, we have sold our birthright for a mess of pottage. We seem to lack a sufficiently compelling idea, or a sufficiently refined taste, for anything else. In short, we lack a philosophy of leisure. Without one, we may never be satisfied.

The late 1700s ushered in what is often referred to as the triple revolution: the American, the French, and the industrial. These revolutions, we were sure, would set us free. They have not, at least not yet. But there is a growing sense that we could be and a growing understanding that we have become gradually disengaged from what is truly important in our lives.

> The important freedom to be left alone, to acquire what one thought worthy of acquiring, to live the kind of life one desired for oneself—these never really had much of a chance, as Alexis de Tocqueville observed, in the first revolutionary, post feudal society—America. Today, there are no longer even Thoreaus or Emersons to give us the needling enjoinder that we can and must be ourselves. The rub is that man needs models of dignity and excellence if he is to pursue them. Without any specifications of things worthy to acquire, models really worthy to follow, things worth doing when alone, man was thrown back on the collective myth: he was harangued from all sides to 'enjoy, enjoy.' He could only give in. As Chekhov lamented, the 'art of enslaving' was being gradually refined. So was launched a race for status based largely on consumption of ever-new goods, a pride of ownership alone and not of excellence—the story is so well known and so constantly aired that it seems hackneyed to repeat it. But it is our story. Worst of all is the gradual disengagement from the sense of community, to shared dedication to larger spiritual goods and common worthwhile goals, from real social challenges, and from the possibilities of continuing interhuman dignity. Responsibility, in a word, is gone. Modern man has learned that acquisitions are fundamentally unsatisfying; that freedom without the knowledge of real choice is a contradiction; that living for one's own pursuits, surrounded by others doing likewise, is not a community. (Becker, 1968: 38-9)

REFERENCES

Aiken, Henry D. (Ed.). 1956. *The Age of Ideology.* New York: The New American Library.

Becker, Ernest. 1968. *The Structure of Evil.* New York: George Braziller Inc.

Darwin, Charles. 1874. *The Descent of Man* (2nd ed.). Boston: Estes and Lauriate.

de Tocqueville, Alexis. 1899. *Democracy in America, Vol. I and II* (Tr. Henry Reeve). New York: Colonial Press.

Duncan, Mary. 1985. "Back to Our Radical Roots." In Thomas Goodale and Peter Witt, *Recreation and Leisure: Issues in an Era of Change* (rev. ed.). State College, Pennsylvania: Venture Publishing.

Durant, Will and Ariel. 1967. *Rousseau and Revolution: The Story of Civilization Part X.* New York: Simon and Schuster.

Galbraith, John Kenneth. 1958. *The Affluent Society.* Boston: Houghton Mifflin.

Heilbronner, Robert. 1980. *The Worldly Philosophers* (5th ed.). New York: Simon and Schuster.

Hofstadter, Richard. 1959. *Social Darwinism in American Thought* (rev. ed.). New York: George Braziller.

Keynes, John Maynard. 1963. "Economic Possibilities for Our Grandchildren." In *Essays in Persuasion.* New York: W.W. Norton.

Linder, Staffan. 1970. *The Harried Leisure Class.* New York: Columbia University Press.

Malthus, Thomas. 1978. *First Essay on Population.* London: Macmillan and Company.

Mandeville, Bernard. 1924. *The Fable of the Bees: Or Private Vices, Publick Benefits.* Oxford: The Clarendon Press.

Russell, Bertrand. 1946. *A History of Western Philosophy.* London: George Allen and Unwin.

Sawell, Thomas. 1985. *Marxism: Philosophy and Economics.* New York: William Morrow and Company.

Smith, Adam. 1937. *An Inquiry Into the Causes of the Wealth of Nations.* New York: The Modern Library.

Sumner, William Graham. 1963. *Social Darwinism: Selected Essays.* Englewood Cliffs, New Jersey: Prentice-Hall.

Tawney, Robert. 1922. *The Acquisitive Society.* London: G. Bell and Sons.

Whyte, William F. 1957. *The Organization Man.* New York: Doubleday Anchor Books.

To the uncritical observer, the record of industrialism has been written in the production statistics, the accomplishments of inventor-heroes, and the rising standard of living of the American people. Even more significant, however, were the less obvious and the less concrete changes: the expansion of economic relationships from personal contacts within a village community to impersonal forces in the nation and the entire world; the standardization of life accompanying the standardization of goods and of methods of production; increasing specialization in occupations with the resulting dependence of people upon each other to satisfy their wants; a feeling of insecurity as men face vast and rapidly changing economic forces that they could not control; the decline of interest in nonmaterial affairs and the rise of the acquisition of material wealth as the major goal in life. These intangible innovations deeply affected the American people; here lay the real human drama of the new age.

(Samuel Hays, 1957: 1)

VI. INDUSTRIALISM, RECREATION AND LEISURE

Among the benchmarks of the emergence of industrialism in North America was Eli Whitney's invention of the cotton gin in 1793. "King cotton" was a commodity as essential to manufacturing in the north as was agriculture in the south, and the cotton gin ushered in the 19th century, a period of rapid and often abrasive change.

THE INDUSTRIAL REVOLUTION

The industrial revolution was aided by revolutions in transportation and communications. The success of the steamboat and the Erie Canal led to a canal building craze in the early 1800s, followed and quickly surpassed in importance by the development of railroads. The ability to move goods is of obvious importance to centralized and specialized production. Coal and ore mines could be linked to steel manufacturers which in turn could be linked to markets. Subsistence agriculture could be converted to commercial production for mass markets, however widespread the consumers.

Communication over these expanding networks was aided by Morse's invention of the telegraph, and Bell's invention of the telephone aided communication as well, especially between the many interdependent components of increasingly large and complex urban industrial systems.

Industrialism also depended upon a revolution in manufacturing technique. Increasingly, sophisticated machinery aided mass production not only of cotton and textiles but also the production in such basic commodity industries as flour and lumber and meat packing. And just as the clock helped standardize time and coordinate the efforts of many men, the calipers, now accurate to one-one thousandth of an inch, helped standardize the production of things (Hays, 1957: 10). Craftsmanship gave way to repetitive manufacture of material goods, each a replica of every other. And not only were goods standardized but also the processes that produced them, as those standardized products included parts of products, including parts of the machinery that produced them. Mass production, assembly line processes, and the division of labor, as Adam Smith illustrated with the manufacture of pins, spread to every form of manufacturing.

Standardized and replaceable parts were first used, again by Eli Whitney, in the early 1800s. It is, perhaps, ironic, that standardized parts were first used in the manufacture of guns.

Standardized parts in the early 1800s were joined by standardized processes as the 1900s approached. To scientific production was added "scientific management." While the science of management has come to pervade all aspects of economic political, and social life, it was first applied to workers on the shop floor. It was the forerunner of what has since come to be called "human engineering."

Frederick Taylor, in 1889, established a company whose product was advice on how to make enterprises more efficient. He is, if not our first, at least our best known efficiency expert. Among Taylor's services were time and motion studies of workers on the shop floor engaged in manufacturing processes. He called his system the "piece-rote" system; each man performed by rote in the most efficient (usually meaning fastest) way. In serving the machinery of industrial capitalism, man, himself, had been turned into a machine—a replaceable one.

The Cult of Efficiency

Taylor's interests were motivated in part by solving the labor problem. The labor problem, throughout the early and middle stages of industrialization, was a shortage of labor, or at least workers sufficiently strong or dextrous to endure hours and conditions which we now consider inhumane. Efficiency, then, became a principal means by which productivity could be increased. Scientific management and human engineering were means to increase efficiency and thus productivity.

Hours of work could be reduced in this way and, coupled with movements by labor and by those promoting sanitation, safety, health and welfare, legislation and negotiation led to significant reductions in average work hours per week. From 1850 to 1950, the average work hours per week decreased from about 70 hours to about 40. That did not, however, result in 30 additional hours of free time per week. Still, this and other benefits of efficiency (lower unit costs thus lower prices, for example) are well known. But efficiency has its costs as well. The "piece-rote system" increased the pace of work and also further alienated the worker from the product of his labor.

It is interesting to note that in the last decade or so, scientific management has seized upon the notion that efficiency and effectiveness are not the same thing. When a process is so efficient that no one works at it, thus having no income with which to buy the product of such processes, how effective is it? While it is more efficient to teach large classes than small, is it more effective? And when efficiency at work or school spills over into free time, the consequences may be even more damaging.

> Where people are involved, one should not worship too long at the altar of efficiency. The work force was sometimes sacrificed at that altar, first by exploitation and more recently by displacement. Dictatorships are more efficient than democracies. And where leisure and recreation are concerned, efficient time use may simply mean we are all more harried. Something important may be lost in playing the Minute Waltz in 30 seconds, or speed reading the novels of Mark Twain in a single evening—without laughing once (Goodale, 1985: 201).

Some Early Reactions

The imperatives of efficiency and productivity fueled changes in every aspect of life. These changes also created much unrest. The division of labor and management, the concentration of wealth and power, and the growing sense of powerlessness produced responses of all kinds. In agricultural areas, the Granger and the Populist movements sought to aid farmers who, no longer self-sufficient, were subject to the economic vagaries of national and international markets and trade. In industrial areas, unions arose, beginning with seamstresses and tailors in textile industries, and spreading among laborers in all fields. The National Labor Union (1866) and Knights of Labor (1869) were forerunners of such later unions as the American Federation of Labor and the Congress of Industrial Unions (later the C.I.O.). Labor unrest surfaced in the late 1800s, in the Haymarket riot in Chicago, the Homestead strike in Pennsylvania, and the Pullman strike, again in Chicago.

History provides few examples of such a great transformation in such a short time. The transformation of economic and social life meant that man, too, was transformed.

The Production of Workers

The transformation of peasants into workers, and the emergence of industrial capitalism which forced them into the worker role, resulted from a number of forces. One important force was the philosophical change in attitudes toward work, at least among those in positions of power. This happened, according to Max Weber, through the development of modern capitalism.

Capitalism had existed for centuries, but it was steeped in tradition and those involved in it had limited financial objectives:

> The number of business hours was very moderate, perhaps five to six a day, sometimes considerably less; in the rush season, where there was one, more. Earnings were moderate enough to lead a respectable life and in good times to put away a little. On the whole, relations among competitors were relatively good, with a large degree of agreement on the fundamentals of business. A long daily visit to the tavern often with plenty to drink, and a congenial circle of friends, made life comfortable and leisurely. (Weber, 1958: 66-67)

This limitedness was lost in the development of modern capitalism. Work became, for many in the emerging, ascetic, Protestant denominations, a God given command. The Puritan conceptualization of God's relation to humans was that the gulf between humans and God was unbridgeable. Mankind was born into sin and was predestined to go to heaven as one of the elect or into eternal hell. Unlike Catholicism, there was no room for "magic" in these ascetic religious movements. One's personal salvation "could not be guaranteed by any magic sacraments, by relief in the confession, or by individual good works" (Weber, 1958: 153). This could only happen "by proof (of salvation) in a specific type of conduct unmistakably different from the way of life of the natural man" (p. 153). For one to feel certain that he or she is among the elect, he or she must deal with God on an individual basis and rationally plan the whole of one's life in accordance with God's will.

Christian asceticism, at first fleeing from the world into solitude, had already ruled the world which it had renounced from the monastery and through the Church. But it had, on the whole, left the naturally spontaneous character of daily life in the world untouched. Now it strode into the market place of life, slammed the door of the monastery behind it, and undertook to penetrate just that daily routine of life with its methodicalness, to fashion it into a world in the world, but neither of or for this world. (p. 154)

Rational labor was, therefore, a religious obligation. The accumulation of wealth was not sinful unless it led one to become a member of the leisure class.

Wealth is thus bad ethically only insofar as it is a temptation to idleness and sinful enjoyment of life; and its acquisition is bad only when its purpose is of later living merrily and without care. But as a performance of duty in a calling it is not only morally permissible, but actually enjoined. (p. 163)

The combination of routine, rational hard work, and prohibitions against spending for pleasure often led to the accumulation of sufficient wealth for each succeeding generation to live a bit more comfortably. Sometimes it led to amounts sufficient to establish industry and many of the "captains of industry," even to this day, trace their lineage to solid Puritan stock.

That ethic and way of life was one which did find a place for recreation, as long as it served a rational purpose such as improving physical efficiency. "But as a means for the spontaneous expression of undisciplined impulses, it was under suspicion; and, insofar as it became purely a means of enjoyment, or awakened pride, raw instinct, or the irrational gambling instinct, it was of course strictly condemned" (p. 167). It has been observed that puritans frowned upon bear-baiting, "not because of the pain it caused the bear, but because of the pleasure it afforded the spectators" (Dulles, 1965: 9). Modern capitalism was partially developed by those who, out of religious conviction, would work unceasingly but would not use their wealth for worldly pleasures. This, of course, was to gradually change and produce a wealthy leisure class.

THE LEISURE CLASS

In a brief description of the history of the wig, Huizinga (1955) pointed out how the wig had gone from serving as a remedy for lack of hair to an "example of the chic run mad, nothing more exaggerated, more stupendous or, if you like, more ridiculous could possibly be imagined" (p. 184). The wig, once functional, became slowly but surely a purely decorative device, sometimes powdered, sometimes full of bows, and nearly always expensive enough that the common person could not afford one. The commoner, however, tried to imitate the fashion by making wigs of yarn or other materials. The wig came to represent a sign of upper social class—one small means of displaying wealth and power. No wonder the custom of wearing wigs temporarily ended during the French Revolution.

The wig served as a means of identifying those of a certain social class or economic status who not only had leisure but also the financial means to display their success. It was one of the trappings of an emerging leisure class.

During many periods of the past, leisure was associated with a class. In some sense, those who led lives of leisure in ancient Athens, native-born males who were citizens, were a privileged, leisure class. Their control of a system of slaves and the very limited rights of women empowered their lives of leisure. In the United States, the first leisure class that evolved did so on southern plantations where plantation owners had none of the prohibitions against pleasure that the Puritans to the north imposed, but did have slaves to do the work. It was in the second half of the 19th century that "society most flagrantly bent its pleasures to display" (Dulles, 1965: 236). Those who became rich after the Civil War, owners of steel plants, copper mines, textile mills, and cattle ranches, "sought to establish social leadership through their extravagance in entertainments and amusements" (p. 23). Capitalism and the processes of urbanization and industrialization had brought about increasing divisions within society. One such division was "The Leisure Class."

Veblen's Theory

In 1899, Veblen launched an attack on the extravagance of the newly wealthy industrial capitalists. In *The Theory of the Leisure Class* he argued that all consumption of goods, as well as leisure behavior, was shaped by the desire to impress others and to distinguish oneself from ordinary people. History, Veblen argued, showed a process by which man, through workmanship, at long last created the material surplus needed for economic security. This surplus, however, permitted a new group of self-centered motives to come into being, and some people "found their pleasure in invidious distinctions at the expense of others" (Riesman, 1953). The primitive balance of production and consumption gave way to a world where too much productivity, in countries like Germany and Japan, put a military surplus in the hands of ambitious dictators while in countries like England and America, too much consumption involved all classes in a meaningless chase to display material goods in an emulative manner. Leisure, as Veblen described it, was:

> ... nonproductive consumption of time. Time is consumed nonproductively: (1) from a sense of the unworthiness of productive work, and (2) as an evidence of pecuniary ability to afford a life of idleness. (1934: 38)

Leisure was thought to be closely related to exploitation, and the achievements of a life of leisure had much in common with the spoils of war or the trophies of economic exploitation. Material goods were such trophies. But, since leisure did not generally result in material goods, those in the leisure class also had to provide evidence of nonproductive, immaterial, consumption of time.

> Such immaterial evidences of past leisure are quasi-scholarly or quasi-artistic accomplishments and a knowledge of processes and incidents which do not conduce directly to the furtherance of human life. So, for instance, in our time there is knowledge of the dead languages and the occult sciences; of correct spelling; of syntax and prosody; of various forms of domestic music and other household art; of the latest proprieties of dress, furniture, and equipage; of games, sports, and fancy-bred animals such as dogs and racehorses. In all of these branches of knowledge the initial motive from which their acquisition proceeded at the onset, and through which they first came into vogue, may have been something quite different from the wish to show that one's time had not been spent in industrial employment; but unless these accomplishments had approved themselves as serviceable evidence of an unproductive expenditure of time, they would

not have survived and held their place as conventional
accomplishments of the leisure class. (p. 91-92)

The use of leisure by the class of society who had it, obviously,
didn't result in self-perfection or the improvement of culture or aid to the
community. Instead, it resulted simply in unproductive uses of time in order
to achieve status.

The roots of the leisure class, Veblen argued, could be traced to the
ancient traditions of predatory cultures in which productive effort was
considered unworthy of the able-bodied male. Thus, a leisure class existed
before industrialism. It was the transition to a "pecuniary" culture, however,
which brought the leisure class into full bloom. The captain of industry and
the tribal chief, therefore, shared some things in common.

The leisure class was, essentially, male. The first ownership of
property was the ownership of persons. The first owners were men: Their
first properties—women. The incentives for ownership of people were "(1) a
propensity for dominance and coercion, (2) the utility of these persons as
evidence of the prowess of their owners, [and] (3) the utility of their services"
(Veblen, 1899). Some women rose above the status of slaves due to the
principle that gentility can be transmitted. Such women and other slaves
became part of that class which no longer did productive work but rather
provided services to the master. Some of these services were of a ceremonial
nature. Many household chores fall into this category. For such domestic
service, which often served a "spiritual" function, there gradually developed
an elaborate system of good form and specialized training. Maintaining
servants (or a wife) who do nothing productive but serve the master displays
the master's high status, said Veblen, since it shows his ability to unproductively consume a large amount of service. Too, the servants consume a large
amount of goods. Those who provide such service have no leisure except
"vicarious leisure," which is leisure only in the sense that no productive work
is performed.

Leisure, Veblen said, had a long history of serving as a means of
documenting one's status and reputation. In archaic cultures there were some
"employments" which were noble and some which were not. Leisure was
honorable, partly because it demonstrated that one was exempt from ignoble
labor. How one used time was either "honorific" or "debasing" and this
distinction became increasingly important, Veblen argued, since leisure could
be used as evidence of wealth just as effectively as goods.

As long as labor was performed by slaves, man's "instinct for
workmanship," which admired efficiency of production and whatever was of

human use, could not come into play. When this "quasi-peaceable" stage of civilization passed to the "peaceable" stage, characterized by wage labor and cash payment, the instinct for workmanship came into play. For the emerging leisure class, this meant that there had to be a reconciliation between reaching out toward purposeful activity and, at the same time, avoiding activity that was productive. "A reconciliation between the two conflicting requirements is effected by a resort to make-believe" (Veblen, 1899: 136). Therefore, ceremonial organizations may be formed or activities undertaken which appeared to be useful but which, in reality, were not. The leisure class, in effect, did pretend work.

Critiquing Veblen

The use of leisure for display and consumption by those who grew wealthy under industrialism certainly had some basis in fact. But even if Veblen exaggerated, he raised the question as to whether leisure must be the result of social class inequities. Marx also raised this issue, envisioning a social class that owned the means of production and profited by requiring those without such means to work excess hours. Both Veblen and Marx saw class oppression leading to superior-inferior economic conditions. For Veblen, this situation led to a purposeful wasting of both time and money among those in the predatory leisure class.

Certainly the leisure class that emerged during the late 1800s was part of an age of extravagance. The newly rich displayed their wealth and used their leisure to show how different and superior they were compared to the working class. And they often used their time unproductively, except as it produced such knowledge or habit as could be displayed.

As David Riesman (1953) pointed out, the portrait painted of the leisure class was somewhat exaggerated. Also, the class basis of leisure and the almost cause-effect relations which Veblen saw were untrue, Riesman said, because of variation which developed within the leisure class. Many in the leisure class, for instance, particularly women, were in the vanguard of modern movements in art and politics. Charity work, however conspicuous, is also useful. *Noblesse oblige.* Veblen, said Riesman, "failed to foresee that many individuals in the better educated strata would be brought into contact with Veblenism, and would learn from him a critique of their consumption which would in turn become part of their conditioning" (p. 176). Veblen made "conspicuous consumption" suspect. That, it seems, was his intent.

The leisure class not only contained people with some diversity in values but also, once exposed to criticisms such as those of Veblen, responded in different ways. That included charity work, urban reform, and championing a variety of worthwhile causes. Also, as consumer goods became widely available to the middle class, there was an ". . . increasing need or desire of people in the upper strata to put on display not as much their purchased possessions as their more subtle qualities of 'personality' and taste" (Riesman, 1953: 170). The arena of display, for many in the leisure class, changed from displaying what one owned to displaying that one had superior taste, and knew both how to do good and live well. Many newly rich, however, still buy the biggest car, house, and boat, at least for the first generation. Perhaps in a world of transients and superficial relationships, it is easier to display economic prowess by the conspicuous consumption of goods, rather than time.

Veblen was in many ways a Puritan and ". . . his books were an attack, not only on spending, but on getting—(since) he saw the race for conspicuous consumption as supporting the race for acquisition" (p. 187). Many in society deplored that race for acquisition. Veblen ridiculed it. Gradually, however, consumerism would become part of the mainstream of American life and the use of leisure without the consumption of goods and services very rare in any social class. Certainly the acquisition and consumption of goods became more democratic and more rational than it was at the turn of the century, but it became, for most, a standard feature of American life. Industrial capitalism was dependent upon it.

THE WORKING CLASS

Not only did industrial capitalism bring about a small "leisure class" which had both time and money, it also brought about a class of workers who often had to be forced to work and, eventually, forced into a model of open-ended consumption which they would eventually come to accept and desire.

Those who lived the rural peasant life were often unwilling factory workers. The Luddite movement, for instance, tried to destroy the machines that were introduced into the work place ". . . until shot, hanged, and deported into submission" (de Grazia, 1962: 313). According to de Grazia, the Luddites were mistaken in their attacks because what really changed and ruled their lives in a revolutionary manner was the clock. "The clock, to repeat, is an automatic machine whose product is regular auditory or visual signals. Who lives by it becomes an automaton, a creature of regularity" (p. 317). Certainly the English villager did not want this industrial life but gradually was forced into it, driven off the land and into the factories. Prior to this,

The life they knew was unpunctual and chatty. A shoemaker got up in the morning when he liked and began work when he liked. If anything of interest happened, out he went from his stool to take a look for himself. If he spent too much time at the alehouse drinking and gossiping one day, he made up for it by working until midnight the next. Like the Lapons or the Trobriand Islanders, he worked in enthusiastic spirits and spent long periods without toil; which, among nonindustrial communities, is a way of working more commonly than is generally supposed. (de Grazia, 1962: 186)

Both the leisure class and the working class were, in many ways, historically new phenomena. The first generation of each group was put at almost opposite ends of the scale: one with plenty of money and plenty of free time but little experience in how to use either; the other with long hours of enforced, standardized, unfulfilling work, but little of the communal leisure they had previously experienced, and little in the way of personal resources to let them adjust to the small blocks of empty time they had. Both groups had great problems in responding to their situations. The working class, in many respects, had been enslaved not only by their dependence upon those who owned the means of production, but also by a world that had sprung up only to accommodate the process of production.

From these initial situations, however, a vast process of transformation would begin. Gradually, through unionization, less brutal management and vast increases in production, the worker would find hours cut and, in many cases, working conditions improved. Also gradually, the worker would begin to accept and then desire the consumption of material goods that was necessary for industrialism to flourish. "The working class has fallen heir to conspicuous consumption, which the leisure class is giving up" (Riesman, 1953). Had the working class not begun to consume in an almost open-ended manner, the world would have unfolded quite differently.

This same process, with some cultural modifications, is going on in many different countries of the world today. In China, Peru, and Japan, some version of this process is unfolding.

For the working class, the meaning and significance of leisure changed somewhere in the fight for shorter hours. Gradually, there took place ". . . a critical change from the nineteenth century vision of man fulfilling himself through the free employment of his own natural gifts that leisure would release. In the new approach, the emphasis was markedly upon a materialistic set of goals" (Glasser, 1970: 52). "The aim was now to exact a price for labor high enough to buy things, a material existence that copied the lives of the leisure classes" (p. 52). Slowly, those in the working class gained the power to actually emulate those in the leisure class, although on a necessarily more modest scale. Leisure began to be the arena for consumption.

Perhaps conversely, some members of the leisure class, having adjusted to the situation of material wealth, became interested in a broader variety of leisure pursuits, from charitable causes to adventures in the out of doors.

Thus, while the huge gaps between classes lessened, the emerging middle class increasingly lived their lives as those who owned the means of production at the beginning of the Industrial Revolution would have wanted them to—as consumers who always desired more and better material things and as good workers willing to sell their labor.

Consumption As Legitimation

Throughout history, leisure has sometimes been suspect and at other times it has been legitimized, for a variety of different reasons. Since the Reformation in the early 1500s, and especially since the emergence of industrial capitalism in the late 1700s, the legitimacy of leisure—or at least free time—has been based on its utility, not for the mass of workers, but for the system of industrial capitalism.

Even today, while there are undoubtedly generous motives based on human welfare, industrial recreation is still rationalized on the grounds of lower absenteeism, lower employee turnover, higher morale and higher productivity. The company picnic and the company bowling league induce a corporate family and corporate community at a time when family and community are besieged.

But industrialism legitimized leisure in another way, in some respects an opposite way. For while leisure is still legitimized for its utility for production, it is now also legitimized for its utility for consumption. Consumption takes money. It also takes time. In fact, as David Riesman (1965) suggested, consuming has become the principal occupation of millions, including teenagers and adults who have no idea what to do with their free time except shop, or at least visit shopping centers and malls. Without evenings and week ends, the entertainment business would collapse; without vacations, so would tourism. In fact, leisure, not work, is driving mature, industrial capitalism. Therein lies its new legitimacy. Unemployment is a problem in such economies not because of the loss of productive work but because the unemployed do not have much money to spend. The modern economic problem is not the inability to produce, but the inability to consume enough to keep everyone at work producing.

Leisure: The End of A Romantic View

The development of a working class and of a Puritan-inspired elite brought about an end to a romantic notion of humans and the role of leisure in their lives. The romantic philosophy had assumed that nature was a guiding principle in life and that human beings were endowed with abilities and motivations which, if allowed free play, would guide them toward "fulfillment." Man in his natural state was good and happy—happy because he was good (Glasser, 1970). The romantics thought humans intuitively understood what was right for their nature. In following one's intuition, both the individual and society at large would assumably benefit. Only the constraints of civilization prevented individual fulfillment. Leisure played a special role in combating the evils of civilization.

> Leisure would provide not an escape route in the cynical
> modern sense but rather a road back, a return to a healthy,
> balanced interflowing with nature, an exalted harmony, in
> which each person would become 'better' and therefore
> happier because he would be truly his 'natural' self.
> 'Better' was understood in these terms alone. (Glasser, 1970: 49)

Leisure was to be fought for and was the medium through which nature would show the way.

The romantic philosophy also assumed a kind of natural equality among all people. This assumption was a rallying point for a series of revolutions in France, the United States, and elsewhere. The romantic philosophy was one of optimistic belief in the capabilities of people and thus directly in opposition to the Puritan Ethic. While the romantic thought that humans, if left to their natural impulses, would benefit both themselves and society due to their innate goodness, the ethic which drove the industrial revolution was one which viewed the natural impulses of humans as sinful and undesirable. Leisure would not be the medium of fulfillment; it would result in activity which was evil and of little value. Humans were not equal; some were chosen by God, predestined to go to Heaven while others were condemned to Hell.

Gradually the working class began to demand leisure, not because it was the arena for self-improvement, the strengthening of family life, or a chance to return temporarily to a state of nature, but merely because the worker was now selling his or her time and wanted the best business deal he or she could make. Unions slowly began to provide the working class with the power to make the best economic deal for the selling of one's work time, but only within the system established by the industrialist. Once the peasant had been taught to want the life of the wealthy, and once given a tiny bit of access to it through the sale of his or her time, the organization of the modern world, including parks, recreation and "leisure services," took shape.

REFERENCES

Burns, Tom. 1973. "Leisure in Industrial Society." In Smith, M. et. al. (Eds.), *Leisure and Society in Britain.* London: Allen Lane.

de Grazia, Sebastian. 1962. *Of Time, Work and Leisure.* New York: Twentieth Century Fund.

Dulles, Foster Rhea. 1965. *A History of Recreation—America Learns to Play* (2nd ed.). New York: Appleton-Century-Crofts.

Glasser, Ralph. 1970. *Leisure—Penalty or Prize.* London: Macmillan and Company.

Goodale, Thomas. 1985. "Prevailing Winds and Bending Mandates." In Thomas Goodale and Peter Witt (Eds.), *Recreation and Leisure: Issues in an Era of Change* (2nd ed.). State College, Pennsylvania: Venture Publishing.

Hays, Samuel. 1957. *The Response to Industrialism: 1885-1914.* Chicago: University of Chicago Press.

Huizinga, Johan. 1955. *Homo Ludens: A Study of the Play Element in Culture.* Boston: Beacon Press.

Lerner, Max. 1948. *The Portable Veblen.* New York: The Viking Press.

Reisman, David. 1965. *Abundance for What?* Garden City, New York: Doubleday and Co.

Reisman, David. 1953. *Thorstein Veblen: A Critical Interpretation.* New York: Charles Scribner's Sons.

Veblen, Thorstein. 1934. *The Theory of the Leisure Class.* New York: Modern Library.

Weber, Max. 1958. *The Protestant Ethic and the Spirit of Capitalism.* New York: Charles Scribner's Sons.

It became clear, as the importance of recreation as a necessary part of normal life was increasingly recognized, that government must assume responsibility for recreation. High governmental officials, prominent organizations, citizens and economists voiced the opinion that public parks and recreation centers were, like schools, essential to the health, safety and welfare of the community. State legislatures passed laws empowering municipalities and counties to conduct recreational activities. Decisions by state and federal courts declared recreation to be an essential governmental function. . . .

Thus recreation has come to be classed with other well-established municipal activities. It is as much a proper subject for collective action as are schools, police and fire protection, sanitation and health, and libraries. Just as the public has learned that to secure a pure and adequate water supply at moderate cost the government must have responsibility, so it is learning that to provide recreation for all there must be governmental responsibility. Government is our means of meeting essential needs collectively. That the government should provide parks, playgrounds, libraries and indoor recreation centers is thus simply a lesson growing out of American experience.

(Weaver W. Pangburn, 1932: 80)

VII. COLLECTIVE RESPONSES

Throughout the 19th century in Europe and North America, the potential for leisure was curtailed both by the terribly long hours of work that factory workers, miners, and other laborers had forced upon them, and by the lack of provision for leisure expression found in cities. Leisure was further limited by the "spread of evangelical principles" (Altick, 1958) which prevented the middle class, on moral grounds, from participating in a wide variety of leisure activities, including most forms of outside entertainment; dance, cards, billiards, most forms of music and singing, "mixed" swimming, and many others.

The working man had little time for leisure on the weekday and, during the weekend, had few alternatives from which to choose. As Altick noted (1958: 45) during weekends the townsmen:

> . . .could get drunk in a public house, or to the accompaniment
> of a song; at a concert room or a dancing saloon; he could
> visit a brothel; he could get into a fistfight or attend a bear-
> baiting; or he could loaf in the streets—and not much else.
> The teaming cities had virtually no provision for decent
> public recreation: few theatres or dance halls; no parks for
> strolling; no museums or art galleries; no free libraries.

For children, the consequences of these conditions were devastating. There was no place to play and many forms of play were condemned as being evil. Often, children were viewed as a cheap labor source and they worked the same long hours as their parents.

THE REFORM AGENDA

From about the mid-1800s until well into the 1900s, reform movements sprang up in every field; labor, child welfare, public higher education, sanitation, health and others. Having been preoccupied, for several decades, with that "peculiar" institution, slavery, Americans discovered that industrialism and urbanization had been proceeding rapidly, leaving a trail of social problems. By the late 1800s, social activists and crusaders had begun to challenge the basic tenets of the economic "laws" of capitalism and the biological "laws" of the emerging social Darwinism.

The progressive movement, populism and socialism became important political and social movements at this time. The philosophical foundations of these movements branched from earlier philosophies of utilitarianism and pragmatism into what John Dewey, by the turn of the century, called "instrumentalism." While accepting the basic notions of evolution, including social evolution, Dewey and others (as did Darwin) believed that man was not simply a biological animal but a social animal as well. In addition, the evolution of society was seen not as the result of inevitable forces but as the product of human values and intelligence.

Instrumentalism, in essence, meant that human intelligence was an instrument that could be used to shape the human condition and to shape social and collective life. Man could intervene on his own behalf and channel the evolution of community and social life. That philosophy is indispensable to interventions and efforts to reform.

THE SPECTRE OF FREE TIME BADLY SPENT

The reformers were deeply concerned about welfare, especially the welfare of children, and they were deeply troubled by the conditions of an urban life bereft of opportunities for healthy exercise and play. The urban churches, in many cases, gradually began to recognize such problems and to come to terms with a new role in regard to recreation. In the last part of the

19th century, there was recognition among many leaders of the church that the church's prohibitions against many forms of recreation, such as dancing, theatre, and "mixed" swimming, would not hold up unless some alternatives were offered. By the 1890s a number of churches had begun to develop libraries, gymnasia, and assembly halls. "It was the era of sociables, fairs, suppers, and strawberry festivals" (Dulles, 1965: 205).

Certainly, a number of church leaders continued to argue that the church should play no role in the provision of recreation. The argument against church involvement gradually lost ground, however, because the increasing leisure opportunities offered by the commercial sector could not go unchallenged.

The settlement house movement was also largely a reflection of urban Christianity's response to industrialization and its problems. Socialism and labor issues had dominated the social gospel by the 1880s, but there had also been interest in problems of immigration, the saloon, the family, housing, and amusements (Knapp & Hartsoe, 1979). Within the urban context, the church often became interested in and involved with social welfare, reform, and character-building.

Almost from the beginning of the industrialization and urbanizing process in both Europe and North America, a number of other reforming movements sprang up to try to improve the recreation and leisure opportunities of urban dwellers. All of these reform movements, although differing in mission and in tactics, dealt more with the concept of recreation than leisure. That is, they were concerned with providing wholesome opportunities for activity after work which refreshed and renewed the worker who was in a cycle of work, recreation, and more work.

These reformers did not all share a common political philosophy or vision of leisure ideals. Far from it. They ranged from radical socialist reformers to conservative businessmen who wanted to help their respective communities. They ranged from those such as Sir John Herschel of England, who promoted books as the answer to the problem of amusing the working man, to Luther Gulick, who, among other interests, was fascinated with determining the qualities essential for a successful game. An athletic game, he decided, should be ". . . interesting to spectators so there would be money to support it, (that) beginners would have some fun in playing; yet, in connection with which, a great deal of skill could be used and (that) would interest year after year." Gulick, an important person in the YMCA movement, urged Dr. James Naismith to create such a game. Naismith did—basketball (Butler, 1965: 9).

Recreation's Social Utility

The evolution that took place with each of those related reform movements was from a voluntary, loosely organized movement to gradual organization and involvement of government until, eventually, government played a primary role. In every case it may be said that each of these social movements was a reaction to many problems created by the abrupt end to rural and small town life which brought with it a loss of sense of community.

A number of the aims of organizations such as the National Recreation Association, or youth-serving agencies such as the YMCA, concerned the use of recreation as a tool for furthering social, intellectual, and moral development. Consider this passage from *Partners in Play*, published by the National Recreation Association and the Young Women's Christian Association in 1934. It describes relations between adolescent males and females:

> Friendship is the accumulation of shared experiences, and it is the chance to have many and varied ones with each other that young men and women need. The hours of leisure, when there is time to do things together, is the time for developing real friendship. Yet it is in the hours of leisure that we segregate adolescent boys and girls. In spite of coeducational schools, we still provide one set of play activities for boys and another for girls and, although some of the activities may be the same for both sexes, we do not make a point of arranging them in such a way that it is easy for a boy and a girl or two boys to play together. They attend occasional dances and parties together, to be sure, but party manners and the convention of pairing off make these the special events of youth and not the every day affairs which afford young people informal and casual contacts with each other.
>
> To learn how to get along with the opposite sex, teenage boys and girls must have opportunities for more varied associations with each other. They must play games together, go on hikes and picnics, take walks and go on camping trips, put on plays and pageants, sing and play instruments, and have the fun of making things together. (p. 7)

This passage typifies the central elements of the leisure philosophy of social reformers. Recreation and leisure are "provided" or "arranged" for the purpose of serving socially useful ends. Opportunity for a variety of wholesome leisure experiences is important and can serve as a vehicle for learning and for socialization. Recreation and leisure also had (and still have, e.g., Reynolds, 1985) an element of social control, since participation in planned recreation of a wholesome nature will discourage or negate the alternative possibility of undesirable or immoral uses of leisure. Recreation and leisure, it was argued, must be both planned and controlled.

The park and recreation movement had a simple answer for a complex question—"Can the world be trusted with leisure?" "No!" No, it could not, because urbanization had provided no place to pursue the rural pastimes of previous generations. No, because industrial capitalism cared nothing about the life of the worker away from the workplace. No, because the leisure alternatives offered by the city—gambling, commercial sport, prostitution, theatre, and saloons—were morally inferior and corrupting. No, because the natural environment was of critical importance in many forms of recreation and this environment was being systematically savaged for economic gain. While the membership in a variety of movements concerned with parks, recreation, sport, play, conservation, and the welfare of youth varied greatly in its political beliefs, from politically right of center to the far left, there was agreement on this issue—the world could not be trusted with leisure, or at least the "wise and constructive" use of free time.

It would be a mistake, however, to characterize this reformist philosophy as one which wished to smother the notions of recreation and play with complete control of the participant. As Joseph Lee wrote in his book, *Play and Education*, published in 1915:

> Do not be forever meddling, interfering, asking questions,
> showing them a better way. Give the constructive power of
> your children scope and elbow room—the temple that it
> builds is invisible to any eye but theirs. If you blur and jostle
> their vision, it is lost. (Butler, 1965: 1)

Play and leisure expression had been seriously damaged by the process of urbanization and industrialization and now had to be rethought if they were to exist in any spiritually satisfying way. Play and the newly rationalized adaptation of leisure—recreation—also had to be more highly organized because work and the rest of life was becoming more highly organized. The perpetual philosophical dilemma of these reformers was that, to resurrect play and recreation, they were forced to use many of the methods of organization, and even adopt some of the goals, of industrialism—goal setting, rationality, specialization, growth, incremented improvement through mastery of technique—even if these values and goals were used to fight the system which utilized them.

Recreation's Reform Agenda

While the various elements of the recreation and park movement all sought basic kinds of reform in regard to the provision of leisure, their interests were often not recreation and leisure as such. Most of the leaders of these movements viewed recreation as part of a broader concern. As Duncan (1985) pointed out, many were interested in a variety of social movements concerning women's suffrage, the abolition of slavery, community use of schools, the plight of the poor, greater involvement of the church in assistance to the community, improving hygiene, the plight of urban youth, conservation, physical fitness, and others. A few of these leaders, such as Joseph Lee, focused on children's play after witnessing children being arrested for playing in the streets. Even Lee, however, viewed recreation as "one important factor in life which also had to be integrated with the educational, political, social, religious and economic realities of neighborhoods and cities" (Duncan, 1985: 412).

The concern, most often, was simply the welfare of people. As Dorothy Enderis, who directed Milwaukee's Recreation and Adult Education Department from 1920 until 1948 stated: "*Leut* is the German word for people, and 'selig' is holy, and to me, the finest attribute with which you could credit a recreation worker is to say that he is *leutselig*, meaning that people are holy to him" (Butler, 1965: 45).

RELUCTANT RESPONSES

Much of the emerging government involvement in recreation and parks was not necessarily due to an increased awareness of the importance of recreation and leisure. In some cases, government involvement represented an unanticipated extension of volunteer effort, as in the case of the Boston sand garden. In 1855, a large sand pile was placed at a children's mission through the efforts of a volunteer group named the Massachusetts Emergency and Hygiene Association. Children played in the sand under the direction of a woman who lived in the neighborhood. Gradually the idea spread and, by 1899, the Boston City Council provided $3,000 toward meeting costs (Butler, 1959). As this process developed, it mirrored other recreation initiatives started by concerned citizens in that it began as a private project and was taken over by government; they were first financed through private philanthropy and later from public monies; the operations moved gradually from private to public property; the recreation activities initially under the supervision of volunteer leaders or matrons were gradually taken over by trained leaders; the first concern was for young children but was later enlarged to include older boys (and still later—girls).

In other cases, such as in much of the involvement of the federal government in the provision of outdoor recreation, involvement was almost forced. The acquisition of land and water by a variety of state and federal agencies for purposes such as conservation, flood control, timber management, irrigation, production of hydroelectricity, and others, created a recreation potential which unwittingly forced many such agencies into the provision of outdoor recreation opportunities. The United States Forest Service, for instance, was literally forced to manage camping and other forms of forest recreation when it became clear that the public could not be stopped from camping in federally owned forested areas and that such unsupervised camping led to hundreds of forest fires. Similarly, the dams created by the Army Corps of Engineers and the Tennessee Valley Authority, although created for flood control and generation of electricity, provided lakes which the public was going to use for boating, fishing, and other forms of recreation. Could the public be trusted with leisure? No, it could not. Uncontrolled use of the federal lands resulted in fires and drownings at an alarming rate.

The Evolution of Public Involvement

The philosophical assumptions made about public recreation and park services evolved steadily from their inception. With regard to urban parks, Cranz (1982) traced their philosophical and political evolution through four distinct phases.

The Pleasure Ground. From the mid- to late 1800s, parks, developed by Frederick Olmstead and others, represented an attempt to regain the rural countryside in the middle of the city. They were characterized by artificial lakes, grass which was regularly mowed, and pathways for carriages. Buildings were considered an evil in these parks, but were sometimes necessary. While such parks were often characterized as existing for passive use, in reality they were full of people participating in unstructured recreation activities such as baseball, bike riding, mass meetings, ice skating, horseback riding, and many others. The ideal was for people to spend the day at the park. Thus, refreshment stands, rest rooms, and other support services were needed. So, too, was the need to create order in these parks, which led to many rules and regulations, enforced by the police. These parks were created largely through the efforts of wealthy community leaders who wanted to create, in Olmstead's words, "a class of opposite conditions" from urban life.

The Reform Park. From the period of 1900 to 1930, children became an important focus of urban park planning. Recreation activities were more highly organized for the masses who were considered incapable of using free time in satisfying ways without guidance. Parks were now designed so that users were segregated by age and gender. The play movement, under the leadership of Joseph Lee, assumed that play developed character. Since children were thought to be imitative, the character and qualifications of play leaders were all important. Playgrounds became a standard feature of parks. Slowly, many playgrounds evolved into recreation centers, combining features of playgrounds and settlement houses.

The reform park was not a substitute for the countryside, but for the street. Reform parks featured swimming baths to promote cleanliness among the working class. Children's vegetable gardens, the sale of pure milk, crafts, folk dancing, library services, and the promotion of athletics were all reform park features designed to improve the physical, intellectual, and moral life of urban dwellers.

The Recreation Facility. During this era of urban parks, park administrators slowly abandoned efforts to use parks for social improvement or social control. Parks had become an expected part of urban life. Park and recreation systems began to be driven by the concept of "demand" rather than a service ethic of moral considerations. Recreation programs were often planned with community groups whose interest was a single activity such as photography, dog-training, or archery. Park design, during this era, became thought of as part of a municipal "package." "Demand" meant what people did or wanted to do during leisure. Cities developed guidelines and standards for open space, facilities and equipment, and master-plans for parks.

The Great Depression led to many public works projects which included the development of many new parks and recreation facilities, in cities as well as the rural outdoors. The Depression also taught us, incidentally, that unemployment is not simply the result of laziness and sloth. Not only did the stock market crash in 1929 but also the life style of the "Roaring Twenties." Widespread poverty taxed municipalities beyond their resources, and senior levels of government took on an expanded role in the provision of social goods, including parks and recreation.

The Open Space System. This era, which began about 1965, was characterized by a philosophical vacuum about what parks are for. Led by New York City's Director of Recreation and Parks, Thomas Hoving, parks became the sites for rock concerts and other mass events. Many parks, which had been abandoned and were considered unsafe, were temporarily shocked back to life by a "Hoving Happening."

This was a period of experimentation, particularly in poverty areas, with the development of some nontraditional kinds of open space such as mini-parks, "play streets" (regular streets where traffic was periodically blocked) and use of abandoned lots for play areas. In addition, linear parks and open spaces, and linear linkages between parks were proposed and developed, with varying degrees of success. Much of this experimentation, however, ended with the decline of support for such experimentation. Many such projects were also ultimately regarded as failures. What remained was the standard approach to parks and open space. In terms of the development of urban parks, in the United States, Cranz concluded:

> Parks have been diffused from city to city and region to region through such media as annual reports, congresses, manuals, national professional associations, and universities. The process has led to design criteria with little living relation to particular cultures, climates, or people. Its antithesis, design with local roots, could introduce regional character into the line of park design options. (Cranz, 1982: 250)

The era of the Open Space System represented, in some respects, an inability to enunciate any ideal which sprang from a sense of space. Open space, often defined simply as "all land and water in an urban area which is not covered by buildings" (Gold, 1973: 320), became an almost generic concept, thought to apply uniformly to all urban areas. As Cranz observed, however, the process of developing urban parks is not so much one of technology but of cultural discovery.

The provision of urban recreation and parks, in summary, had come from one philosophically extreme position—i.e., parks and recreation are an important means to be utilized in the prevention of juvenile delinquency, the improvement of citizens' physical fitness, the strengthening of family life, etc., to another philosophical extreme in which parks and recreation are an important end simply because people want them. Since people want them, the process of providing which services is merely one of technology—how to do so efficiently and effectively. Put another way, the emerging profession of recreation and parks became removed from consideration of philosophical questions concerning recreation and leisure or answered any question raised by responding that, since the public wanted such services, they were automatically worthwhile.

Public and Private Interests Merge. This change in mentality signaled an end to the antagonism between those who provided public leisure services and those involved in commercial leisure services. Both sectors were now driven essentially by demand as measured by the willingness of participants to spend money. Public leisure services, at all levels, increasingly used fees and charges as a means of financing their operations. The marketing techniques of commerce were increasingly utilized. The old slogan of marketing: "See what the lady wants" became central to the management of government leisure services. Certainly this change reflected other changes in society; higher levels of education, greater discretionary income, improvement in urban conditions. There also appeared to be an increasing philosophical assumption that people could take care of themselves. In effect, people really were assumed to be free, or, if not free, at least sovereign. If they were poor or ignorant they had, in effect, chosen to be so. This change of philosophy toward society meant the answer to a fundamental question had changed: Could the world be trusted with leisure? Yes! Yes, because people were no longer slaves to those who owned the means of production. Yes, because individuals were exposed to a variety of leisure activities and, in effect, voted for what was worthwhile during leisure by their actual participation and other expressions of interests and desires.

Responding to Need. The following table describes different concepts of recreation need which have been utilized by public recreation and park officials. These differing concepts mirror the changes identified by Cranz. Both normative and comparative concepts of recreation need assume that some minimum level of recreation is necessary within the context of a work-recreation-work cycle. Neither of these concepts assume that individuals must be asked about their recreation desires. The comparative need model further assumes that government must give priority to those who are most dependent recreationally, e.g., the poor. Normative measures reflect the beliefs of those who began fighting against the loss of common playing grounds in Britain and advocated a park within walking distance of every household. Comparative need corresponds to the reformist recreation movement which sought to improve city life for the poor and change the distribution of wealth and the balance of power.

Expressed need and felt need represent a fundamental change in the philosophy of public recreation and park agencies. Both express a marketing approach. The important determinants of recreation are what people say they want to do and what they actually do. Expressed need, in particular, seems to assume a world with no need for reform—people can do what they wish during leisure so government must merely measure what they are currently doing for recreation, make population projections into the future, and provide more of the same. This concept of recreation need, which has been particularly popular with state and federal agencies which manage resources for recreational use, comes full circle from a reformist mentality. Not only can the world be trusted with leisure, but the entire universe is no doubt unfolding as it should. What is needed, therefore, in terms of recreation, is more of what exists.

The Return to Community. The economic conditions of the 1970s which led public park and recreation agencies to behave increasingly like their counterparts in commercial recreation had another effect as well. Increasing demands for municipal services, without equal increases in financial and other resources, necessarily meant that public agencies could not meet the new demands. In some cases, municipal park and recreation agencies could not even maintain their present levels of service.

This was coupled with a change of philosophy among those in the leisure services field. Concerns had been voiced about the likelihood that, by providing so many facilities and services, individuals and groups in the community were becoming dependent on others, particularly local government agencies, for their recreation. This was seen to be directly counter to the objective of making individuals and groups as self-sufficient as they could become. Agency staffs shifted their thinking, and in many cases their roles, from providers of programs and services to community developers seeking to enable and facilitate others to provide for themselves. The new task was defined as developing and capitalizing on all the resources in the community, including its human resources, to assure ample recreation opportunities for all.

Commercial Forms of Leisure. If the excesses of industrialization brought about a reformist response in regard to recreation, so too did it eventually bring about new opportunities for commercial leisure. Dramatic improvements in income, a gradual reduction of working hours, child labor laws, advances in the technology of communication and transportation brought about a broader range of choice. Recreation activities undertaken by the rich began to trickle down to the rest of society. Low-cost train and

RECREATION NEEDS

	Conceptualizations of Recreation Need	Definitions of Recreation	Value Assumptions	Information Needs
Expressed Need	• Individual's need for leisure is determined by individual's current leisure activity patterns.	• The expression of individual values through participation in freely chosen activities.	• Government should be a culturally neutral provider. There is a relatively just distribution of recreation resources. • Individuals have a relatively easy and equal access to recreation resources. • Individuals don't have a similar need for publicly sponsored recreation services. • Variation in need is expressed through differences in participation rate.	• Determining what people do during leisure: activities participated in, duration, frequency, sequencing, and scheduling.
Comparative Need	• Need for leisure services of government as systematically related to both supply of leisure resources available to an individual and his/her socioeconomic characteristics.	• High autonomy in non-work activity which is the prerogative of an elite; a right to pursue happiness which is systematically inequitably distributed.	• Government should not be a culturally neutral provider. • People do not have similar need for public recreation resources. • Those wth low socioeconomic statuses have higher need.	• Studies of participation and nonparticipation and relationship to socioeconomic variables. • Studies of relationship of supply of recreation resources to socioeconomic status.

| Created Need | • Leisure need is determined by individual choosing to participate in activity after being taught to value it. | • Any activity in which, after sufficient introduction, an individual will freely and pleasurably participate. | • There may not be a relatively just distribution of recreation resources.
• Individuals may have relatively difficult and unequal access to public recreation services.
• Government should not be a culturally neutral provider.
• Individuals often don't know what they want to do during leisure and are happier if given guidance.
• Leisure activities are substitutable since the individual seeks certain environmental conditions, not specific activities.
• It is legitimate to use recreation to promote the desired goals of the state. | • Case studies examining reasons for participation among various subcultures.
• Pre- and post-testing of behavior and attitudes as a result of participation in public recreation services. |

RECREATION NEEDS (continued)

	Conceptualizations of Recreation Need	Definitions of Recreation	Value Assumptions	Information Needs
Normative Need	• Experts can establish precise, objective standards to establish desirable minimum supply in quantitative terms. Implies physiological need for leisure.	• A set of physiologically necessary yet pleasurable activities undertaken during nonwork time which restore and refresh the individual and prepare him/her for work again and otherwise contribute to his/her well-being.	• Government should not be a culturally neutral provider. • Individuals have similar need for public recreation. • Certain well-established kinds of recreation resources are inherently in the public interest. • Recreation resources should be equally distributed through space.	• Testing of assumptions of standards; i.e., accuracy of service radii. • Testing relationship between perceived satisfaction and social quality indicators; e.g., crime rate, and having met standards.
Felt Need	• Individuals need for leisure activity as a function of individual belief, perception, and attitude.	• What an individual would choose to do given a minimum of constraints or high autonomy. • It is a set of personally ideal activities in the mind of the individual which, given the opportunity he/she will undertake.	• Government should be a culturally neutral provider. • Many individuals desire to participate in activities which they currently do not. • There may not be a relatively just distribution of recreation resources.	• Attitudinal research concerning people's desire for recreation experiences and environments and intensity of desire.

- Individuals often have legitimate reasons for not using public recreation resources.
- Individuals may not have relatively easy or equal access to public recreation resources.
- Individuals will be happier participating in what they "perceive" they want to do than in what they are currently doing.

Source: David Mercer, "The Concept of Recreation Need." *Journal of Leisure Research.* Winter, 1973, p. 39; and Geoffrey Godbey

streetcar fares, for instance, made day-long excursions possible for many. Amusement parks, developed at the end of trolley car routes, drew the masses. Many forms of sport began a process of democratization. Technology, shaped by the commercial sector, brought about the phonograph, radio, movies, and automobile. Not only were a broader range of leisure opportunities coming about but, by the 1930s, the two-day weekend was becoming prevalent in North America. Prohibition against many forms of recreation on the Sabbath has loosened. The prohibition of alcohol informed us of the limits of reform-ist zeal.

Because of these changes, historian Gary Cross noted that "Despite efforts of governments, employers and trade unions to organize mass leisure in the interwar period, in the West, at least leisure increasingly became privatized as well as more democratic and commercial" (1985: 5).

The various reformist movements in recreation and parks were not a failure; far from it. They were, however, reactions to specific societal situations and, to the extent these situations changed, the impact of these movements lessened. The Depression and world wars brought about new sets of social emergencies which placed the agendas of recreation and park reformers temporarily in the center of community life. With each new era of prosperity, however, commercialized forms of recreation became increasingly important. What societal situations we will face in the future, and how we will respond, is anyone's guess. We now have a new industry, the "futures" industry, seeking to inform our guesswork. Meanwhile, look what we've done to our time.

REFERENCES

Altick, Richard D. 1958. "The Spread of Reading." In E. Larrabee and R. Meyersohn (Eds.), *Mass Leisure*. Glencoe, Illinois: The Free Press.

Breen, Mary J. 1939. *Partners In Play—Recreation for Young Men and Women Together*. New York: Barnes and Noble.

Butler, George. 1959. *Introduction to Community Recreation*. New York: McGraw-Hill.

Cranz, Galen. 1982. *The Politics of Park Design—A History of Urban Parks in America*. Cambridge, Massachusetts: MIT Press.

Cross, Gary. 1985. "Leisure in Historical Perspective." (Unpublished).

Dulles, Foster Rhea. 1965. *A History of Recreation: American Learns to Play* (2nd ed.). New York: Appleton-Century-Crofts.

Duncan, Mary. 1985. "Back to Our Radical Roots." In Thomas Goodale, and Peter Witt (Eds.), *Recreation and Leisure: Issues in An Era of Change*. State College, Pennsylvania: Venture Publishing.

Enderis, Dorothy. Quoted in Butler, George. 1965. *Pioneers In Public Recreation*. Minneapolis: Burgess.

Godbey, Geoffrey. 1985. *Leisure In Your Life: An Exploration* (2nd ed.). State College, Pennsylvania: Venture Publishing.

Gold, Seymour. 1973. *Urban Recreation Planning*. Philadelphia: Lea and Febiger.

Knapp, Richard F. and Hartsoe, Charles E. 1985. *Play for America: The National Recreation Association*. Arlington, Virginia: National Recreation and Park Association.

Pangburn, Weaver W. 1936. *Adventures in Recreation*. New York: A.S. Barnes and Co.

Reynolds, Ron. 1985. "Leisure Services and Social Control." In Thomas Goodale, and Peter Witt (Eds.), *Recreation and Leisure: Issues in An Era of Change*. State College, Pennsylvania: Venture Publishing.

Into this problem, I do not think our inner sense of duration—psychological time—takes us far, at least not on the level on which it is usually examined. Of course it is important and must be discussed, for it is the time we really live with. Clock time is our bank manager, tax collector, police inspector; this inner time is our wife.

Notice how inner time behaves, as if it had centuries of chronological time at his disposal. As soon as we make full use of our faculties, commit ourselves heart and soul to anything, live richly and intensely instead of merely existing, our inner time spends our ration of clock time as a drunken sailor his pay. What are hours outside seem minutes inside. Yet no allowance is made for this prodigality; our calendar time is not extended as a reward for living generously. If we wanted to stretch out our allotment of outer time, to make the most of it in a miserly fashion, we would take care to keep ourselves only half-alive, spend yawning hours (they would be like whole days to our inner time) with boring and mechanical people or with dreary little pursuits.

Failing that, we might do what many important and successful men always appear to have done: appoint a kind of policeman from outer time to control the antics and vagaries of our inner time. When one of these important and successful men awards us 15 minutes of his outer time, we can often see that policeman in his eyes, hear him in the guarded voice. But although his control of inner time might bring more success and importance, few of us feel it would enrich experience and make for a good life. These seem to demand a certain recklessness in our relation with our inner time, as if as we move inward we can defy outer time, the clocks and calendars, like immortal beings. We are not immortal beings, but we should often behave as if we were.

(Joseph Priestly, 1964: 66)

VIII. TIME AS COMMODITY

In commenting on the research methods used in a twelve-nation study of people's use of time, the German sociologist Erwin Scheusch (1972: 77) stated:

> A main problem in recording the use of time derives from the fact that many people during a large part of the day do more than one thing at one time. Our pretests suggest that the more a person is part of an industrial society with a very high density of communication, and the more educated a person, the more likely he is to do a number of things simultaneously. While it is generally true that everyone—regardless of status or nationality—has merely the same 24 hours at his disposal there is actually something like 'time deepening' (to coin a term in analogy to capital deepening): if a person develops the ability to do several things simulta-neously, he can crowd a greater number of activities into the same 24 hours.

This finding reflects the changes which modernization and increased education have brought about in the way we conceive of time and of leisure. These changes have been so drastic that the notion of leisure among many today is almost in direct opposition to its ancient meanings.

TIME ANCIENT . . .

The oldest meanings of time were rooted in the changes which took place in the natural, physical world. The sun rose and set, the tides came in and went out, the moon orbited the earth, the earth orbited the sun, vegetation and the color of the sky changed with the passing of seasons. These changes produced the basis for measurement and shaped a concept of time which may be called naturalistic. To a great extent, this concept was cyclical. That is, the sun circled the earth (the ancients believed) the seasons followed one after another in a perpetual reoccurrence, crops were harvested time and time again. While humans have always been unique among animals in their ability to predict their own deaths, and thus can see some aspect of time as being limited and moving in a straight line, even the knowledge of death was incorporated into the concept of time as a recurring cycle of birth, life, death, and rebirth which repeated endlessly. To ancient peoples, who viewed themselves and their lives with less seriousness than we, humans were the playthings of the gods. Humans were dust in the wind; time was a cycle of ashes to ashes, dust to dust. The individual was a small part of existence whose significance was bound up in the endlessly repeating cycle of nature. Time could not be lost since the events that made up time would return again, forever. Humans did not control time since most measures of time came from nature and even those guidelines concerning time which came from society, such an annual festivals or celebrations, had tradition and cultural necessity attached to them and were, therefore, largely beyond individual control.

If one were the plaything of the gods, however, whose meaning was wrapped up in natural events over which one had no control, time was a phenomenon which humans did not expect to shape or control. Indeed, in many cultures it would have been considered the height of arrogance to expect to interfere with the passage of time in the natural world. Given these beliefs, it was natural to speak of time as "passing." Time was not within one's ownership, not much shaped by human desires or behaviors.

. . . And Modern

It is hard for us to understand the ancients' concept of time. While we still use the word "pastimes," it is almost impossible to think of letting time pass or to be "passive" in regard to time. While the original conceptualizations of time may have been naturalistic, cyclic, or circular, time gradually became thought of as linear; proceeding in a straight line. This change occurred for many reasons which cannot be completely represented here or even completely conceptualized. It was, perhaps, the most important change in the spiritual lives of humans which has yet taken place. Time became linear, that is, proceeding in a straight line. It became finite, capable of being measured in terms other than those provided by nature, and standardized across cultures and among individuals. It also, somehow, has come to rule our lives.

Linear time, which refers to time measured mechanically, was made possible by the invention of the clock. While sun dials and the ringing of bells in monasteries were used to signal the time in preindustrial cultures, the clock made it possible for everyone to "keep" the same time with great accuracy. As de Grazia (1962) put it:

> Though its original contribution as a model was great, the clock's main function became to give frequent signals, auditory and visual, to enable men to start or stop an activity together. Before the clock there was the bell tower which from far off could not only be heard but also be seen for orientation. Then there was, and still is in some places the factory whistle. But both these devices were limited for work in the big, noisy cities. The clock, first placed in a tower and later hung up wherever work was to be done, provided the means whereby large scale industry could coordinate the movements of men and materials to the regularity of machines. (p. 395)

The measurement of time by clocks signaled the completion of a conversion to linear time in society. Time now could be measured without regard to natural events. Seconds and minutes ticked off one at a time, as if in a straight line. Once gone, a second would never return.

The measurement of time was now controlled by humans instead of nature but linear time, as measured by clocks, soon became a new form of human enslavement. As de Grazia (1962) observed, humans rejected the tyranny of man while submitting to the tyranny of the clock. A number of factors, of course, helped set the stage for this to happen.

THE CREATION OF WANTS

One of the great hopes that accompanied industrialization was that there would eventually be more leisure for all. As John Kenneth Galbraith wrote in 1967, however:

> The notion of a new era of greatly expanded leisure is, in fact, a conventional conversation piece. Nor will it serve much longer to convey an impression of social vision. The tendency of the industrial system is not in that direction. (pp. 365-6)

At the present time, the percentage of people in the labor force in the United States, Canada and elsewhere is, in fact, at an all-time high. It has become clear that the emerging industrial state has led, not only to the situation in which time is treated as a scarce commodity, but to the increasing scarcity of that commodity. While conventional wisdom continues to assume that increases in productivity will lead to more time for leisure, almost no case can be made, over the last 40 years, that this assertion is correct. In fact, a case can be made that people do not want more leisure, or that desire for more leisure is distinctly secondary to desire for more material goods. Consider the evidence:

> In the advanced industrial countries, the creation of wants, and therewith the need to work, is a matter of considerable sophistication, but the principles are the same. It is also a task of great importance. In 1939 the real income of employed workers in the United States was very nearly the highest on record and it was then the highest of any country in the world. In the next quarter century it doubled. Had the 1939 income been a terminal objective, work effort would have been cut in half in the ensuing twenty-five years. In fact, there was a slight increase in weekly hours actually worked. This was a remarkable achievement. (Galbraith, 1967: 272)

Such a situation, in which the desire for more money, primarily for the satisfaction of wants rather than necessities or savings, came about, Galbraith contended, because of the persuasive power of the industrial system to inculcate belief in its needs. The production of goods came to be the primary test of social achievement. Indexes such as the Gross National Product, Dow-Jones Industrial Average and the Consumer Price Index became the measures of our well-being. Economic theory has supported this by assuming that consumer wants are all equally valid and that they are insatiable. "If all wants are of equally good standing, it follows that the moral and social obligation to work to fill them remains undiminished in power no matter how much is produced" (p. 273). Such a line of reasoning ensures that time will remain a valuable commodity and that reducing the workweek length will not necessarily be viewed as worthwhile social policy.

Advertising, of course, has become a very important stimulator of wants and it has been argued that without advertising wants would not be stimulated and the economy would decline. This, as Galbraith observed, flies in the face of the idea that wants are insatiable or that all wants are the same. Nonetheless, advertising is amazingly pervasive in our society and has been one of the means by which, as we observed earlier, the working class was persuaded to work longer hours in exchange for more things.

Goods Cost Time

As de Grazia (1962) observed, what we want today are things, things cost money, money costs time. The increasing accumulation of goods also means that more time will be spent in the consumption and maintenance of them, unless short cuts can be found. As Linder (1970) pointed out, when increases in the productivity of goods occur faster than increases in the productivity of services, maintenance will be increasingly expensive in relation to goods. Since this appears to have happened, we try to purchase goods which require less maintenance and also cut back on the time spent maintaining goods. Replacement becomes cheaper than repair, and shortcuts are sought for personal maintenance. Goods are substituted for time, which is thought to be increasingly scarce.

In such a situation, as the amount we own, consume and maintain increases, advertising becomes increasingly necessary since we no longer have as much time to acquire complete information on each item we purchase. Advertising both informs and persuades in a highly capsulized manner.

In addition, as more and more goods are owned, the time spent in consumption per item will decrease since goods are becoming cheaper in relation to time. Consumption will become more "commodity intensive" (Linder 1970). That is, people will try to speed up consumption since time is both more "limited" and more "expensive" in relation to things. Accelerating consumption, according to Linder, may be done by maximizing the time spent through using a more expensive version of a commodity, simultaneous consumption in which more than one thing is consumed at a time, or by consuming more rapidly.

Some activities, of course, are very limited in their ability to be combined with things; eating, for instance, or making love, or all those activities which involve the cultivation of the mind. These activities, Linder believed, would have less and less time devoted to them since they cannot be substantially enhanced by things.

The result, then, is not only a speed-up or attempt to speed up many leisure behaviors to save the increasingly valuable commodity of time, but also a change in how we prefer to "spend" our leisure. Among the activities that will be minimized are contemplation, writing poetry and political debate which the ancient Athenians, 23 centuries ago, believed to be the essence of leisure.

The creation of wants under industrialism, then, led to the increasing scarcity of time and to changes in leisure behavior.

THE INCREASING SCARCITY OF TIME

If we assume that time is subject to economic laws, then the scarcity of time will be determined simply by the demand for time in relation to the supply. The demand for time may be shaped by what our time is worth economically and by what and how much we want to do for personal satisfaction. The increases in production brought about a situation described by Linder (1970: 4) as follows:

> The yield on time spent working increases as the result of economic growth. Productivity per hour rises. This means that the time allocation which has represented equilibrium at our previous level to other activities must also be raised. We are aware that time in production becomes increasingly scarce with economic growth. What we will now claim in addition to this is that changes in the use of time will occur, so that the yield on time in all other activities is brought into parity with the yield on working time. In other words, economic growth entails a general increase in the scarcity of time.

The implications of this statement are enormous. First, it confirms what we have found elsewhere—our institutions of work shape leisure and the rest of life in essential ways. Second, as Bell (1973) and many other sociologists have told us, thinking of "scarcity" only in terms of material goods is an obsolete notion. Linder claimed we have cultures which suffer from food famine and cultures which suffer from time famine. Because our culture still measures well-being based primarily upon economic indicators, we ignore the scarcity of time which produces stress, perhaps the greatest killer in our society.

Third, the most important way we think about time is our perception of it, that is, "psychological" time. Just as gold is valuable because we believe it to be, so is time. Clock time, in effect, can be severely lengthened or shortened by our perception of it which, in turn, is greatly shaped by our economic valuing of it.

Fourth, just as time spent in work became more carefully regulated as the yield on it increased, so too did leisure time become regulated. Such regulation changed the very nature of what leisure is. While leisure had historically carried connotations of tranquility, peacefulness, timelessness and an opposition to materialism and action, these characteristics were now not only lost but opposed by what leisure had become. It had become, for many, highly time-conscious periods for the consumption of goods and services which materialism had brought about. Leisure was now not a halt from action but rather pleasurable action undertaken within the constraints of the ultimate scarce resource—time. The idea of leisure, much less the prospect of leisure, as a permanent condition, was lost. While individuals might still experience timeless states during leisure, leisure itself was slotted between periods of work, whose values washed over into it continuously.

Time in the Age of Computers

Since time is not so much a tangible thing but rather an idea or concept which reflects our values, the way in which the concept of time is being shaped by the computer revolution may tell us a number of things about how our values have changed. Computers, according to Rifkin (1987) aren't just tools; they represent a new time orientation. The basic electronic pulse beat of the computer, the "nanosecond," is one-billionth of a second, far less that any human can consciously perceive. "Never before has time been organized at a speed beyond the realm of consciousness" (p. 28). While the clock sped the flow of work and synchronized it, the computer may push this speeding up process to an extreme. The average secretary, for instance, once did 30,000 keystrokes an hour but today the average VDT operator does 80,000. "The tool that was designed to allow us to catch up accelerates the flow of activity of the society (thus) requiring us to try to catch up even quicker" (Rifkin, 1987: 28). What will voice recognition technologies do?

Computers have pushed the idea of efficiency and doing things as quickly as possible to such a remarkable extent that these values have become unquestioningly accepted in both capitalist and socialist countries. Work, increasingly, is of value only according to the volume produced. With this mentality, the drive for efficiency is unending. Work will always take too long. Time will become increasingly scarce. Researchers will have more and more data spewed forth from computers and less and less time to analyze, think about, or even read it all. According to Rifkin, computers will push the issue of time saving and efficiency to its logical extreme, forcing us to confront central issues. How efficient is efficient enough? How fast is fast enough? Certainly these questions are related to the question of what level of ownership of material goods is sufficient. How much information is enough? The questions here involve production, consumption, time, leisure and happiness. They are of central importance to our society and, as many observers have noted, there is a remarkable absence of debate concerning not only where the limits are but even what constitutes the good life.

Certainly one part of any such debate will be concern over the way in which time is defined. Will we define time in human terms or terms which machines have created? What does progress mean and how is it related to the amount of things produced, distributed and consumed or discarded? (Notice that "goods" very easily comes to mean material things.) Is good health, which is almost assuredly related to happiness, related to the production of things and, if so, how?

While we cannot presume to answer all these questions, it seems obvious that the answers will, in some form, involve a slowing down of daily life. We may be happier if the pace of our lives is slowed down but we may not know how to do that. If you drive on many of the tollroads in North America, for instance, you find only fast food restaurants. Such establishments encourage you to hurry. Park the car as close as possible. Hurry to the shortest line. Watch the great beehive of activity behind the counter where employees scurry about, speaking in a language code designed to shorten communication time. Receive your food fully cooked and prepared for eating in two or three minutes. Eat your meal within ten minutes and leave. Or order everything "to go." Eat and drive at the same time, and save ten minutes. The fast food restaurant will get you on your way faster, but why? For what purpose have you rushed and, if you rush through dinner, might you also rush through other activities and, eventually, your life? If you rush through life, will you be more or less happy?

Decadence in Abundance

Similarly, if we own more and more material possessions and work long hours so we can purchase them, will this lead to more or less happiness? Linder (1970) said that the acceleration of consumption has led to a situation wherein the marginal utility on each possession we own, while not reaching zero, continued to decline but we became more attached to material goods in general. We are, Linder said, in a period of decadence. Without some change, the following will continue to happen just as they have since 1970, when he wrote this:

There will be an increasingly hectic tempo of life marked by careful attempts to economize on increasingly scarce time.

There will be an expanding mass of goods, which will make great demands on time in the form of such maintenance and service tasks that cannot very well be mechanized. This will happen in spite of a decline in maintenance per item.

Since affluence is only partial, there will be increasing hardships for those whose welfare does not primarily require abundant goods but the scarce time of their fellow creatures. While the aged, in the beginning of the growth period, lacked bed and bread, they will toward the end of the growth mania period lack a nurse.

There will be a curious combination of an increasing attachment to goods in general and, owing to a low degree of utilization and a rapid turnover, an increasing indifference to each of them in particular.

There will be a declining competitive position for time devoted to the cultivation of mind and spirit and for the time spent on certain bodily pleasures. *Dolce far niente.*

There will be a declining utility of income but not an
exhaustion of wants; in order to achieve some addition to
material well-being, increasingly attention will, therefore, be
given to further economic advances.

In the name of economic progress, there will be increasing
emphasis on rational economic policies and behavior, but
for this very reason also—as stated by the rationale of
increasing irrationality—there will be a growing number of
ill-considered decisions.

There will be a new form of economic "unfreedom," marked
not by a fight for economic survival, but an obsession with
growth that sometimes forces us, in the name of registered
increases in economic growth, to allocate our economic
resources, including time itself, in destructive ways—to
destroy God-given bases for life, i.e., air, water, earth,
natural beauty, and our heredity. (pp. 143-144)

It looks as though these predictions are coming true, not only in
North America, but in the rest of the industrializing world. Within the human
body there is a name for the uncontrolled growth of cells—cancer. Surely our
own growth, which has forced a view of the world in which usefulness and
efficiency are the test of almost everything, must be changed. Surely we must
slow down. Surely we must recapture our time not by clinging to it and
counting it more precisely but by loosening our grasp on it, like we would a
small bird held gently in our hands, and, eventually, let it fly.

Can We Change Our Pace?

How to slow down time and de-commodify it is a difficult question.
Linder and others think it will require a change of the human heart: perhaps a
simple recognition that enough is enough. But there is little evidence, so far,
that enough will ever be enough. In spite of record amounts of stress, pathological behavior and a continuing increase in the tempo of life, enough is not
yet enough. North Americans have come to admire Japanese ways of work
and are seeking instruction in the kind of total dedication to work and total
efficiency which the Japanese have utilized to greatly increase their production of goods. Brazilians, South Koreans, Mexicans and others are all

attempting to follow suit. The biggest employer of teenagers in North America is the fast food industry which teaches that rushing through meals (and by implication, through life) is a preferable form of behavior. Time "saving" devices, from microwave ovens to drive-in oil change stations for automobiles, flourish. How many people have all of us observed, impatiently waiting the few seconds required to heat (such as it is) their meals? How many of us do that too? And also for elevators and traffic lights and super-sonic planes? Network television stations cut away from broadcasts of sports events if they take an unexpected long time to finish; bringing prepared food to your door has become a huge business; the average length of magazine and newspaper articles continues to decline. Life continues to speed up.

It may be argued, as did Rifkin (1987) and others, that the sped up way of life will become a political issue which will be raised by the younger generation. But they, too, so far at least, get impatient with microwave ovens. The issue may, however, be forced upon them.

NEW DILEMMAS

Time has always been the source of many ironies. Perhaps the major irony concerning time today is that, while we can document that the percent-age of our lives spent at work has declined considerably during the last century (see, for instance, Owen, 1969; Kreps, 1971), in our minds time has become more scarce. In effect, the more we have, the less we seem to have. This is somewhat like what happens to money in periods of inflation. If we are going to change the situation, however, our analogies to time must not concern money but, perhaps, the human body.

All living things are subject to both daily (diurnal) and annual cycles and processes. Humans are not exempt from such processes.

> For the planning of working hours and sleeping time, which also means for the planning of free time, the biological diurnal cycle must be taken into consideration. Because of technology, man has freed himself much more from the influence of seasons than he has from the influence of the diurnal cycle. Nevertheless, the biological annual cycle has not completely disappeared. It thus remains to be seen whether or not it also has a role to play in the planning of free time. (Aschoff, 1974: 127)

All the organs of the human body are subject to the influences of the biological diurnal clock. "The biological diurnal cycles are not caused by the alteration in sleeping and waking. They are rather, just as the sleeping-waking cycle itself, an expression of the inborn time programme" (Aschoff, 1974: 129). As much research shows, our performance ability is greatly influenced by the time of day. With industrial workers, for instance, performance reaches its first peak in the morning and then another slightly lower one in the afternoon, following a midday low. Performance in the evening drops off quickly and reaches a pronounced low in the early hours of the morning. This pattern applies to both day and night shift workers. Other examples abound. Alcohol is absorbed by the blood stream faster at some times of the day than others. Suicide rates, the conception of illegitimate children, the number of books loaned by libraries, even the effects of exercise vary by the time of year (Aschoff, 1974).

All of these examples demonstrate that, while leisure may be thought of as time which is free, we are always shaped by time. This influence is a positive thing.

> Temporal pressure is constricted, but it is also the framework within which our personality is organized. When it is absent we are disoriented. There is nothing to bind the sequence of activities; we are alone. . . . Human equilibrium is too precarious to do without fixed positions in space and regular cues in time. (Fraisse, 1964: 141)

There are, in other words, advantages to time pressure. It is a natural and healthy part of our nature and our lives. There are also time patterns in the natural world which shape us because we are a part of nature. We must recognize them and behave accordingly.

Having more or fewer blocks of free time thrown into a style of living in which time is treated like so many identical units which are extremely scarce will not change the problems brought about by the commodification of time. The solution will not be found by devaluing time but rather by changing our values. Primary among such changes must be the acceptance of a consumption maximum. Since our open-ended attitude toward consuming leisure experiences, which results in the need to do more work to pay for what we want, the cycle can only be broken by consuming less and setting some limits on what it is justifiable to own. This is not a new discovery of course; the Athenian philosophers reached it long before the birth of Christ.

It may be argued that to limit ownership of material goods is to limit personal freedom. While that may be true, the utter lack of tranquility in much of modern life, the stress and the extraordinary cost to our environment brought about by unlimited materialism are also forms of unfreedom with more serious negative consequences. Not only is freedom never absolute but more freedom in one realm often means less in another. And more freedom in one generation may mean less freedom for generations to come. Those who defend the absolute right to the unlimited ownership of things are not defending freedom, only their preference to be free in one realm of living at the expense of freedom in other, more essential realms. Greed is a poor substitute for freedom.

TO EVERYTHING . . .

Time viewed as a commodity makes our lives shorter and less tranquil, but in the ancient meanings of time, tranquility is foremost. Contrast the commodification of time with the words of Ecclesiastes, The Preacher (Eccl. 3: 1-8).

> To every thing there is a season, and a time to every purpose under the heaven:
>
> A time to be born, and a time to die; a time to plant, and a time to pluck up that which is planted;
>
> A time to kill, and a time to heal; a time to break down, and a time to build up;
>
> A time to weep, and a time to laugh; a time to mourn, and a time to dance;
>
> A time to cast away stones, and a time to gather stones together; a time to embrace, and a time to refrain from embracing;
>
> A time to get and a time to lose; a time to keep, and a time to cast away;

A time to rend; a time to sew; a time to keep silence, and a time to speak;

A time to love, and a time to hate; a time of war, and a time of peace.

REFERENCES

Aschoff, Jurgen. 1974. "Free-time Within the Framework of Biological Programme." In *Leisure Activities in the Industrial Society.* Brussels, Belgium: Foundation Van Cle.

Bell, Daniel. 1973. "The End of Scarcity." *Saturday Review of the Society* (May).

de Grazia, Sebastian. 1962. *Of Time, Work and Leisure.* Glencoe, Illinois: The Free Press.

Ecclesiastes. *The Holy Bible* (authorized King James' version). 3: 1-8.

Fraisse, P. 1964. *The Psychology of Time* (English Translation). London: Eyre and Spottiswoode.

Galbraith, John Kenneth. 1967. *The New Industrial State.* Boston: Houghton Mifflin Company.

Kreps, Juanita. 1971. *Lifetime Allocation of Work and Income—Essays in the Economics of Aging.* Durham, North Carolina: Duke University.

Linder, Staffan. 1970. *The Harried Leisure Class.* New York: Columbia University Press.

Owen, John D. 1969. *The Price of Leisure.* The Netherlands: Rotterdam University Press.

Priestly, Joseph. 1964. *Man and Time.* London: Aldus Books Limited.

Rifkin, Jeremy. 1987. *Time Wars,* reviewed by Jonathon Rowe, "In Hock to the Clock; A Call for 'Slow is Beautiful.'" *The Christian Science Monitor* (August 24) p. 1, 28.

Scheucsh, Erwin. 1972. "The Time Budget Interview," In Alexander Szalai (Ed.) *The Use of Time—Daily Activities of Urban and Suburban Populations in Twelve Countries.* The Hague, The Netherlands: Mouton.

What so many students today 'want' out of college is graduate school. Or, alternatively, a Good Job. Most of them seem to be majoring in initials—embarked on the lockstep course to gain an M.D., a Ph.D., or a V.P.

This is what is called being 'hardheaded about life,' looking at the 'bottom line' and making sure that college is 'cost-effective.' In accounting terms, they say, a liberal arts degree and 25 cents (in 1977) will get you a cup of coffee.

I have nothing against earning a living, but using college as an employment agency seems like the ultimate extravagance to me. Rather than being 'sensible,' this notion is motivated by fear—fear of the future—and by a profound misconception that the best armament against uncertainty is a life plan that reads like a Piece of the Rock.

Colleges are urged to 'get on with the business of life,' as if life were a business, and thousands of families will break the bank in order to prepare their children for a future that is myopically limited to the day after graduation. It's short-term insurance of the most expensive kind.

If I were one of Alan Watts's tutors (and I am eminently qualified, having planned my future once and for all half a dozen times), I'd point out that majoring in what Gail Sheehy labeled 'The One True Course' will lead inexorably to a crash.

They can get there by following in the footsteps of professors who are in one stage or other of the midlife crises, or of parents who are currently feeling locked in. They are being expensively prepared for their own middle-aged discontent, and may end up as the next generation of consumers for self-help books, divorce lawyers and employment agencies specializing in second careers.

The only adults I know who are still merrily marching along their one true course are boring, insensitive or lucky. The rest of us are survivors, survivors of crises, reverses, life changes. What you need to survive is a sense of humor, some joy, flexibility and a philosophy to hang your hat on.

(Ellen Goodman, 1980: 241-2)

IX. EDUCATION, FREE TIME AND LEISURE

When they wrote about education, the early Greek philosophers were very clear about its nature and purpose. Plato was intent on producing those wise leaders who he referred to as philosopher-kings. In the *Republic* he proposed a detailed program of education which would produce them. Aristotle, too, spelled out a program of education designed to prepare citizens for the responsibility of citizenship. That his discussion of education is found in his writing on *Politics* is revealing. To these philosophers, the citizen and the state were one. So, too, were morality and legality. Education was the basis of citizenship and statesmanship in the Greek city-state. It led to membership in the community of citizens.

Aristotle, particularly, was insistent that education not lead to a profession and not prepare one to earn an income. One engaged in gymnastics and music, for the benefit of body and soul, as an amateur. To apply those skills in a practical way, that is to earn an income from them, was regarded as illiberal and degrading. Instruction which did not lead to enlarging the spirit and developing insight was beneath the dignity of man. Instruction served to free man by making his actions rational and, with spirit and insight, making possible an advance to original action (Davidson, 1904: 11).

Our ideas and ideals about education spring from these distant sources. But the spring ran dry. The context and circumstances which gave rise to philosophy in Greece's golden age gave way to other contexts and circumstances, but theirs is a compelling philosophy still.

In earlier chapters, we noted the interpenetration of education and religion. For many centuries, education was confined almost exclusively to monastery schools and monastic orders, the exceptions being tutors for the nobility and local priests for their parishes. Significant roles were played by the Franciscans and Dominicans, as was noted previously, along with that of the Jesuits since the time of the Counter Reformation.

In a sense, if we take priests as educators, then professional education has a very long history. The earliest universities, which helped set the stage for the Renaissance, were, in the main, professional schools preparing students for careers in law, medicine, translation and religion. Cambridge University in England, which dates to the early 1300s, prepared students for careers in the church and also careers in government. That tradition carried over to the universities established during the colonial period in the United States, most of which were founded by one or another Protestant denomination. But there were other developments during the 1600s, developments which have gradually led to education systems and institutions as we know them.

EDUCATION FOR ALL

With the spread of Protestantism and the Protestants' democratic leanings and desire for followers to have direct access, through reading, to the Bible and other religious thought, education for everyone, including children and youth, had its start. Further impetus was added by the Puritans reaction to the educational practices of Elizabethan England. That was probably our best example of a system for the education of a gentleman, a person of taste, refinement and courtly manner. The austere and practical puritans would have none of that and they set out a course not of three R's but four: reading, 'riting,' 'rithmatic,' and religion.

Among the first of many education reformers was John Comenius. By the mid-1600s, he was championing a common, democratic education for everyone up to age 12. Beyond that, by merit and aptitude, students might then continue to "Latin school" and to university. His philosophy was based on the suppositions of unity of knowledge and particularly unity of mankind; the Christian brotherhood of man. To him, learning developed the intelligence and that, in turn, was the basis for piety and virtue. That is quite similar to Aristotle's understanding though with religious and democratic purposes added.

During the following two centuries, a number of well-known education philosophers, practitioners and reformers followed Comenius's lead. Most were influenced by Rousseau's romanticism but not his rejection of civil society and its institutions. Some of his ideas, but not his proposed applications, influenced Pestalozzi, Herbart, Froebel, Fichte and Montessori—all champions of public education, all reformers seeking to improve social conditions, all concerned to make learning an active process, and all concerned with morality as an aim of education.

Education For Democracy

In the United States, three names stand out and deserve mention. Thomas Jefferson championed education for two reasons. First, the political freedom of citizens in a democracy required education for all. Liberty, he believed, was only safe in the hands of the people; its preservation depended on their discretion and intelligence in decision making. So, in a democracy, everyone must be educated.

> I know of no safe depository of the ultimate power of the society but the people themselves; and if we think them not enlightened enough to exercise their control with a wholesome discretion, the remedy is not to take it from them, but to inform their discretion by education. (In Huchins, 1952: 81)

Second, Jefferson sought to cull from the populace a "natural aristocracy" based on talent and virtue who would take leadership and devote themselves to the welfare of the people and the nation. John Dewey, one of the greatest U.S. philosophers and certainly its most influential in the field of education, spelled out his philosophy in scores of publications, one of the most important of which he entitled, *Democracy and Education* (1916). Before turning to Dewey, however, a brief mention must be made of Horace Mann, the first secretary of the Massachusetts Board of Education and, prior to Dewey, the leading spokesman and promoter of public education. Mann believed in public education which would be free, universal, democratic, and nonsectarian. He ended his career as president of Antioch College, unique in its democracy and its provision of equal access and opportunity for women and blacks.

Massachusetts led the education movement in the U.S. in a number of ways: the first university (Harvard, 1636); the first public high school (1821); the first state-wide public school system (1837); the first "normal school" for training teachers (1839). Horace Mann, William James, John

Dewey, and more recently James Conant, all New Englanders, are among our best known and most influential educators. To that group must be added Robert Huchins, a New Yorker who spent several years at Yale as student, professor and dean of the Law School before becoming, at age 30, president of the University of Chicago. Huchins devoted much of his life to championing liberal education.

DEWEY'S PRAGMATISM AND INSTRUMENTALISM

Though one of its leading spokesmen, Dewey did not found the pragmatic school of philosophy but rather inherited it from Chauncy Wright, James Pierce, and particularly William James. Simply put, pragmatism was a way of defining truth. To pragmatists, the truth and meaning of a concept is expressed and tested by its practical consequences. It is experimental and empirical like natural science but it also extends to include social science and ethics and values. Contrary to the philosophy of Spencer and Sumner, which are largely fatalistic and laissez faire, pragmatism was a philosophy of experiment and observed consequence in an effort to improve social conditions. Instrumentalism is an outgrowth of pragmatism. William James' approach to instrumentalism was largely religious in seeking ways to improve moral behavior. To that Dewey added a more scientific approach. This philosophy holds that learning, intelligence, thoughts and ideas are instruments to be used to consciously shape and improve individual and social life. Thus, "instrumentalism."

This is the philosophy of reformers. Dewey, in addition to his work in education and philosophy, was involved in a number of "causes" and he was influenced by such other reformers of the time as Upton Sinclair, Lincoln Steffans, and Thorstein Veblen along with Jacob Riis and Jane Addams, both early champions of parks, playgrounds, community centers and recreation services. To Dewey we attribute the movement referred to as progressive education which in its truest sense meant education as an effective instrument for progress, and faith in knowledge as a basis for experimentation and action. Dewey's philosophy also influenced the progressive era in government and politics, an era characterized by faith in democratic processes and in progress through political action.

Most of the reforms Dewey sought had been sought by others before him but he provided a needed synthesis and a more careful and thorough rationale. He sought to make the school a scaled down model of society. That meant democracy in the classroom and the school, more self-discipline than tyrannical rule, active participation in class activity, group involvement in projects and problem solving, work and play as well as the three R's, and it meant exposure to a variety of occupations.

Unfortunately, this was not always understood and applied as Dewey intended. He was often opposed to things that were done in the name of progressive education, and spoke forcefully in favor of intellectual rigor (Dworkin, 1959: 13). The matter of exposure to occupations offers a good illustration of the misunderstanding and misapplication of Dewey's ideas. It sometimes resulted in vocationalism and job training. Dewey's interest, however, in exposing students to occupations, was merely to provide an opportunity for students to explore their own interests and aptitudes as a way of discovery and self-direction. He recognized vocations as an important part of life and believed they should be a rewarding part, but the purpose of such exposure was to broaden experience and not provide vocational training. In outlining his "Pedagogic Creed," Dewey argued that with democracy and industrialism, it was impossible to foretell circumstances to be faced 20 years hence. Thus, he argued, the best preparation for young people was not the command of particular knowledge or skill, but rather command of themselves. That was before the turn of the century.

Since that time, pragmatism has lost some of its philosophical foundation and intellectual sophistication. At the present time, pragmatism often means no more than expedience and, with time discounting, expedience in the short run rather than the long. Instrumentalism has suffered the same fate and, in addition, its essentially social and collective progressivism has been narrowed to the personal and individual. Dewey had seen that evolving, and as early as 1936 observed that the multiplicity and superficiality of education programs reflected social aimlessness, dispersiveness, and atomization. "A society," he argued, "that is largely held together by the aim of many individuals to get on as individuals is not really held together at all" (Dewey, 1936: 7).

THE OLDEST ANTITHESIS

For the past 300 years or more, we have embraced democracy and equality. Additionally, our belief in equality (and experience) has brought us to believe that our abilities and talents are determined more by education and experience than by biological inheritance. The nature-nurture issue was weighted mostly on the nurture side. John Locke suggested the ratio was ten percent nature and ninety percent nurture, a ratio which many, today, dispute.

Still, those beliefs led inevitably to insistence upon equal opportunity and to free, universal education. Thus has evolved the institution of education which, like government, is expected to be all things to all people. Education was to be a great leveler, an equalizer.

In speaking of universities, though perhaps applicable to other levels as well, Kerr noted that because of being all things to all people, the university must, "of necessity, be partially at war with itself" (1963: 8). Perhaps war is too strong a term but certainly the educational system is pulled in many directions, sometimes opposite ones. A dozen or more opposite thrusts, or at least dichotomies, come readily to mind: elite-egalitarian; aristocratic-democratic; material-spiritual; theoretical-practical; vocational-cultural; classical-modern; general-special; broad-narrow; liberal-servile; education-training; individual-social; work-leisure; worker-citizen. Of the above pairs, the last two are of particular interest though nearly all these pairs are implicated in each other. As Dewey (1916: 293) wrote:

> Probably the most deep-seated antithesis which has shown
> itself in education history is that between education in
> preparation for useful labor and education for a life of leisure.

The roots of this antithesis are found, of course, in the Greek social, political and economic class structure of citizens and slaves. But as Dewey observed, social distinctions of a similar nature are still made.

> The idea still prevails that a truly cultural or liberal
> education cannot have anything in common, directly at
> least, with industrial affairs, and that the education which
> is fit for the masses must be a useful or practical
> education in a sense that opposes useful and practical to
> nurture appreciation and liberation of thought. . . .
>
> (Now) cultural and utilitarian subjects exist in an inorganic
> composite where the former are not by dominant purpose
> socially serviceable and the later not liberative of
> imagination or thinking power. The outcome of the
> mixture is perhaps less satisfactory than if either principle
> were adhered to in its purity. . . . It would be hard to find a

subject in the curriculum within which there are not
found evil results of a compromise between the two
opposed ideals. . . .

It will generally be found that instruction which, in
aiming at utilitarian results, sacrifices the development
of imagination, the refining of taste and the deepening of
intellectual insight—surely cultural values—also in the
same degree renders what is learned limited in its use.
(Dewey, 1916: 298-303)

Dewey's inclination toward what we might call education for life is
quite clear. But if asked to choose education for work or education for leisure,
he would not choose except as to choose both. And so must we. As he
argued, if work and leisure were equally distributed among people, there
would be no evident conflict and the task of education would be to prepare for
both. Education should bridge the gaps between all of the apparently anti-
thetical pairs noted above.

These distinctions between the liberal-cultural and the servile-
utilitarian, Dewey argued, are historical and social but they are not necessarily
distinct as they are neither inherently nor absolutely distinct. We are committed to equal opportunity and to education for all, but that is not incompatible
with developing the mind. That is most fortunate. Nearly all of us have to
work. And all of us have a variety of other roles and responsibilities. We also
have time, often more than we realize, during which we can choose what to
do. There is no alternative to preparation for both and so it seems futile to
take sides. There may be issues of balance, emphasis and the like. But there
can be no either-or; there can only be both.

Although unemployment and underemployment are more serious
problems than in the past, most of us, regardless of the amount and nature of
our formal education, earn at least a minimally adequate "living" through paid
employment, including those educated in the liberal arts as well as those
trained for vocations and professions. For some occupations, a long period of
training may be particularly advantageous if not also quite necessary. For
most jobs, however, a brief period of apprenticeship, even as little as a few
hours, is often all that is needed to develop the essential skills. Beyond that,
what is needed is education more so than training. It is curious, then, that so
many cannot conceive of liberal education as useful after all.

It is also curious that we think of liberal education almost exclusively
as subject matter; some arts; humanities, social sciences, natural sciences,

math, native and foreign language in some mix. That is not inappropriate. But the manner in which the subject is taught may be as important, perhaps more so. A "liberal" subject can be taught in a dogmatic and thoroughly illiberal fashion. Conversely, even the most narrow vocational subject can be taught in a manner that leads to all of those outcomes which a liberal education is expected to provide (Green, 1968). Given the continual and perhaps inevitable growth of specialization and vocationalism, which includes the professions, there may be some hope in noting that such programs and courses can be so construed as to produce liberal education outcomes. Perhaps the saving grace of our education institutions is that any young person who is sufficiently earnest and intelligent cannot be prevented from getting a good education (Huchins, 1956: 27).

ALL THINGS TO ALL PEOPLE

Because education institutions are expected to be all things to all people, they have been charged with a burden under which they can only stagger and sometimes fail. Just as recreation and leisure are often expected to compensate for lives otherwise devoid of purpose, meaning, and satisfaction, so schools are expected to fill voids created by the default of other institutions. Such institutions as the family, the church and the community have usually played key roles in the education of young people. In many cases and places, they still do. But often they do not, and their functions are passed on to the schools.

One consequence of this is that schools undertake too many things. As early as 1829 the faculty at Yale declared: "There are many things important to be known, which are not taught in college, because they may be learned anywhere" (Huchins, 1956: 91). The unfortunate reality is that that is often no longer true. Schools are expected to provide instruction in health, fitness, guidance, counseling, socialization, sex education, recreational activities and much more, not to mention vocational training and preparation for college. Learning often becomes secondary to getting along, getting out, and getting a job. The severest critics of education argue that its principal function is to accommodate young people for an extended period and delay entry into the labor force. Youth have no place except in school and no role except as students. Too, adjustment as an objective of schooling is profoundly conservative; adapting reinforces the status quo. Yet growth, development, progress, improvement and the like are among the expected outcomes of education. But as Huchins argued, "If we have to choose between Sancho

Panza and Don Quixote, let us by all means choose Don Quixote" (Huchins, 1953: 20).

Another consequence is that education has come to be equated with schooling and we have no other way of measuring or even discussing education without reference to years of school completed. Education is equated with time spent in school. Diplomas, certificates and degrees are earned (a thoroughly work-oriented notion) when a certain number of a certain kind of credits have been completed. Since we have no clear, qualitative understanding of what an education is, we think of it quantitatively. And lacking an understanding of what education is, we have no measures of the effectiveness of our schools and programs of instruction. Consequently, we focus not on effectiveness but efficiency. A student makes "normal progress" by accumulating a certain number of credits in a given period of time. School boards fight with teachers' unions over student-teacher ratios. Universities evaluate departments according to costs per student contact hour and various other measures of efficiency. With this product orientation (how often do we speak of graduates as a product of this or that school) and business efficiency evaluation, it is little wonder that success in getting jobs, particularly well paying ones, has come to be the measure of success in education, both for students and for schools.

There are a thousand books and at least that many arguments about why schools fail and what is wrong with our educational system. Perhaps the major problem has been the guiding philosophy. When such philosophies as utilitarianism and pragmatism are degraded to individualism and expedience, the aim of education is a low one. Education may be successful in meeting its aims, but its aims may be too low.

The preceding discussion is but an illustration of the enormous task and difficulty facing the institution of education. But it does point out the context in which any discussion of education for leisure or leisure education must take place. It suggests, at a minimum, that one should not expect too much too soon. We certainly support the philosophical base of education for leisure, although we conceive that in two ways and have a decided preference for one. Equally, we support leisure for education since education has so much in common with leisure as we have defined it. In addition to those arguments in favor of the leisure orientation are those which point out the inadequacies of an education slanted toward narrow specializations and to vocationalism and professionalism. Highly specialized training is, of course, essential for some occupations. We want our physicians to make us well when we are not, and we want our buildings and bridges to withstand the stresses placed upon them. But those highly specialized fields employ but a small minority of the labor force and a much smaller portion of the adult population. And even for those in highly specialized fields, a liberal education background is desirable.

EDUCATION FOR JOBS

Choice of the word jobs rather than work is a deliberate one. It points out once again the problems we encounter when our concepts are confused. It could be argued, for example, that a job is what provides you with a livelihood, thus enabling you to get on with your work. The Christian religion's conceptualization of work equates one's work with God's. The concept of "calling" refers to that work which God calls upon you to do. Work, by this conception, is infused with the highest spiritual purpose. Occupation and employment can be something different from either work or job. One can be occupied or employed without working or having a job, occupied without being employed, or vice-versa, and so on.

Among us are many whose work is also their job. For them, leisure is not so much a problem—or opportunity—as for those whose work and jobs are different. For them, their work has to be rescued from their job, just as does leisure. In fact, work and leisure, when we define them with words like purpose, meaning, intuitively worthwhile, love and faith, are seen to be quite similar. In that case, we become advocates of education for work which, in fact, we are. It can also be seen that philosophers are right when they demand that conceptual clarity which some dismiss as mere semantics.

For a number of years, sociologists have been interested in people's "central life interest," often using work and leisure as loci of centrality. Work seen also as a calling is surely one's central life interest. Too, the Protestant ethic's infusion of morality and salvation into work, and even jobs, is bound also to focus one's central life interest around work. And for several generations, work was the central interest not for its intrinsic worth or its role in salvation but to make life better for the next generation. Given our misgivings about the future and weakened institutions of religion and family, work has lost some of its centrality of life interest and leisure has gained. We will not know the consequence of that shift until some time in the future, a few decades at least, if not a few generations.

Meanwhile, we have a dilemma. If work is only a job, which is the case for many, devoid of inherent worth, salvation, or better future prospects for our children, then lack of commitment and all of its consequences are as understandable as they are lamentable. Fear of losing one's job is not the most desirable motivation for good performance, but it may be effective. Indebtedness adds motivation of a similar kind. On the other horn of the dilemma, the expectation of finding a job that also is intrinsically important and worthwhile work, may lead to disappointment and a necessary but painful disillusionment as well (Terkel, 1972: xi-xxiv). That dilemma, it seems, is one of the major reasons why leisure, not jobs, must have centrality as a focus of education.

Contrary to official pronouncements, many jobs, perhaps most, do not require long periods of training. From the standpoint of both efficiency and effectiveness, an extensive apprenticeship program would provide better job preparation than can be expected from high schools and universities whose principal task should be not training but education. Long before compulsory public education systems, there were apprenticeship laws, as early as 1562 in England and 1642 in Massachusetts. Parents, or in their failure, other craftsmen, tradesmen, or husbandmen, were charged with providing children with "learning and labor and other employments which may be profitable to the commonwealth" (Good & Teller, 1973: 26). These laws assured not only a skilled labor force but also were measures to police youth and prevent vagrancy and idleness, a function which modern school systems still perform. Since those early dates, laws and public support of schools have been mainly vocational in intent, including public, often land-grant, universities dating to the Morill Acts of 1862 and 1890, and the Smith-Lever and Smith-Hughes Acts in the early 1900s.

More recently, schools have been under attack for producing a nation of scientific illiterates. That was the case after the Soviet Union launched "Sputnik" in 1957, shaming us into space. Now there is fear of falling behind a number of nations in economic competition. As a 1982 National Commission on Excellence in Education proclaimed (1983: 5):

> Our nation is at risk. Our once unchallenged preeminence
> in commerce, industry, science and technological innovation
> is being overtaken by competitors throughout the world. . . .
> We have, in effect, been committing an act of unthinking,
> unilateral, educational disarmament.

The report then goes on to be critical of the educational system, particularly high schools, for their minimum requirements in science, math and other subjects.

The commission argued: "These deficiencies come at a time when the demand for highly skilled workers in new fields is accelerating rapidly" (p. 10). They mentioned computers, lasers, robotics and technological transfers to and from various fields. That is no doubt true, but the number of jobs in those fields is limited and there is stiff competition for them. Everything else points to a service sector economy in which most growth in the labor force is in jobs that are not highly skilled. Worse, they are not highly paid. Various surveys, including those done by governments, point to job growth in such areas as fast food service, clerical, custodial, waiting on tables and bartending, and police and security work.

Further, whether because of a response time that is too slow, too many competing demands, or too rapid and unpredictable shifts in the labor market, the fit between the schools' products and labor force needs is usually a poor one. There always seem to be too many of this and too few of that. As Sidney Hook related, it is a fundamental error to build programs with focused concentration on transitory environmental circumstances. Relevance, usually equated with job preparation, he regarded as mere pretext for passing fashions or predicaments. "The doctrine of relevance is valid only in a perfectly stable world where the future is easily predictable" (Hook, 1946: 73-4). We have neither the stability nor predictability that relevance presumes.

Those whose education has not been oriented to particular specialties or fields of employment get jobs, large numbers trained for particular fields do not get jobs in those fields, and those who do find work change jobs and fields as much as mobility permits. Moreover, employers who hire those particularly trained for their fields regularly complain about the lack of competence and skills of recent graduates.

There are, to make matters worse, forces which regularly diminish the skills needed by workers. Mechanization, automation, cybernation, and human engineering all lead to less worker involvement in industrial processes. Bureaucracy, red tape, and endless rules and regulations have a similar effect for those who presumably work with their heads more than their hands, yet who cynically refer to themselves as paper pushers, number crunchers, and worse. And for several decades at least, there has been some cynicism about working hard at your studies to get a good job when "pull," influence, contacts, connections and luck are perceived as being more useful. Phrases like "being at the right place at the right time" or "its who you know rather than what you know" reflect that. No doubt there is some "scapegoating" among those dissatisfied with their job situation. But given high expectations created by all the pronouncements about education leading to good, high-paying jobs and a reality in which many jobs are not as inherently meaningful or as financially rewarding as expected, there is bound to be more than a little skepticism.

There are other problems with education attempting to perform functions best left to employers: credentialism, arbitrary standards and requirements, the promotion of occupational snobbery and the like. Our schools may be serving employers better than students. Though not wishing to prolong the critique of vocationalism and job preparation, one more point must be made. Such preparation is profoundly conservative. Education should develop the intellect and imagination for what could be, rather than prepare people to work with what is, or worse, what was. It should extend to the human community and to the distant future and not be limited to individuals finding jobs as soon as they graduate. At best, training is preparation for the present; sometimes it is preparation for the past. That is partly the result of rapid change. But it is also partly the result of a faulty aim. John Dewey's aim was higher than that as was that of all reformers and philosophers, or at least all we know of.

> The problem of American education is not, therefore, that of teaching the young the routines of jobs: nobody knows what their jobs will be. The problem is to help them learn what to do with themselves, how to be citizens of a well-ordered state, and how to become human beings. (Huchins, 1956: 95)

EDUCATION FOR LEISURE

The merits of leisure, in contrast to job preparation, as a focus for education are seen, in part, in the demerits of job preparation. Education must be seen in reference to things other than the job market. Noting those demerits may be one-sided. But it is not nearly as one-sided, or misleading, as most pronouncements of business and industry, and often governments. They pay, with our money, as consumers and taxpayers, for the messages we receive about education and jobs. True leisure, as de Grazia (1962) well argued, is not embraced by business and industry or by governments, including democratic ones, except as we use free time to buy goods and services and pay taxes for them.

Still, there are merits to education for leisure, of which there are two orientations. We will label them modern and traditional and briefly speak to both. And while supporting both, our preference for the traditional conceptualization will be eminently clear. A philosophic approach does not, in all cases, incline one to the traditional rather than the modern but in this case the foundation of tradition seems stronger.

Leisure Education—Modern

The modern concept of education for leisure has, nonetheless, a history of many decades. A report of the Federal Bureau of Education made it a "cardinal principle" of high-school education as early as 1918. Perhaps the report's authors anticipated the decade which, for the era, many regarded as mindlessly hedonistic—"the roaring twenties." Perhaps leisure education would have progressed more rapidly had there been no stock market crash in 1929, followed by a decade of severe depression, high unemployment, soup lines and shanty towns. The nation was preoccupied with getting the economy back on its feet and people back on the job. The Second World War followed fast on the heels of the economic recovery from the depression. So it was not until the late 1940s that the importance of education for leisure received the attention called for in the Bureau of Education report. Here, the objective of and rationale for leisure education, in a modern sense, was first expressed by a high level public agency.

> Aside from the immediate discharge of these specific duties (home membership, vocation, citizenship), every individual should have a margin of time for the cultivation of personal and social interests. This leisure, if worthily used, will recreate his powers and enlarge and enrich life, thereby making him better able to meet his responsibilities. The unworthy use of leisure impairs health, disrupts the home, lessens vocational efficiency and destroys civic-mindedness. The tendency in industrial life, aided by legislation, is to decrease the working hours of large groups of people, while shortened hours tend to lessen the harmful reactions that arise from prolonged strain, they increase, if possible, the importance of preparation for leisure. In view of these considerations, education for the worthy use of leisure is of increasing importance as an objective. . . .

Education should equip the individual to secure from his
leisure the re-creation of body, mind and spirit, and the
enrichment and enlargement of his personality. This
objective calls for the ability to utilize the common means
of enjoyment such as music, art, literature, drama and
social intercourse, together with fostering in each individual
one or more special avocational interests. Heretofore the
high school has given little conscious attention to this
objective. . . .

The school has failed also to organize to direct the social
activities of young people as it should. One of the surest
ways in which to prepare pupils worthily to utilize leisure
in adult life is by guiding and directing their use of leisure
in youth. The school board should, therefore, see that
adequate recreation is provided both within the school
and by proper agencies in the community. The school,
however, has a unique opportunity in this field.
(Bureau of Education, 1918: 1-5)

These statements reflect the mood of the era, the emerging playground and recreation movement at the turn of the century, the influence of
the progressive education movement, and the assumption by the schools,
along with other agencies in the community, of responsibility for the social as
well as intellectual development of youth. Leisure, as understood by the
report's authors and as is commonly understood today, was equated with free
time.

Following World War II, leisure education reemerged, though not so
much in secondary schools as in colleges and universities. Programs to
prepare students for careers in the growing field of parks and recreation
emerged throughout the country. The number of such programs and students
enrolled in them continued to grow for about three decades, apace with
developments in the field of park and recreation services, particularly in the
public sector and more particularly at the local government level.

Most of these programs were geared not to leisure education per se
but to preparation for careers. College and university park and recreation
educators did, however, recognize that responsibility and, in a paper on
Education for Leisure, accepted the task of creating, "an understanding in all
university students of the challenges, problems and opportunities of leisure as
it will affect their lives individually, and the fabric of their local, national, and

world communities" (Storey, 1972: 2). In practice, however, career preparation of students enrolled in these curricula remained the major thrust.

Since that time, leisure education has been approached in a more
methodical fashion. Major aspects of leisure education include: (a) the
provision of information to assure that people are acquainted with available
and potential opportunities; (b) through formal and informal instruction,
provide for the development of the intellectual, social and physical skills
requisite to satisfactory participation in any of a myriad of activities, and
(c) by clarifying interests and values, providing guidance and counselling so
as to match an individual's interests and values with those activities most
likely to produce the satisfactions sought. In all of these areas, the level of
sophistication has gradually increased. Research, analysis and marketing
skills have contributed to this, along with increasing use of available technologies such as computers, video, and public and commercial broadcast media.

Leisure education, conceived and approached in these ways, offers
useful advantages in a society in which leisure has increasing centrality in
people's lives. More attention is paid to the individual than to the masses.
Additionally, more importance is attached to the individual than the activity.
Just as each activity has a nature of its own, each person has a nature of his or
her own, and leisure education develops and utilizes knowledge of this type.
But the emphasis upon individual experience may be carried too far. No
experience is exclusively personal and individual. If it were, there would be
no collective in social and political life, no community, no culture. The
growth, development and enrichment of individuals are not ends in themselves. We desire it because the collective is enriched thereby.
Experientialism, including experiential education, may be carried too far.
Surely no one would suggest that the route to learning the dangers of fire is to
play with matches. We must learn all that we can from the experience of our
ancestors and our contemporaries. Part of the experience of an educated
person is books—good ones and in great numbers.

As a counterweight to the demands of remunerative employment,
particularly in jobs which are not inherently meaningful or satisfying, leisure
education in this modern sense can play an important role providing a better
balance and perhaps greater discretion in the use of that discretionary time we
refer to as leisure. But in thinking about education for leisure, we may wish to
go beyond that. Perhaps we will have to.

The limiting element here is the equating of leisure with free time.
Recent textbooks which focus particularly on education for leisure use free
time as a starting point (cf., Mundy & Odum, 1972; Verduin & McEwen,
1984). This seems partly the result of the delimitation of one's "turf" required
of a professional or vocational perspective which is not required from a

philosophical one. Education for the use of free time is really founded on the idea that something should be done that is compensatory, that in other segments and roles in one's life there are elements lacking, elements that can be provided during free time. That may not be the case. That is too heavy a burden for leisure to bear. That was Paul Goodman's argument, as we note later, in calling for a life of significance for the individual and community.

Leisure Education—Traditional

For all of these reasons and more, we are directed back to the earliest understandings of leisure and education. Leisure has always been related to freedom and the purpose of education has always been to make men free. Liberal arts, in contrast to servile arts, has no other meaning than liberation from ignorance and from enslavement to irrational passions and fears. An education which does not do that is not, then, education for leisure. Perhaps free time should be used to provide an education for leisure.

In the opening chapter we used Pieper's concept of an educated man as a way of defining philosophy, that is, "a point of view from which to take in the world." Many others have noted the important link between education and philosophy. As Dewey argued (1916: xi):

If we are willing to conceive of education as the process
of forming fundamental dispositions, intellectual and
emotional, toward nature and fellow men, philosophy may
even be defined as the general theory of education.

If philosophy can be defined as the general theory of education, then it must also be the general purpose of education. Alfred North Whitehead, one of the greatest philosophers of our century, argued that our society cannot succeed until general education provides us with a philosophic outlook (In Huchins, 1959: 23):

The essence of education is that it is religious. A religious
education is an education which inculcates duty and reverence.
Duty arises from our potential control over the course of events.
Where attainable knowledge could have changed the issue,

ignorance has the guilt of vice. And the foundation of
reverence is this perception, that the present holds in itself
the complete sum of existence, backwards and forwards,
that whole amplitude of time, which is eternity.

Duty and reverence are integral parts of Aristotle's concept of
leisure. They are also the foundation of those acts undertaken out of internally
compelling love, the central phrase in our definition of leisure. At the
junctures of philosophy and education, and particularly those also joined by
leisure, the language of meaning and purpose is clear and consistent. Robert
Huchins (1963: 22) spoke of the necessary relation between education,
morals, intelligence, and metaphysics; John Dewey (In Dworkin, 1959: 19)
argued that "all education proceeds by the participation of the individual in the
social consciousness of the race;" William Arrowsmith (1970) spoke of
education guided by value and vision and moral responsibility for intellectual
skill; Bertrand Russell (In Layford, 1970) noted that education is supposed to
develop minds sensitive enough to perceive and feel the shock of tragedy and
communicate those feelings to the heart; Charles Brightbill (1966) spoke of
learning for leisure in terms of the highest social values, the good of humanity,
freedom, dignity, justice, benevolence, and humaneness; Henry Rosovsky
(1978) described an educated person as one capable of making discriminating
moral choices.

Education which aims at lesser ends simply will not do. Both our
work and our leisure will be trivialized and our success at either will be
hollow for want of enduring meaning and purpose. The essence of education
is freedom, and the essence of freedom is the opportunity—more importantly,
the necessity—of choice. Education which does not make us more free or
inform those choices we are free to make may leave us a situation like that in
which the Italian people found themselves in 1939. The government was
fascist and about to side with Germany in the Second World War. But the
trains were on time; Mussolini insisted. And they were the World Cup
champions in soccer. But man does not live by train schedules alone. Or by
trophies. Education must constantly and insistently remind us of that.

REFERENCES

Arrowsmith, William. 1970. "Idea of a New University," *Century Magazine* (3: 2) (March-April).

Brightbill, Charles. 1966. *Education for Leisure-Centered Living.* New York: John Wiley and Sons.

Bureau of Education, Commission on the Reorganization of Secondary Education. 1918. *Cardinal Principles of Secondary Education.* Bulletin No. 35, Bureau of Education, Washington, D.C.: U.S. Govt. Printing Office.

Davidson, Thomas. 1904. *Aristotle and Ancient Educational Ideals.* New York: Charles Scribner's Sons.

Dewey, John. 1916. *Democracy and Education.* New York: The Macmillan Company.

Dewey, John. 1936. *Education and the Social Order.* New York: League for Industrial Democracy.

Dworkin, Martin. 1959. *Dewey on Education.* New York: Teachers College, Columbia University.

Good, Harry and Teller, James. 1973. *A History of American Education.* (3rd ed.). New York: Macmillan Publishing Company.

Goodman, Ellen. 1980. Close to Home. New York: Fawcett Crest.

Green, Thomas. 1968. *Work, Leisure and the American School.* New York: Random House.

Hook, Sidney. 1946. *Education for Modern Man.* New York: Dial Press.

Huchins, Robert. 1963. *On Education.* Santa Barbara, California: Fund for the Republic.

Huchins, Robert. 1956. *Some Observations on American Education.* Cambridge: The Cambridge University Press.

Huchins, Robert. 1953. *The Conflict in Education.* New York: Harper and Brothers.

Huchins, Robert. 1952. *The Great Conversation: The Substance of a Liberal Education.* Chicago: Encyclopedia Britanica Inc.

Kerr, Clark. 1963. *The Uses of the University.* New York: Harper and Row.

Layford, Joseph. 1970. "In My Neighborhood, An Adult is a Dead Child," *Century Magazine* (3: 6) (November-December).

Mundy, Jean and Odum, Linda. 1977. *Leisure Education: Theory and Practice.* New York: John Wiley and Sons.

National Commission on Excellence in Education. 1983. *A Nation at Risk: The Imperative for Educational Reform.* Washington, D.C.: U.S. Gov't Printing Office.

Rosovsky, Henry. 1978. In an address to the National Forum of the College Board.

Storey, Edward H. 1972. *Education for Leisure. National Policy and Position Statement,* Society of Park and Recreation Educators. Washington, D.C.: National Recreation and Park Association.

Terkel, Studs. 1972. *Working.* New York: Random House.

Verduin, John and McEwen, Douglas. 1984. *Adults and Their Leisure: The Need for Lifelong Learning.* Springfield, Illinois: Charles C. Thomas.

Whitehead, Alfred North. 1959. *The Aims of Education and Other Essays.* New York: The Macmillan Company.

In play, all that is gay, lovely and soaring in the human spirit strives to find the expression which a man of the spirit and of enthusiasm is ever seeking to attain. There is a sacral secret at the root and in the flowering of all play: it is man's hope for another life taking visible form in gesture.

To play is to yield oneself to a kind of magic, to enact to oneself the absolutely other, to pre-empt the future, to give the lie to the inconvenient world of fact. In play earthly realities become, of a sudden, things of the transient moment, presently left behind, then disposed of and buried in the past; the mind is prepared to accept the unimagined and incredible, to enter a world where different laws apply, to be relieved of all the weights that bear it down, to be free, kingly, unfettered and divine. Man at play is reaching out . . . for that superlative ease, in which even the body, freed from its earthly burden, moves to the effortless measures of a heavenly dance.

(Hugo Rahner, 1972: 65-6)

X. BEING AT PLAY

The surest sign of mature adulthood—and this will surprise many adults—
may be the ability to be as a child; to be able, as a child, to play. That is not a
new discovery but rather a rediscovery. A century of observation and reflection has provided us with mounting evidence of what people through all time
have always known. Man must play.

AN EVOLUTIONARY VIEW

Anyone who has ever visited a zoo has a favorite story about what
the monkeys, baboons or chimpanzees do, including showing off for or
"putting on" their human observers. But one need not visit a zoo to know that
play is not unique to man. Many an arm has been worn out throwing balls,
sticks, and more recently frisbees for the family's pet dog. Many an hour has
been spent watching squirrels playing in the backyard or in the park. Literally
hundreds of studies of dozens of animals have demonstrated that play is found
throughout the animal kingdom. It has been well argued that play is the basis
of, and therefore necessarily precedes, culture. In fact, play precedes man.

As with so many other terms we have encountered, play is difficult to
define. There is not even agreement that play is a distinct category of behavior, so some prefer to use the adverb "playful" to describe a way of behavior
rather than a type of behavior which is recognizably play. One advantage of
using the adverb "playful" is that we are not forced into quite arbitrary
distinctions between, for example, work and play.

Animal (Including Human) Play

Yet there are certain characteristics of play, about which there is much agreement, that inform us of its essential nature. One of the most frequently cited summaries of the characteristics of play in animals, including but not limited to man, suggests five characteristics. First, play is characterized by an emotional element of pleasure. That is difficult to demonstrate objectively but reason suggests that if play were not pleasurable there would not be any. Too, it usually appears to be pleasurable. Second, play is usually regarded as characteristic of the immature. Adults may play but they appear to play less frequently than do the young. Third, play does not seem to have any immediate biological result, although modern science has provided some evidence of results that are both biological and immediate, in addition to long-term beneficial results. Fourth, the observable forms of play are species specific. That is, dogs play in certain ways, cats in others, and so on. Fifth, the amount, diversity and duration of play is related to phylogenetic position (Beach, 1978: 325-6).

This, the fifth characteristic, points particularly to the link between play and evolution. The lower the phylogenetic position, the less the amount, diversity and duration of play. There is some evidence of play among some species of fish, though of a very limited and rudimentary form. Mammals play more, and humans play most of all. The word mammal really means nurturing the young, particularly nourishing the young, and parental care of offspring. Those animals low in phylogenetic position provide less care for their offspring. The reproduction rate is very high; the survival rate very low. Survival of the species requires, then, the production of thousands of eggs annually. Those fish which appear solicitous of their offspring lay fewer eggs, perhaps fifty or so. Birds care for their young and typically produce from about five to twelve eggs annually. As the amount of parental care increases, the fertility rate decreases and the survival rate increases. So does the duration, diversity and amount of play.

Similarly, the role of nurturance and of play in evolution parallels the growth and function of the brain. This pattern is clear in comparing primates to other mammals or mammals to birds. Even among birds, play is more prevalent among some species, corvids for example, than among other species of birds with smaller brains.

Play's Costs and Benefits

There is one other argument to be made about the link between play and evolution. The process of natural selection leading to "survival of the fittest" can only lead to the conclusion that play provides a selective advantage. We have evolved to extended periods of nurturance and play rather than shorter. Because play involves certain costs, the benefits must be large enough to outweigh those costs. We will note some of the benefits presently; but first, the costs.

The most obvious cost of play is time. In humans as well as in the juvenile members of most animals, play is the principal activity of the young. In our own case, play time absorbs several years. Secondly, play often involves considerable expenditures of energy. It is not uncommon for children and adults to play to a point of exhaustion. That hardly appears useful to survival; certainly not in any immediate sense. Survival in an immediate sense would suggest conserving energy or at least not exhausting oneself, thus leaving oneself vulnerable to environmental contingencies. Time and energy costs, then, are very significant.

There are, in addition, two other costs of playing. Related to the vulnerability noted above is the danger of exposure. Although more obvious among animals living in the wild but, sadly, not unknown in human communities, there are predators to which, when playing, young members of the species become exposed. Restricting territory, providing surveillance and other means are used to reduce the risk, and potentially high cost, of exposure. Finally, there are potential costs of play because there are risks of injury. Scrapes and bruises are inevitable but play can also involve risk to life and limb. Again, we do what we can to minimize those risks; some suggest we do too much. But in any case, injury and sometimes even death are other costs of play (Smith, 1982: 141).

Yet despite these costs, and despite those historic episodes during which attempts were made to stifle play, thousands upon thousands of years of evolution have demonstrated the importance of play. Though it may grate against the remnants of puritanical attitudes, play is fun, play is pleasurable, and pleasure seems clearly to have selective advantages for the survival of the species. We should not be surprised at that. The species would not survive if sex were not pleasurable, nor would individual members survive if eating were not pleasurable (Smith, 1985: 60). Play, too, is pleasurable. Play, too, is important to survival. Moreover, it is the basis of our culture and thus civilization as we know it.

Other animals have organizations, sometimes quite elaborate ones. Other animals work. We sometimes chide—or pride—ourselves about being busy as a bee or conscripts, as if ants, in an industrial army. But no other animal plays as long, or as hard, or in so many ways as does man. And no other animal produces art, science, philosophy, spinnakers, model trains, violins, and castles in the sand or in the sky.

PLAY—THE BASIS OF CULTURE

Our heading appropriates Pieper's argument that leisure is the basis of culture. Substituting the word play does not alter the argument but rather substantiates it by adding historical and anthropological evidence and insight to the religious base of Pieper's essay.

As Durant observed, "the games of the young are as old as the sins of the fathers" (1939: 288). Anthropologists, as they peel back layer after layer of human development, find not just tools but also toys of all kinds: rattles, dolls, clay figures, hoops, carts, swings, seesaws and pieces for games like marbles and dice. Our ancestors, as deep in the historic past as we have gone, were ingenious toy makers. It may be that the wheel and the sail first appeared as playthings; the bow as a musical instrument; domestic animals as pets; clothing as ornamentation for a cosmic drama. Some of this remains speculative though both reason and careful documentation support the central idea.

We know that among the early Greeks, inventions arose from and were objects of play. Leonardo was a painter by vocation, an inventor by avocation, and Hoffer (1963), among others, suggested that most inventions, including the microscope and telescope, were conceived and born as toys. The revolutionary scientific discoveries of Gilbert, Harvey, Galileo and Kepler, like the mathematics of Descartes, Desargues, Fermat and Pascal, were of no immediate practical use. Freedom, rather than necessity, was the principal power behind the scientific revolution (Nef, 1958: 64).

Hoffer also indicated why that would be the case:

Men never philosophize or tinker more freely than when
they know their speculations or tinkering leads to no
weighty results. We are more ready to try the untried,
when what we do is inconsequential. . . . It is highly doubtful
whether people are capable of genuine creative responses
when necessity takes them by the throat. (1963: 13-14)

Necessity is not, it seems, the mother of invention. Rather it is the freedom to play afforded by leisure and the freedom to try the untried (and to fail) afforded by play. The word play derives from the old English word *plegen*. The old English meaning included taking risks and exposing oneself to danger or failure.

But we must think of invention in ways beyond the reach of the government patent office. Government, too, is an invention, as is everything subsumed in the grand inventions of culture and civilization. The classic exposition of their foundation in play is Johann Huizinga's *Homo Ludens* (man the player) which he subtitled, *A Study of the Play Element in Culture*. He sadly noted that the play element in culture has been on the wane for nearly three centuries and that civilization is no longer playing. But that, surely, requires a brief explanation for any unfamiliar with Huizinga's classic study.

Characteristics of Human Play

In essence, he argued that culture and civilization arose in the form of play. That becomes evident if we reflect upon the characteristics of play as he described them. They are, in the main, self-explanatory. Play is characterized as:

> . . . a free activity standing quite consciously outside 'ordinary' life as being 'not serious' but at the same time absorbing the player intensely and utterly. It is an activity connected with no material interest, and no profit can be gained by it. It proceeds within its own proper boundaries of time and space according to fixed rules and in an orderly manner. It promotes the formation of social groupings which tend to surround themselves with secrecy and to stress their differences from the common world by disguise or other means. (1953: 13)

In play, Huizinga believed, the outcome was always in doubt. If the ending could be predicted, such as a contest between two highly unequal sports teams, the play element was lost but might be restored by selecting more balanced teams. Often play was highly competitive and utterly absorbing. The winning in play, however, was only gaining glory, not money or power, and this glory was shared with other players, who were honored and considered equals. In play, there was always some tension: something risked. Luck or fate has a role in play, so pure talent, skill or desire to excel can never completely dominate the play. Play is always, in some senses, a testing of fate.

True play, according to Huizinga, is always limited in its objectives. The player, even though absorbed by the play, understands that it is not real life.

All this is evident in highly organized sports, games, dramatic (re)presentations and the like. But it is also evident in the informal play of children, though the rules, boundaries and order may not be so readily evident to the observer. Given these characteristics, we can understand how culture and civilization emerged in play form. Play, remember, came first.

Culture—Play's Progeny

Huizinga pointed out the presence of the play form in a variety of aspects of culture and civilization: law, war, philosophy, knowledge, poetry, art and more. We can only briefly illustrate his analysis. In law, for example, we have all the elements of drama and contest. Judges wear robes and in many countries wigs as well, as do also lawyers presenting cases and representing clients. Sometimes jurors, too, have some kind of identifying sash or insignia reflecting their special role in the drama and contest. Territory is clearly demarcated and scrupulously respected; a place for participants and spectators and among participants a place for judges and jurors, accuser and accused. The docket sets out the time and place where the ritual of civilized justice is enacted.

Prose is an outgrowth of poetry, and all poetry is born of play. Is not poetry a form of playing with words and meanings, of allusions and illusions, and of rhyme and rhythm and meter? Poetry, Huizinga noted, arises in sacred ritual, martial contest, disputations of bragging and mocking, jest and wit, or the rites of courtship, marriage and passage (Huizinga, 1955: 129). It has been said that America is a place where one could earn a good living converting poetry into prose. That exemplifies the sad conclusion that the play element in culture has long been on the wane.

A third illustration of the play element in culture is found in religion. In religion, we find poetry and song, music and dance and actors in dress and decoration acting out the drama of life. Order prevails in a clearly demarcated sacred ground; sacred ground which is truly the playground. As Walter

Bagehot noted, "Man made the school, God the playground" (In Hoffer, 1967: 76).

Play is outside ordinary life because it is limited in space and time, and is nonrational because it serves only its own ends. It is not simply outside ordinary life but, rather, transcends it. As there is no profit or material interest, it is innocent. It is absorbing because, being extra-ordinary, it is filled with wonder and enchantment. Hugo Rahner, in *Man at Play*, has well expressed the transcendent nature of play. As noted at the outset (1972: 66): "Man at play is reaching out . . . for that superlative ease, in which even the body, freed from its earthly burden, moves to the effortless measure of a heavenly dance." Can anyone who has observed children at play deny the transcendence of the dance?

CAN PLAY BE EXPLAINED?

Attempts to explain play are of recent origin. Some set the date in the late 1800s when William Newell, one of the founders of the American Folklore Society, published *Games and Songs of America's Children* and George Johnson became Professor of Play at the University of Pittsburgh (Mergen, 1975: 401-07). It was also at the turn of the century that Karl Groos wrote *The Play of Man*, one of the early formal efforts to develop a theoretical understanding of play.

Prior to that, play was conceived only in traditional and religious terms, sometimes encouraged as a way of preventing idleness for the devil's hands, sometimes discouraged on the grounds that "those who play when they are young, will play when they are old" (In Lehman & Witty, 1927: 1). A book published in 1744 (*A Little Pretty Pocket Book Intended for the Instruction and Amusement of Little Master Tommy and Pretty Miss Polly*) related in rhyme the morals taught by various games, the up and down flight of the shuttlecock in badminton teaching the ups and downs of life's fortune, for example. We still moralize about play, or at least rationalize it. We should not have to. We must play.

By the mid-1800s, the kindergarten movement had spread to the United States and there was growing acceptance of the importance of play in the lives, and particularly education, of children. The playground and community center movements were soon to follow. Since that time, the work of Jean Piaget and many others have detailed the importance of play in intellectual development.

Theorizing About Play

The first theory of play, though with more philosophical tone than scientific, should probably be attributed to Friedrick von Schiller. In his essays (or letters) on aesthetics he proposed that two instincts, the sensuous and the formulative, combined to produce a play instinct; its object is to produce living form or, in other words, beauty. Man, he argued, only plays with beauty and "the whole edifice of art and the still more difficult art of life . . ." is supported by that principle.

Perhaps science will have more to say about beauty and the art of life some day. But by the late 1800s, Darwin's theory of evolution guided speculation along the lines of biology and human evolution. The Protestant work ethic was infused with biological notions of competitive struggle. These tendencies are reflected in the early theories of play. In *Why People Play*, Michael Ellis (1973) provided a concise but comprehensive review and analysis of 15 theories which have been postulated to explain play. We need, then, only briefly review the evolution of our thinking about play, including the social and intellectual developments which have influenced our thinking.

The early theories, dating to about the first quarter of the century, were based mainly on instinct, genetic inheritance, and on levels of energy. One theory argued that play resulted from having energy in excess of that needed for survival; another held that play resulted from the need to relax from the expenditure of energy in work and other nonplay activities. One argued that play was a rehearsal of skills needed in the future, clearly including work, while still another held that in play one repeated the past practices of evolving man. The ties to biological evolution and the work ethic are clear in these theories. Yet they all helped to explain at least some of the observable forms of play, despite being based on assumptions which were often not valid and sometimes quite contradictory. They were, as to be expected, not as powerful as more recent theories in that more recent theories can be generalized to encompass much more of the phenomenon of play.

Since the early 1900s, much of our theoretical speculation about play has developed in keeping with the growing interest in the fields of sociology and anthropology, but particularly in psychology, especially as it relates to growth and development and learning. These theories are still discussed in the literature, explored in studies of various kinds, and remain credible in different quarters and different ways as partial explanations of at least some forms of play. The theories which we label generalization and compensation refer mainly to the influence of work and other obligations: generalization being the carry over to the world of play those experiences found pleasing; compensation the attempt in play to obtain pleasurable experiences not found in other aspects of life. These are mainly sociological theories viewing play in reference to work. There is, of course, the old saying that one man's work is another man's play, expressing the problem with such categories and thus problems with such theories.

The influence of psychology, including the work of Sigmund Freud among others, is evident in the psychoanalytic theories and in the cartharsis theory. The latter, which is not supported by research findings, deals mainly with aggression and supposes that play provides an acceptable outlet substituting for socially unacceptable, aggressive behaviors. The psychoanalytic theories suggest that play is essentially therapeutic in that it allows one to overcome unpleasant experiences and emotions either by purging or by gradually assimilating them.

Learning, Competence, and Arousal

Those theories which are most current and appealing to us explain play in terms of mental growth and development and learning. We are generally familiar with these concepts, even if not in the precise and particular ways described by Piaget and others. The competence—effectance theory is less familiar. In essence it refers to a need to produce effects, to be a cause of things taking place or being produced, and to derive positive feelings from the effects one produces. This is a more sophisticated formulation of certain elements in the early thinking of Schiller, Groos and others who recognized the joy of being a cause.

The most intriguing theory, and perhaps the most powerful to date, is the theory of arousal. It derives from the fascinating explorations in recent decades of the physiology and chemistry of the brain. Fascinating, but also technical and complex. In brief and nonscientific terms, play is thought to occur because of a need to stimulate activity in the brain. While different for every individual, and for each individual at different times or in different circumstances, there is a level of arousal or neural activity which is best. By best is meant the level of activity in the brain which leads to the individual functioning at his or her best. Optimal arousal equals optimal performance, the importance of which, in evolutionary terms, is obvious. It seems also that at the optimal level of brain activity, the individual feels the best, perhaps in part because of the positive feelings, indicated in the theory of competence effectance, derived from optimal performance.

Perhaps an analogy will help. Students and former students who have written more than one term or theme paper know how difficult it is when one does not have enough information. Some know the reverse is also true;

there is just too much information. The result, in either case, is usually less than one's best performance and that is reflected in how one feels about the result (before the paper is graded and returned, of course).

Play, then, is motivated by the need to maintain the optimal level of arousal according to this theory. And play and optimal arousal are pleasurable. There is in the brain, an area which is commonly referred to as the pleasure center. We know that it can be stimulated by electrical energy. We know, too, that the brain produces chemicals far more potent than the opium, heroin and other drugs for which there is a multi-billion dollar commerce in legal medicine and illegal traffic. Those "natural opiates" influence the flow of electrical current in the brain and contribute to our feelings, positive and negative, pleasurable and painful. Laughter produces these natural opiates as do also delight, joy, amusement and so much else that is found most often in play (Cousins, 1979).

We are also aware of what is known in medical and allied fields as the placebo effect. Placebos, often just sugar pills, have no medicinal effects, yet "cures" resulting from taking placebos are often reported in 30 to 35 percent of the patients "treated." The active ingredient is the self. Self-healing seems the result of faith, hope, optimism and feeling positively about oneself and one's future (Tiger, 1979). We have known of psychosomatic illness for many decades. Now we know of psychosomatic wellness. Fun, or the pleasurable feelings characteristic of play, is good for your health.

THE FUNCTIONS OF PLAY

Play does not take place because it is functional or useful. In play, the activity itself, rather than any useful outcome, is the motivating and energizing force. But play is functional in many respects, and provides many benefits to the player and to the entire species. In the most immediate and individual sense, as just noted, play is emotionally positive and that is important for mental and physical health.

Of course, play often takes the form of vigorous physical activity. How frequently observers of people at play remark that it makes them tired just watching. Other forms of play involve playing with objects and materials of almost every kind. In these activities, dexterity, coordination and other skills are developed. The physical and skill development outcomes of play are well known and readily observable.

Play also contributes to social development in many ways and at many levels of complexity, from bonding between the very young and their nurturers to understanding the roles and dynamics of all sorts of social situations. Not all play is social, though much of it is, and this necessarily involves communication and the continuous taking into account of those others involved. Play cannot take place without shared understanding and mutual expectations. Competition in games and contests of every kind requires first and foremost consensus and cooperation. There are commands and prohibitions and rules and penalties which provide order and make sense. In their absence, or the absence of agreement and understanding, there can only be the frustration Alice found in Wonderland. The play group and the game, then, as much if not more so than parents and teachers, are principal agents of socialization (Mead, 1934: 153-164).

A third general category of functions or benefits of play is that of intellectual development. One can often, if not quite literally, see or hear the players' minds engaged with the intellectual content of play. Players are frequently engaged in the same intellectual activity as scientists. They test hypotheses with contingency statements of if—then. "If I do this, then that will occur." As players learn and develop intellectual skills, the process shifts to higher levels of abstraction and complexity. Once a certain level of mastery is achieved, players deliberately make the play more challenging by adding obstacles and complexity to their play (Miller, 1973: 87-98).

There is, then, in play, a strong element of problem solving, not so much in an applied sense as in the theoretical sense of formulating and testing hypothetical propositions. But in addition to cause-effect sorts of problem solving, the variety of play experiences and the freedom to explore and experiment, because outcomes are inconsequential, makes play a progenitor of creativity. Play induces responses labeled variously as flexible, adaptable, bi-associative, combinational or thinking which is divergent as well as conver-gent. Play provides the learning and experience from which novel responses may flow. Novelty is an essential element in creativity: a necessary element but not sufficient in itself as creativity also requires a response appropriate to the situation at hand (Bishop & Jeanrenaud, 1985). Without further elabora-tion, it is clear that play produces the raw materials for adaptability, flexibility and creativity. This function, as well as the other noted above, are obviously significant for the individual and, in evolutionary terms, the species.

From this brief review, it is evident that there are ways parents, teachers, and other adults in positions wherein to influence play can have an increasingly positive influence. The environment should be sufficiently rich in materials and opportunities so that players can pace themselves according to their respective skills, interests and levels of development. The "kitchen-sink" approach is intuitively attractive but also strongly recommended by empirical observation. The amount of direction provided by adults should be moderate; too much or too little stifles creativity, the former by encouraging responses that are appropriate but not novel, the later by encouraging responses that are novel but not appropriate.

While high levels of skill and performance should be encouraged and recognized, sharply peaked pyramidal structures discourage too many from participation at too early a time. This is particularly true of sports but not limited to sports. More emphasis should be placed on participation rather than outcomes, and more recognition should be given to a much broader range of activities which begin and should remain as intrinsically rewarding play.

Beyond some words of recognition and encouragement, we should not burden play with rewards and punishments. When we do, the motivation for play switches from the intrinsic pleasure of playing to the extrinsic, external reward of performance. Maria Montessori, who sought to reform education, railed against the discipline imposed in classrooms of her era, a discipline which equated good with silence and immobility. For that, benches bolted to the floor and facing front had much the effect of a galley for slaves. Rewards and punishments, she said are "the benches of the soul" (Montessori, 1912: 16-21).

CAN PLAY SURVIVE GROWING UP?

Do you ever play at games? Or is your idea of life breakfast, lessons, dinner, lessons, tea, lessons, bed, lessons, breakfast, lessons, and so on? It is a very neat plan of life and almost as interesting as being a sewing machine or a coffee grinder. (In Blake 1974: 11)

Charles Dodgson, in writing to a young friend, provided that delightful summary of the hazards of growing up. Dodgson's style and tone mark him as the man who wrote, as Lewis Carroll, *Alice's Adventures in Wonderland, Through the Looking Glass*, and other tales for adults as well as children.

Play can survive growing up, and sometimes does. But it does not often flourish. Too many lives become as neat and as interesting as being a sewing machine or coffee grinder. How revealing that we sometimes speak of our work as a grind and as something we crank out. Surely the oft-voiced imperative "grow up" does not mean that. The meaning "don't be childish" is bad enough. But there is a world of difference between being "childish" and being "childlike" and our language reveals deeply rooted values and attitudes. There are enough obstacles to play without adding jaundiced and moralistic views.

Often we live in environments which are noisy, cluttered and hectic. Complete absorption in activity, whether paid or unpaid, is difficult when elements of the environment so often intrude and interrupt. Such environments may "overload" our sense systems, particularly of sight and sound, causing levels of arousal exceeding the optimal and pleasant and reducing our sense of competence and thus the positive feelings of effectance. We may, then, seek to reduce arousal through some kind of mental passivity, the kind which television often induces.

Lack of feelings of competence is undoubtedly reinforced by the professionalization of activity, and constant media exposure to the highest standards of performance. In addition, much of the growing service industry is based on the notion that we are incompetent in almost every sphere and thus in need of the services offered. We have more avocational counselors than vocational ones. We are trained to be incapable of and at play.

The imperative to consume also forecloses opportunities to play. Consumption not only costs the time to earn the money required but also the time required to choose just the right item at the right price. Consuming is hard work. It is also cumulative; the purchase of one item necessitating the purchase of many others. A set of golf clubs, or even a moderately priced tennis racquet may wind up costing many hundreds, if not thousands, of dollars in more equipment and supplies, apparel, books, videotapes, lessons, fees and club memberships. Such investments, to say nothing of yachts and summer homes or cottages, demand one's time and attention if the investment is to pay off.

A particularly difficult obstacle to play is our penchant for creating mutually exclusive categories, including categories like work and play. These categories do not exist at the theoretical level. Theories of growth and development, learning, competence-effectance and arousal all recognize that these motivating needs can be satisfied by any activity, irrespective of categories. Perhaps work and play should be regarded as a continuum along which there is a great deal of overlap. It is everyone's desire to find work that is interesting and rewarding in itself; work which, if one did not need the income, one would do anyway. As with play the reward is in the activity itself and many of the characteristics of play are present. The ordinary is transcended by complete absorption in the activity. But unfortunately, much work is not inherently worthwhile and satisfying. In those cases, workers will take what opportunities they find to incorporate some elements of play and games, in "horseplay," "kidding," jest and wit, practical jokes and celebrating any occasion.

In addition to what is problematic about jobs which are not inherently interesting and intuitively worthwhile is the problem of attitudes about work and play. We continue to believe that work is somehow virtuous. We never think of play that way because play is pleasurable and pleasure, if not down right sinful, is at least not virtuous. We cannot find virtue in those enjoyments to which we seem by nature inclined, denying entirely the wisdom of nature. The evidence is quite to the contrary.

If work is fun, pleasurable, enjoyable and the like, we would be shorn of what is probably our principal source of virtuousness. Work is supposed to be work; difficult, unpleasant, hard, taxing, demanding. Otherwise, why should one be paid in money, benefits and time free from work? This attitude blinds us to the possibilities of play in work. The notion that work is the serious business of adults depreciates the value of play in adult life. As Russell suggested, "The morality of work is the morality of slaves, and the modern world has no need of slavery" (Russell, 1935: 17).

Play cannot be born of slavery, it can be born only of freedom. But we make a grim business of even that. Freedom is something that has to be earned, and that takes hard work. Freedom, the heart of leisure, we refuse to accept as a gift. Freedom must be won in glorious combat or virtuous work—then and only then can adults, in good conscience, play—as long as they are not childish, of course.

But again, childish is not the same as child like, and it is possible for us to be as a child. In adult life it is not as easy for there are restrictions, including roles to play and responsibilities to meet. There are limits, then, to our ability to range freely and without regard to time according to what attracts and interests us. Our environments become too familiar and we impose a uniformity and sameness upon them. They lose their inherent interest. And so we shut ourselves off from them with autos and earphones.

Too, growing up means that we know a great deal, and thus there is much less about which we are, therefore, curious and desirous of exploring. But our pragmatism and utilitarianism, limited as it is to the immediate and self-centered, blunts our curiosity and interest in things in themselves. Rather than seize opportunities for play, we search for ways to make all our time useful.

> We are all of us compelled to read for profit, party for
> contacts, lunch for contracts, bowl for unity, drive for
> mileage, gamble for charity, go out for the evening for

the greater glory of the municipality, and stay home for the
weekend to rebuild the house. Minutes, hours and days
have been spared us. The prospect of filling them with the
pleasures for which they were spared us has somehow come
to seem meaningless, meaningless enough to drive some of
us to drink and some of us to doctors and all of us to the
satisfactions of an insatiate industry. (Kerr, 1962: 39-40)

We may derive some pleasure or satisfaction from all that although,
as Kerr suggested, activities which are not practical, useful and motivated by
ends outside themselves have come to seem meaningless. The inability to find
meaning in activities in themselves drives us to drink and to doctors and
purveyors of amusement and entertainment and escape.

The most serious obstacle we face may be the result, as Pieper noted,
of making work of all intellectual activity. Play is an intellectual activity
which is then, though not always, made manifest in observable behaviors.
Learning and understanding often take place in play, without effort, and in
that sense they are gifts. But again, there is no virtue in what is acquired
effortlessly. Even as adults, we learn simply by being participants in life, as if
by magic. But adults do not believe in magic, and that is one reason why it is
so difficult for them to play.

With rationalism, empiricism and Cartesian doubt, we have abandoned explanations and understandings of a metaphysical or religious nature.
We enclose ourselves completely in a world of the known and the knowable,
governed by necessity and the laws of cause and effect. But as Keen suggested (1969: 167):

Philosophies of life . . . reflect a pathological orientation to
life whenever they conspire to destroy wonder and freedom
by picturing the world as a closed system which may be
understood and explained without remainder.

Children live in a world of remainder, a world filled with wonder and
enchantment, mystery and magic. Adults, partly coerced and partly voluntarily, have found themselves exiled from the child's world. Yet they carry with
them a longing for the freedom, spontaneity, innocence and joy of being as a
child. Those who live most authentically and joyfully are those who have

always kept at least one foot in a child's world and never stopped playing. Like Socrates, Plato and Aristotle, they seem to know that philosophy is born of wonder and that life should be lived as play.

HOMO FABER OR HOMO LUDENS?

"There is a minority report throughout the course of history that play is the chief end of man" (Neale, 1969: 15). It is a sizeable minority, perhaps it is also a growing one. The literature in many fields, anthropology, education, philosophy and others is replete with evidence and argument which gives primacy to play. Educators like John Dewey and Joseph Lee argued that work and life are raised to the level of art and reach their pinnacle when they are most fully infused with play. Huizinga, with the support of many other anthropologists and historians, attributed culture and civilization, surely man's greatest achievements, to play. Karl Marx believed adults should be taught by their children. Daniel Defoe agreed. Thoreau said one need not live by the sweat of one's brow: his friend Emerson believed that, to the wise, life is a festival. Mark Twain insisted he never did a day's work in his life; that everything he did he did because it was play.

The primacy of play, in fact even reverence for play, was clear to the early Greek philosophers. In the *Laws*, Plato wrote (In Huizinga, 1955: 212):

> God alone is worthy of supreme seriousness, but man is
> made God's plaything, and that is the best part of him.
> Therefore every man and woman should live life accord-
> ingly, and play the noblest games, and be of another mind
> from what they are at present. . . . What, then is the right
> way of living? Life must be lived as play, playing certain
> games, making sacrifices, singing and dancing, and then a
> man will be able to propitiate the Gods.

Friedrick von Schiller was of the same mind. "Man," he wrote, "only plays when in the full meaning of the word he is a man, and he is only completely a man when he plays" (1905: 71).

Philosophy and biology, ethics and aesthetics, anthropology and education, science and religion find common ground in play. Man plays longer and in more diverse and complex ways than any other animal and is the

only animal that produces culture. We should not be surprised to find so
much agreement in so many quarters. All were born in play and all are
sustained by play. And play, in turn, is born in freedom, pleasure and wonder.
These are gifts of which the child, unless somehow deprived of them, makes
perfect and joyful use. Does adulthood mean nothing more than adulteration
of these gifts? It appears so but it does not appear necessarily so. The hobo
turned longshoreman turned philosopher, Eric Hoffer, summarized the case
very well (1963: 116):

> My feeling is that the tendency to carry youthful characteris-
> tics into adult life, which renders man perpetually immature
> and unfinished, is at the root of his uniqueness in the
> universe, and is particularly pronounced in the creative
> individual. Youth has always been called a perishable
> talent, but perhaps talent and originality are always aspects
> of youth, and the creative individual is an imperishable
> juvenile. When the Greeks said, 'Whom the Gods love die
> young,' they probably meant, as Lord Stankey suggested,
> that those favored by the gods stay young till the day they
> die; young and playful.

REFERENCES

Beach, Frank. 1978. "Current Concepts of Play in Animals." In Dietland Muller-Schwarze (Ed.), *Evolution of Play Behavior*. Stroudsburg, Pennsylvania: Dowden, Hutchison and Ross.

Bishop, Doyle and Jeanrenaud, Claudine. 1985. "Creative Growth through Play and Its Implications for Recreation Practice." In Thomas Goodale and Peter Witt, *Recreation and Leisure: Issues in an Era of Change* (2nd ed.). State College, Pennsylvania: Venture Publishing.

Blake, Kathleen. 1974. *Play, Games and Sport: The Literary Works of Lewis Carroll.* Ithaca, New York: Cornell University Press.

Cousins, Norman. 1979. *Anatomy of an Illness as Perceived by the Patient.* New York: W.W. Norton.

Durant, Will. 1939. *The Life of Greece: The Story of Civilization, Part II.* New York: Simon and Schuster.

Ellis, Michael. 1973. *Why People Play.* Englewood-Cliffs, New Jersey: Prentice-Hall.

Hoffer, Eric. 1963. *The Ordeal of Change.* New York: Harper and Row.

Hoffer, Eric. 1967. *The Temper of Our Times.* New York: Harper and Row.

Huizinga, Johann. 1955. *Homo Ludens: A Study of the Play Element in Culture.* Boston: Beacon Press.

Kerr, Walter. 1962. *The Decline of Pleasure.* New York: Simon and Schuster.

Lehman, Harvey and Witty, Paul. 1927. *The Psychology of Play Activities.* New York: A.S. Barnes and Company.

Mead, George F. 1934. *Mind, Self and Society.* Chicago: University of Chicago Press.

Mergen, Bernard. 1975. "The Discovery of Children's Play." *American Quarterly* (XXVII: 4) (October).

Miller, Steven. 1973. "Means, Ends and Galumphing: Some Leitmotifs of Play." *American Anthropologist* (75: 1) (February).

Montessori, Maria. 1912. *The Montessori Method* (Tr. Anne George). New York: Frederick A. Stokes.

Neale, Robert. 1969. *In Praise of Play: Towards a Psychology of Religion.* New York: Harper and Row.

Nef, John. 1958. *Cultural Foundations of Industrial Civilization.* Cambridge: Cambridge University Press.

Rahner, Hugo. 1972. *Man at Play.* New York: Herder and Herder.

Russell, Bertrand. 1935. *In Praise of Idleness and Other Essays.* New York: W.W. Norton.

Schiller, Friedrich von. 1905. *Essays Aesthetical and Philosophical.* London: George Bell and Sons.

Smith, Peter K. 1982. "Does Play Matter? Functional and Evolutionary Aspects of Animal and Human Play." *The Behavioral and Brain Sciences* (5:1) (March).

Smith, Stephen. 1985. "On the Biological Basis of Pleasure," In Thomas Goodale and Peter Witt. *Recreation and Leisure: Issues in an Era of Change* (rev. ed.). State College, Pennsylvania: Venture Publishing.

Tiger, Lionel. 1979. *Optimism: The Biology of Hope.* New York: Simon and Schuster.

In the modern world institutions are more or less independent, each serving its own proximate purpose, and our culture is really a collection of separate interests each sovereign within its own realm. We do not put shrines in our workshops, and we think it unseemly to talk business in the vestibule of a church. We dislike politics in the pulpit and preaching from politicians. We do not look upon our scholars as priests or our priests as learned men. We do not expect science to sustain theology, nor religion to dominate art. On the contrary we insist with much fervor on the separation of church and state, of religion and science, of politics and historical research, of morality and art, of business and love. This separation of activities has its counterpart in a separation of selves; the life of a modern man is not so much the history of a single soul; it is rather a play of many characters within a single body.

(Walter Lippman, 1964: 105-6)

XI. LEISURE AND THE REST OF LIFE: HOLISM AND SEGMENTATION

A major series of philosophical questions concern what parts of life are or should be separated or segmented, what has or should have unique identity or be a part or an aspect of something else. Many such philosophical questions exist. Should we think of the self as something unique or as a part of a larger system? (If we think of "my" mind or "my" arm, then who is the "me" who is contemplating his or her possessions?) There is philosophical debate concerning the dualism of mind and body, the separation of humans from other animals or the whole of "nature," the separation of knowledge from belief, of the rational from the emotional, of perception from objective reality (if there is an objective reality), of groups of people from each other due to geographical location (or culture, race, gender, age, income, educational level, military strength, etc.), the separation between teacher and learner, giver and receiver, and other bases for segmenting existence. All these distinctions are of great philosophical importance, but in this chapter we focus upon only one aspect of the segmentation question: the segmentation of life into leisure and nonleisure.

Interest in this question has grown out of observations that work and play are becoming more and more alike, that they are becoming, in a sense, fused. As Wolfenstein (1959) noted:

> There has been a mutual penetration of work and play.
> Work tends to be permeated with behavior formerly
> confined to after work hours. Play conversely tends to be
> measured by standards of achievement previously applicable
> only to work. One asks oneself not only in personal
> relations but now also at work: Did they like me? Did I
> make a good impression? And at play, no less than at work,
> one asks: Am I doing as well as I should? (p. 93)

The lingering, nagging questions about such a fusion are: What are the consequences for work? What are the consequences for play? What are the consequences for people? Riesman (1963) expressed the hope that individuals could find self-directed autonomy in play and that play could be rescued if we could overcome obstacles to becoming autonomous in play. But he concluded we may also have to do something about the nature and conditions of work. Should play be fused with work or should play be rescued from it?

Leisure, we have seen, is often conceptualized as a segment of life, i.e., time periods in which one may pursue what he or she wishes in relative freedom, or as a quality or condition of life which is a continuous or permanent condition, that is, the absence of the necessity of being occupied. Leisure may also be thought of as being segmented from the rest of life due to other considerations, such as the inability to celebrate, the inability to find meaning, or lack of faith. Leisure may be segmented or separated from other activity by conceptualizing leisure as "serious" activity, as activity which leads to self-knowledge, or activity which is virtuous or pleasurable or tranquil.

BASES FOR SEGREGATING LEISURE

The most important way of segmenting or distinguishing leisure from other activity in the industrial world, of course, is to divide our time and activity into categories of leisure and work. But there are a number of other ways of separating leisure from nonleisure.

Leisure as a State of Salvation

Some authors, most notably the Swiss Catholic philosopher Josef Pieper (1952), have viewed leisure as a condition of the soul.

> Leisure, it must be clearly understood, is a mental and
> spiritual attitude—it is not simply the result of external
> factors, it is not the inevitable result of spare time, a
> holiday, a weekend or a vacation. It is, in the first place,
> an attitude of the mind, a condition of the soul. (p. 40)

This condition is essentially a state of grace which some people achieve and others do not. Those unable to achieve leisure suffer from a despairing refusal to accept their place in the world; an inability to celebrate existence and their place in it. The proletariat, therefore, seeks refuge in work. Its members prefer to work, are willing to suffer without a rationale being given for their suffering, and do not want to be freed from their work. Rather, they want to enmesh those who attain leisure in their world of work. In summary, the proletariat are incapable of celebration in a spiritual sense; they lack religious faith. Because of this, they lack the condition of the soul needed to transfer ordinary experience into leisure.

A person cannot make leisure happen simply because he or she wants it. According to Pieper:

> The ultimate root of leisure is not susceptible to the
> human will. Absolute affirmation of the universe cannot,
> strictly speaking, be based upon a voluntary resolve.
> Above all it cannot be 'done' for the sake of a purpose
> lying outside itself. There are things that we cannot do
> 'in order to . . .' or 'so that. . . .' Either we do them not at
> all or we do them because they are right in saying that
> lack of leisure makes for illness. But just as certainly
> it is impossible to attempt to engage in leisure for health's
> sake! Such a reversal of the meaningful order of things
> is more than just unseemly; it simply cannot be done.
> Leisure cannot be achieved at all when it is sought as a
> means to an end, even though that end be 'the salvation
> of western civilization.' (p. 62)

In spite of this, Pieper does point out the conditions under which it is likely that leisure will be given.

Leisure is not the attitude of mind of those who actively
intervene, but of those who are open to everything; not of
those who grab and grab hold, but of those who leave the
reins loose and who are free and easy themselves—almost
like a man falling asleep, for one can only fall asleep by
'letting oneself go.' Sleeplessness and the incapacity for
leisure are really related to one another in a special sense,
and a man at leisure is not unlike a man asleep. (p. 41)

Play as Segmentation

The industrial revolution resulted in a more extreme partitioning of
not only production and consumption but also of work and play. The values,
social organization and goals of industrial work and play became much more
highly differentiated. For most workers, the characteristic feature of their
work was constraint. Those few who owned the means of production led lives
of comparative privilege and elevated work to a religion. For laborers, work
was slavery; for management it was identity. The chief characteristic of play,
for most workers, was its decidedly secondary role in the social system, if not
in their own personal interests. One need read only a handful of historical
accounts of the play behavior of such workers to understand that such behavior proceeded from values that were far different from those values which
were rewarded in their places of work. While at work, planning, goal-setting,
seriousness, rationality, time consciousness, incremental improvement through
mastery of technique, activity as means to an end, earnestness, efficiency,
effectiveness, precision, inferior-superior social relationships, feedback,
evaluation, and profit were valued; these changed during play. Play, very
often, met the criteria and was imbued with the values described by Huizinga
(1955). It was outside ordinary life, limited in time and space, voluntarily
entered into, served as its own end, created its own meaning, was contained by
rules freely accepted by players, was nonrational, created its own morality,
was surrounded by an air of mystery, exaggeration, spontaneity, celebration,
and illusion; was "fun"; was characterized by equal social relationships and
promoted social groups when the play was over. The differences between
play and work were not possible to reconcile. Thus, the values and meanings
of daily life for many such workers could be considered segmented. Such
segmentation was most easily characterized as springing from the tremendous
variation in the level of personal constraint experienced at work from that
experienced at play.

Much of the argument made by Huizinga rests in the belief that, except in the earliest stages of a culture, play must remain separate from the rest of life. Play, being inherently limited in its objectives, limited in time and space, and serving no ends but its own, cannot be integrated into a culture where aspirations are essentially unlimited and most behaviors serve as means to other ends. Also, Huizinga saw play as being in the realm of the nonrational and outside conventional morality. Play contained its own meaning and its own morality. As a culture became increasingly rational, play could not be integrated with the rest of life without destroying it.

Work as Constraint

Because work has often been thought of as behavior which is, essentially, constrained, leisure has been thought of in many societies as existing only in a different segment of life. A major philosophical question concerning leisure is whether it is desirable for leisure to be segmented from work and other obligated activities or whether it is better for leisure to be integrated into the rest of life. The latter, integration, is a major component of what is referred to as "holistic living." Parker (1972) described the ideal as follows:

> In this (holistic) fusion, work may lose its present feature
> of constraint and gain the creativity now associated mainly
> with leisure, while leisure may lose its opposition to work
> and gain the status—now associated mainly with the product
> of work—of a resource worthy of planning to provide the
> greatest possible human satisfaction. (p. 229)

Since it is relatively easy for us to recognize some of the harm done to people by their industrial work in society (and perhaps more difficult to recognize the many benefits), there is a great tendency to philosophically support any notion of "holistic" living, health, medicine, or religion. Holistic philosophies reject not only the dualism of mind and body but also reject dividing life into work and play or dealing with each other in ways which limit our options or self-expression because of some forced constraint.

Holism, to some extent, indicates an end of scarcity or constraint. It is in keeping both with Maslow's notion of "self-actualization" being at the top of a hierarchy of needs as well as with the ancient Athenian notion of "leisure" in the sense that it implies the absence of the necessity of being occupied: having nothing you must do.

Segmentation, conversely, assumes that it is often necessary for us to be occupied and to be occupied in ways which do not allow us to do as we please or act as we would in other situations. One line of reasoning assumes that our work-leisure roles have been increasingly segmented from hunter-gatherer societies to farming societies to those based upon trading (mercantilism) to those based upon industry. At each succeeding phase of economic evolution, work roles became more specialized and separated from the rest of life. The barbaric consequences of industrialism, it is argued, in which workers became little more than slaves or living machines, will gradually disappear and a holistic mode will once again emerge in postindustrial society.

The belief that work and leisure were totally integrated in less technologically advanced societies is not shared by many historians. Clayre (In Cunningham, 1980), for example, argued that:

> . . . except in primitive societies, people have always been
> aware of a separation between work and leisure, and have
> put a high value on leisure. Leisure itself, a harvest
> celebration, for example, may have been inextricably
> bound up with work, but to pretend that participants
> were unaware when they were working and when they
> were not is sheer romanticism. (p. 57)

Perhaps it can be said that the process of industrialism increased the differences between work and leisure by changing the nature of work and, hence, the rest of life. Industrial work, in which the worker was often no more than an extension of or replacement for a machine, needed to be segmented from the rest of life.

Part of the process of segmenting work and leisure undoubtedly came from managers of industries where newly mechanized work needed to be coordinated and regulated. As historian Gary Cross determined, however, many laborers readily accepted a strict segregation of work and leisure as a way of containing work and making it more predictable. In discussing the development of the eight-hour day in France, which many workers attained in 1919, Cross (1965) stated:

Workers sought not only a regular workday defined as
time at the disposal of the employer, but accepted a
compression of time at the workplace. Some unions
negotiated away the casse-croute, a 15-30 minute rest and
food break, generally 8:30 a.m. and 4:00 p.m. This custom
disappeared in numerous trades without much protest
after the war. Apparently workers preferred breakfast
with family and an earlier dinner at home to food and rest
breaks with workmates. This indicates an important shift
from a work-centered to a leisure- and family-centered
mentality. (p. 202)

Thus, many union workers whose jobs were disagreeable and
sometimes dangerous accepted increased segmentation of work and leisure to
diminish the pervasiveness of work and claim some predictable intervals of
leisure. It may be argued, of course, that this was merely making the best of a
bad situation. Ideally, these workers may have wanted to change the qualities
of their work but, that being impossible, pushed for a containment of work.
Too, for those whose work was merely onerous toil, work probably never was
a central life interest but simply what one had to do to survive, support one's
family, and perhaps assure a better future.

Segmentation may be thought of as a compromise brought about by
industrialism which is characterized by workers viewing their work as a
necessary evil and a means to an end. Such workers will push for more pay
and shorter hours initially and, only later, for more humane working conditions. Part of this compromise was the reordering of "leisure" to become
"recreation." "Recreation," which was often conceptualized as physical and
emotional restoration or re-creation, became a segment in a cycle of work-
recreation-work. As Margaret Mead (1958) stated:

The word recreation epitomizes this whole attitude of
conditional joy in which the delights of both work and play
are tied together in a tight sequence. Neither one may ever
be considered by itself, but man must work, then weary
and 'take some recreation' so he may work again. (p. 12)

Work and recreation, then, are highly segmented but both part of an
unending cycle designed to accommodate the demands of work.

While work and recreation may have become more segmented under industrialization, recreation during this period began to take on some of the characteristics of work. That is, recreation changed in nature to become more planned, rational, and done as a means to an end. Popular recreation in Britain and elsewhere prior to the industrial revolution was usually "public, improvised and inconclusive" (Delves, 1975: 7), much of it taking place in the street. As the mercantile class of the 17th century and then the owners and managers of industry in the 18th century realized the economic necessity of instilling a "work ethic" among laborers, idleness had to be eliminated. Along with the attack on idleness came attempts by some moral reformers, with the help of economists and government, to eliminate or change the nature of the recreation pursuits of the peasants. Cunningham (1980) characterized the leisure pursuits of this class as possessing a live-and-let-live indifference with no vision of improvement or long-term ideal. This had to change if the peasants were to become dedicated workers. The change was brought about not only by taking economic advantage of them so that they had no choice but to work, but also by reforming their leisure habits.

> Those radicals who pushed for working class improvement
> in all its guises—teetotalism, Owenism, chartism, trade
> unionism, benefit and educational clubs, socialism, secular-
> ism—all had their own particular sincerities, but equally
> they all also had the destruction of the old popular culture as
> integral to their ends. (Colls, In Cunningham, 1980: 94)

Recreation activity, then, was pressured to fit into the plans of both those who wished to accumulate wealth and would use the peasant as a slave in order to do it, as well as those who wished to "improve" the peasant through altering his or her use of leisure.

Specialization at Work

Among the more important causes of segmentation has been the development of specialized work roles in which individuals are highly limited and specialized in the tasks they perform. This specialization was really the hallmark of the industrial revolution. Adam Smith, in *The Wealth of Nations*, stated that specialization had been more responsible for improvements in production than any other factor. The development of assembly lines for automobiles and other machinery coincided with workers being responsible for only a tiny part of the total production. Henry Ford's Model T, for instance, was built on an assembly line which required 7,882 separate specialized jobs. Of these tasks, Toffler (1980) quoted Ford as saying that 949 of these specialized tasks needed men with strong bodies, 3,338 needed men of only ordinary strength, and the rest could be performed by women or older children.

The worker, to a great extent, had become merely an extension of the machine. It was the worker who was left to fit into the process of production rather than accommodating the process of production to the needs and desires of the worker. Not only were many manufacturing jobs specialized but they were also designed to be capable of being performed by almost anyone, regardless of their talent or training.

The rise of the professions also represented specialization, but specialization based upon training. Those in the professions also maintained segmented relations with their "clients," increasingly dealing with them only in regard to their occupational specialty. Professionalism became a way to elevate the status of a whole occupational group and specialized knowledge and skill, which further segmented relations with clients, became traits of the professions. As the professions became more highly specialized, the distinction between worker and professional became more rigid. Those who were capable of doing the specialized work (or sanctioned to do it) were separated from the rest of society. For all specialized workers, the constriction or focusing of work made it increasingly distinguishable from the rest of life.

Leisure as a Prerogative of an Elite

From the time of Athens before the birth of Christ, leisure has often been reserved for an elite in society. Indeed, the Athenian notion of leisure was extremely elite since the privileges of leisure were reserved for native born males. A slave system and the near-slave status of women were necessary to provide leisure.

In many other cultures, work and leisure roles have been segmented by social class. Often, leisure has had different connotations for rich and poor, powerful and powerless. As Hall (1963) commented, in regard to the industrializing period in England: "Leisure in a poor man is thought quite a different thing from what it is to a rich man, and goes by a different name. In the poor it is called idleness, the cause of all mischief." Marx (In Cunningham, 1980: 515) was even more explicit "In capitalist society . . .

leisure time for a privileged class is produced by converting the whole lifetime of the masses into labor time."

In its most oppressive beginnings, industrial capitalism forced work requirements on those without financial means, requirements to which they were not accustomed and which they resisted. Certainly this situation has been evident in many periods of history in which one group has been able to make slaves or near slaves of another. The slaves of plantation owners in the southern United States allowed their owners to become the first "leisure class" in the United States. The justification for such segmentation in a society assumes the capability of those who have leisure to benefit from it, or assumes their entitlement to it because of power, financial success, or accidents of birth. In Britain in the 1830s and 1840s, many of the public areas which provided recreation for the working class and the poor began to be taken over by the rich. That, presumably, was their entitlement.

Public bathing (which the working class often undertook in canals while naked) was widely banned; footpaths were closed to all but the rich; open fields which had served as public "commons" were fenced off. "The enclosure of the open fields was a visible sign and symbol that rampant family and individual power had gained a complete victory over the civic community" (Cunningham, 1980: 13). Even many public gardens (allotments) disappeared. Most cultural activities were generally too expensive for the poor or thought of as inappropriate. Zoos, botanical gardens, libraries, museums and art galleries, which were part of many towns, were almost exclusively private ventures run for profit or through subscription and were beyond the means of the common people. One consequence of this blocking off of public rights may have been to drive the poor to the alehouses for their recreation.

A similar situation took place in the United States and Canada. Thorstein Veblen (1899) believed the rich had formed a "leisure class" for whom leisure represented not an opportunity for self-improvement but merely the chance to consume conspicuously, to display wealth and to increase social distance from common people. The leisure class, predatory by nature, maintained its style of life by continually taking advantage of those less affluent and powerful. Thus, it is clear that leisure, in the sense of participation in a range of pleasurable and freely chosen activities, has been segmented—by wealth, by class, and by power. Leisure was, in all these cases, the prerogative of an elite.

BASES FOR INTEGRATING LEISURE

Most of the ideas and beliefs about integrating leisure have to do with the changing nature and meaning of work. There are some exceptions.

The Search for the Authentic

As noted elsewhere, the rise of existential philosophy, with its belief that human nature was not fixed or predetermined, made the distinction between work and leisure a meaningless one. People, without fixed definitions of who they are, feel compelled to act in order to define themselves. They experience anxiety in doing so, whether or not their activities earn money or are compelled on other bases. While people may be free, the consequence of such freedom is dread, anxiety, and a sense of being alone in the world. To the existentialist, our lives are not so much divided into free and nonfree segments as they are unified by the condition of being free and alone and undefined in an irrational world.

The Humanization of Work

Another of the ways in which leisure and work are thought to be integrated is due to the increasingly positive conditions under which individuals are thought to work. Work and leisure are, therefore, thought to be more and more alike. Parker (1972: 44-49) identified the sources of work satisfaction as: (1) creating something—a feeling that one has put something of oneself into a product, (2) using skill—whether the skill is manual or not, (3) working wholeheartedly—not being arbitrarily slowed down, (4) using initiative and having responsibility—freedom to make decisions, (5) mixing with people—social contact, and (6) working with people who know their job—competent bosses and associates. Work was not satisfying, Parker found from reviewing research, because of the following: (1) doing a repetitive job, (2) making only a small part of something—making the worker an appendage of the machine, (3) doing useless tasks, (4) feeling a sense of insecurity, and (5) being too closely supervised.

Thus, if work is to become more satisfying and, perhaps, more like leisure, work would have to become increasingly creative, skilled, and involve social contact and freedom. There would need to be less repetition, less specialization, more security, and less supervision on the job. The belief among many is that work has become increasingly so characterized since the early periods of industrialization. Workers are more likely to be protected from unsafe conditions by laws and more likely to have a greater say in the conditions under which they work than they were a few decades ago.

Today, higher education levels among workers, a shift in jobs from manufacturing to the service sector, the rise of professionalism, and other factors have made work less like slavery for many and more like leisure for some. But this is a broad assertion and there are many examples to the contrary. There are many unskilled and low-skilled jobs in the labor force. Too, while conditions may be more pleasant and even more gregarious, the work is not necessarily more meaningful.

Broadening Participation in the Labor Force

In most preindustrial societies everyone had some work role— children, old people, sick people—everyone contributed. The industrial revolution began to change that. Children at first worked incredibly long hours in the factories, right along with adults, but gradually the inflexible work schedules and intolerably hard working conditions changed when child labor laws were passed. Similarly, peonage laws were enacted to prevent the mentally retarded, emotionally disturbed, and others committed to institutions from being forced to perform what amounted to slave labor. During the 1930s, the retirement age of 65 for men and 60 for women was selected by the federal government to serve as a base for paying social security. These ages were chosen for political expediency, in part to reduce unemployment among younger workers during the Depression.

All these situations, combined with the continuing attitude that a woman's place was in the home and that those who engaged in technical work had to have specialized training, restricted those who worked for money to adult males under the age of 65 and a small percentage of women. A common life cycle was legislated. One went to school, by law, during the first two decades of life, worked full-time the next four (or became a homemaker), and then retired for the next decade. This "linear life plan," as it has been called by Best (1980), has had profound impact on work-leisure relations. Recreation on weekday evenings, weekends, holidays, or vacations was the reward for the full-time worker who had earned the chance for refreshment.

Today, this linear life plan is breaking up, for various reasons. Among these are the changing role of women, the changing age composition of our society, expanding continuing education, changes in attitudes toward work, and other factors. Today almost one in six employees voluntarily works part time. Often, such workers are homemakers, students, or those who have "retired from a full-time job." "Flextime," the use of flexible hours for employees, allows many part-time workers to plan their work schedules so as to accommodate other duties, rather than the reverse. Thus, a mother with school-age children might put in thirty hours a week, electing to work from 9 to 3 daily so she can return from work when her children return from school. The changing role of women also contributes to the breakup of the linear life plan. About 60 percent of adult women are now employed for pay and the number enrolled in higher education continues to rise. Of course many people work part-time for lack of full-time work. Others may be employed on a seasonal basis or on short-term contracts. And in the recent past we have been faced with high rates of unemployment. All these influences erode the linear life plan.

Removing Work From the Workplace

The industrializing process in society took work out of the home and field and put it in the factory. Slowly, however, this process is reversing. Today, as Naisbitt (1982) pointed out, the majority of the labor force is involved in some aspect of the creation, processing, and dissemination of information. Many such jobs, thanks to the microcomputer, communication satellite, and other technological advances, can be done almost anywhere at almost any time. Thus, the segmentation between "workplace" and "home" may partially disappear. The home "work station" may be next to the Ping-Pong table and surrounded by paperback novels, merchandise catalogues and children's art. How this trend develops will be interesting to watch. There are already signs that working at home is less idyllic than it first appeared. Work at home may often be in addition to the regular work week at the office. In any case, work and leisure get mixed into schedules in different ways. The advent of social institutions such as the workers' "conference," in which employees travel to some distant city for both meetings and tourism, helps combine aspects of work and leisure in the same experience. The business lunch and golf game with prospective clients or buyers has many parallels.

Under industrialism, "workers" were usually males who worked full time until they retired. Women, of course, also did hard work, but often as homemakers and, hence, not for pay. The "workforce" consisted of those who worked for pay. Retirees were not in the workforce, nor were students or the unemployed. Hence, the segmentation between "worker" and "nonworker" (or, more properly, wage earner and nonwage earner) was a critical distinction. This distinction, it may be argued, is slowly diminishing.

THE NEED FOR SEGMENTATION

Certainly there are legitimate arguments that can be made both for and against the segmentation of leisure from the rest of life. Nonetheless, we would argue for one of these positions—segmentation—realizing that in doing so we may be accused of pessimism. But segmentation seems both more realistic and more desirable.

The Incompatibility of Play and Technology

Play cannot be made a part of ordinary life in a technological society without killing it off. Play has links to the sacred and these links are easily destroyed. No one has ever been able to force children or adults to play. When it occurs it is a gift and one we do not understand. Not understanding it makes little difference to the player. In all play the outcome is in doubt, and play is a celebration of the unknown. Technology celebrates the known and seeks to remove all doubt from outcomes. Play cannot become a part of ordinary life—nor should it. Play, like leisure, is transcendent. In a learned, technological society, in which we have the capacity to do great harm to one another, to play all of one's life would surely be a symptom of nihilism. Not to have an important place for play outside of ordinary life, conversely, would cause us to die spiritually.

The Need for Segmented Behavior

The segmented self is functional. We cannot always insist that we be allowed complete independence or consistency in our roles and behavior. To insist upon such is an extreme form of greed. (Remember Ayn Rand's novel *The Fountainhead*, in which the "hero," an architect, blew up a building which had not been built to his precise specifications?) If we are to live among others, we must accommodate, which is another way of saying segment. The four letter expletives of the locker room or tavern may offend the company at the concert hall and the family picnic. Presentation of self varies situationally and it does so for good reason. Many impulses must be controlled. We have to live with each other. Except for hermits, there is no other way.

This does not mean we should always alter our behavior to fit other people's wishes. It does mean we must select the degree to which we allow ourselves to behave and act the way we choose. To trade discretion for holistic consistency is a bad bargain. Our very survival requires discretion and will likely continue to require it.

Much of the argument favoring holism assumes that the segmented lifestyle was a product of industrialization which will disappear as our civilization becomes decentralized. Toffler's (1980) "third wave" and Bell's (1973) "postindustrial society" assume a breakup of standardization and massification of culture and of work, a heightened use of information in individual decision-making and a diversity of lifestyles and energy sources. Even the rhythm of life could become more complex as the linear life plan breaks down and computers invade the home. (Many of these pages were composed, "processed" and printed at home. Conspicuous consumption has a counterpart—conspicuous production.)

Certainly such a future appears to be upon us right now. The signs of the end of industrial society are everywhere. There are signs that the meaning and role of leisure in our society are expanding and diversifying. Our potential for leisure has increased and the extent to which leisure values permeate our lives appears to be on the rise. In spite of this, the previous arguments for segmentation appear to be valid.

Much of the argument favoring holism also assumes something about the nature of people. We are not simple beings in the sense of consistency or uniformity in perception or behavior. Just as there are many roles and situations, there are many selves. Walt Whitman, in *Song of Myself*, wrote: "Do I contradict myself? Very well then . . . I contradict myself; I am large . . . I contain multitudes" (In Allen & Davis, 1955: 126). Do we not, as did the essayist Montaigne, consider ourselves variously?

> If I speak variously of myself, it is because I consider myself variously; all the contrarities are there to be found in one corner or another; after one fashion or another; bashful, insolent; chaste, lustful; prating, silent; laborious, delicate; ingenious, heavy; melancholic, pleasant; lying, true; knowing, ignorant; liberal, covetous, and prodigal. I find all this in myself, more or less, according as I turn myself about, and whoever will sift himself to the bottom will find in himself and even in his judgment this volubility and discordance. I have nothing to say of myself entirely, simply and solidly without mixture and confusion. (In Cotton, 1870: 214)

The Benefits of Constraints

Work will continue to be constrained, albeit in different ways than previously. Existing under different sets of constraints will still be valuable. The work ethic will continue to be necessary to master the very technology which we have already let loose. There will still be an "ordinary life" and play should still be outside that sphere. Work, play, and other parts of life are all constrained but in different ways and to different extents. Such variation in constraints can be a positive thing. It is folly to think that only work is constrained. As Bennett Berger (1962: 38) said, "If sociology has taught us anything it has taught us that no time is free of normative constraints." No time, in short, is "free." All human behaviors are constrained and, in a post-industrial society characterized by rapid change, the types of constraints are changing constantly and from situation to situation.

To be constrained is to be limited and we are limited by time, by our imagination, and by the capacity of our environment. We are also constrained, as Bell (1973) observed, by the tremendous amount of information we must absorb and by the extensive coordination necessary for us to function. The essential difference between work and leisure for most in our society is the extent to which various constraints impinge and the process by which such constraints are established.

That there are different constraints in different situations is a positive thing. We learn much about ourselves and about the rest of the world from operating under different sets of constraints. This is not to argue that we must suffer "pain" to grow, only that we are complex, multifaceted beings with only partial understandings of ourselves. Operating under different sets of constraints may teach us to determine what we think is important or show us our limits. To be without constraints would mean we were godlike, and we still hope that a God exists other than ourselves.

It should also be recognized that constraint has different meanings in different societies. For instance, while many in North America no longer think leisure should be earned by constrained work, in other industrialized nations such as Japan, South Korea, or Taiwan, this belief is very strong. Every Japanese school child is taught his or her country's historic ethic—*Senyu Koraku*—"Struggle first, enjoy later." Not only do the Japanese defer their leisure, but they often refuse to accept leisure after they have earned it. Many government workers in Japan, for instance, do not take off the one free Saturday a month they are offered. The Japanese Government's Leisure Development Center reports that only three percent of the public prefer leisure to labor.

If the argument made for holistic living is that work is constrained, oppressive, and needs to be reintegrated into the rest of life, how does one explain those who prefer work and, given a choice, voluntarily select more work? There are surely several sensible reasons.

One thing this situation tells us is that what constraint is and how we view it are bound up in our cultural heritage. While it may be easy to think of the Japanese work ethic as being a product of their culture, so are all other ethics. The Japanese place greater importance upon collective identity while our culture is built upon individual identity. (A Japanese doctoral student, frustrated at trying to explain how the Japanese could incorporate parts of conflicting religions into their culture, finally said: "You must understand; being Japanese is the real religion.") What is constraint viewed at an individual level may be thought of as an honorable duty joyfully accepted at another level. Thus a culture oriented to the individual, such as our own, is very aware of the large, government-induced, collective constraint in the Soviet Union which prevents freedom of speech, but does not similarly recognize the widespread, individually created constraint against freedom of travel in urban areas which high crime rates have produced in the United States and elsewhere.

The arguments for an end to separating work from play, recreation or leisure are almost always undertaken from a national rather than an international perspective. They argue for the transformation of one nation-state or another, but not all together. Increasingly, however, the nation-state is not an independent political and economic unit. Economic, social, and political influences cross borders. Many nations are now entering a period of widespread industrialization, such as South Korea and Taiwan, and putting the work-recreation-work model into place. The increasing access to technology which these nations possess means that they can challenge the position of economic privilege of North America, Western Europe and Japan. As this challenge becomes greater, it will become more and more evident that our fate is tied to their fate.

The rest of the world wants what we have and, in the coming decades, will take steps to obtain it. During this period, holism may remain as an ideal but one for some era in the future when we are wiser—much wiser.

REFERENCES

Allen, G. and Davis, T. (Eds.). 1955. *Walt Whitman's Poems.* New York: New York University Press.

Bell, Daniel. 1977. "The End of Scarcity." *Saturday Review of the Society,* (May).

Berger, Bennett. 1962. "The Sociology of Leisure: Some Suggestions." *Industrial Relations* (2: 1) (February).

Best, Fred. 1980. *Flexible Life Scheduling.* New York: Praeger.

Cotton, C. (Tr.). 1870. *The Essays of Michael Seigneur de Montaigne* (3rd ed.). London: Alex Murray and Son.

Cross, Gary. 1965. "The Quest for Leisure: Reassessing the Eight-Hour Day in France." *Journal of Social History* (18:2).

Cunningham, Hugh. 1980. *Leisure in the Industrial Revolution.* London: Croom Helm.

Delves, A. 1975. "Popular Recreations and Their Enemies." Paper presented at the Conference for the Study of Labor History, London, England (November).

Huizinga, Johan. 1955. *Homo Ludens.* London: Paladin Books.

Lippman, Walter. 1964. *A Preface to Morals.* New York: Time Incorporated.

Mead, Margaret. 1958. "The Pattern of Leisure in Contemporary American Culture." In Eric Larrabee, and Rolf Meyersohn (Eds.), *Mass Leisure.* Glencoe, Illinois: The Free Press.

Naisbitt, John. 1982. *Megatrends.* New York: Werner Books.

"One Secret of Japan's Success" 1985. Intelligence Report. *Parade Magazine* (November).

Parker, Stanley. 1972. *The Future of Work and Leisure.* New York: Praeger.

Pieper, Josef. 1952. *Leisure: The Basis of Culture*. New York: New American Library.

Pollard, S. 1963-4. "Factory Discipline in the Industrial Revolution." *Economic History Review (16)*.

Riesman, David. 1963. *The Lonely Crowd—A Study of the Changing American Character* (abridged ed.). New Haven: Yale University Press.

Terkel, Studs. 1974. *Working*. New York: Pantheon Books.

Toffler, Alvin. 1980. *The Third Wave*. New York: William Morrow and Co.

Veblen, Thorstein. 1899. *The Theory of the Leisure Class*. New York: B. W. Heubsch.

Wolfenstein, Martha. 1959. "The Emergence of Fun Morality." In Eric Larrabee and Rolf Meyersohn (Eds.), *Mass Leisure*. Glencoe, Illinois: The Free Press.

In America I saw the freest and most enlightened men, placed in the happiest circumstances which the world affords: it seemed to me as if a cloud habitually hung upon their brow, and I thought them serious and almost sad in their pleasures. . . . [They] are forever brooding over advantages they do not possess. It is strange to see with what feverish ardor the Americans pursue their own welfare; and to watch the vague dread that constantly torments them lest they should not have chosen the shortest path which may lead to it. . . . Their taste for physical gratification must be regarded as the original source of that secret inquietude which the actions of the Americans betray, and of that inconstancy of which they afford fresh examples every day. He who has set his heart exclusively upon the pursuit of worldly welfare is always in a hurry, for he has but a limited time at his disposal to reach it, to grasp it, and to enjoy it. . . . Besides the good things which he possesses, he every instant fancies a thousand others which death will prevent him from trying if he does not try them soon.

(Alexis de Tocqueville, 1899: 144-5)

XII. WANDERLUST OR LEISURE?

The end of World War II found the United States and Canada in an enviable position compared to most of the industrialized world. Although both countries had suffered greatly from this nightmare for humanity, the war had not taken place on North American soil. Partly because of this, economic recovery and expansion occurred first in North America. A period of rising incomes and optimism followed during the fifties and sixties. People began to marry younger, have larger families and move out of the cities into the suburbs. Houses built in "developments" had lawns and yards and an increasing number of mechanical conveniences, such as clothes washers and dryers, dishwashers, air conditioners and vacuum cleaners. Television, by 1950, had transformed Americans' use of time and had become an important part of our daily lives and character. The world it portrayed had several things in common.

THE WORLD ACCORDING TO TELEVISION

Television not only rejected the tragic view of life, it also was responsible for the notion of the "quick fix." Within one hour or, more usually, one-half hour, solutions would be found to a broad array of predicaments. Things happened quickly on television, since commercial sponsors wanted the widest possible viewership, many of whom had short attention spans and wanted little complexity from the "Boob-Tube." Television generally made attention spans even shorter. Even the half-hour programs were broken up by commercials and station identification.

The "quick fix" on television often happened as a result of dramatic confrontation. The individual assertion of will, often accompanied by the use of violence or sexuality, was a favorite problem-solving technique. And it was the individual, usually, who solved problems. Television served to reduce the increasing complexities of life in ways which were easy to accept. One exception to this was attempts to bring legitimate theatre to television. Soon, however, the only drama which appeared on television was movies which were "made for television" along with soap operas.

Even the interview techniques used by newscasters on television encouraged the person being interviewed to provide brief, concrete answers devoid of reflection or doubt. Television made the world smaller, faster, and simpler.

An endless variety of attractive material goods was brought to the attention of the viewer through advertising, and success and happiness, particularly during leisure, were equated with the use of these products. Television also made us observers rather than participants. It meant, in many ways, that we did not have to take responsibility for our own free-time. Once the set was on, we could live passively and vicariously. Television also showed us a world which unfolded somewhere other than where we were. It was a retreat from life. But the ghost images of television, dancing in another world, filled us with new kinds of longing for things and experiences. Because television, from the start, was sponsored by commerce rather than government or nonprofit groups, one-fourth to one-third of the time people spent watching was spent watching attempts to sell them things and experiences, often with great success. Programming (with some notable exceptions) was designed to attract the maximum possible audience.

Television revolutionized our collective psyche. While our economic and religious heritage taught us that anything worth having was worth waiting, working and saving for, "commercials" implied we could have it now, no waiting, with an easy payment plan. Television showed us other worlds and made us want to live in them. It told us things could be better without too much sacrifice. In general, Americans came to want—and want now—the world they saw on television.

If television began to define the world for the "Baby Boom" generation, the automobile became the accepted way to get it. Automobiles, which after the war became an increasingly common possession of the middle class, were the machines for freedom: freedom to live farther away from where one worked; freedom for teenage couples to have privacy beyond the control of parents; freedom to leave Point A when one wanted and arrive at Point B at a predictable time; freedom to drive just for the pleasure of it. Driving for pleasure, in fact, became the most popular form of outdoor recreation, according to Federal surveys (ORRRC, 1962). Americans are in love with automobiles. Neighborhoods were divided so roads could take people where they wanted to go. "Customizing" cars, racing or "dragging" cars, naming them, polishing them, and identifying with them became part of a national obsession. Cars let millions of teenagers act out their wanderlust, endlessly cruising the town, lapping the blocks, escaping the family in favor of temporarily finding somewhere else; almost anywhere else would do. And, if not going anywhere, at least being on the move. If television was the harbinger of the coming good life, the automobile was the only way to get it.

AN OPEN-ENDED SOCIETY

The "good life," which was characterized by television, big cars, and movement to the suburbs, was increasingly assumed to be an "open-ended" one. This meant that life was characterized not by recurring cycles or defined limits but by growth and improvement, and this growth and improvement was potentially unlimited. Some of the types of growth that Americans came to expect (but not always obtain) during this era were a higher material standard of living, a better medical system, increasing scientific achievement, rapidly growing population, more and more services from government, increasing "professionalization" of employees, increasing control over the future, increasing longevity, bigger houses and, of course, more free-time. Many began to accept, however unwittingly, the philosophies of positivism, empiricism and pragmatism. These philosophies were rooted in the methods of scientific analysis. They held that facts were only meaningful if they could be verified through experience. All beliefs outside the realm of such scientifically verifiable proof were rejected (Theodorson & Theodorson, 1969). These philosophies, combined with the optimism of the American public, produced a great faith in science as the key to open-ended growth and improvement. Humans were thought of as rational and potentially capable of perfection. Every problem had a solution; the challenge was the use of the correct technique to discover it.

One consequence of this faith in science and, especially the future, was a challenge to the idea of deferred gratification. Traditionally, most Americans had been taught to take care of their responsibilities first. Work comes before play. Don't buy something until you have the cash to pay for it. Suppress your desires for pleasure until the time is appropriate and your duties have been fulfilled. Part of the idea of deferred gratification came from the necessities of agrarian life. Part came from the notion that humans were born sinful and needed to atone for their sinfulness through hard work. Recreation, as Margaret Mead (1958) observed, had to be earned and re-earned. But our great faith in science, along with rising incomes and expectations, raised questions about deferring gratification. Since the future, we believed, would get better and better, perhaps it was no longer necessary to defer all pleasure until after work. Perhaps it was not necessary to earn money in advance of making a purchase. Perhaps it made sense to develop nuclear power plants to give us more energy even if we had (and still have) no idea what to do with the extraordinarily toxic waste. Perhaps it was not necessary to wait for many of life's pleasures since the world was going to get better and better. Fate, we began to think, was largely in our hands. It is the environment which shapes us rather than our heredity, and we could increasingly control our environment.

Certainly government contributed to this mentality. The gradual emergence of Keynesian economics, which advocated deficit spending as a legitimate means of economic expansion, helped legitimize the increasing doubt about the necessity of deferring gratification. Both government and private borrowing began to be rewarded. Saving began to be penalized. Because economic expansion was seemingly assured, being in debt was not so bad. In fact, it became the American way; an individual and collective statement of faith in the future.

Yankelovich, Skelly and White (1982) observed that these new values manifested themselves in many ways. By 1960, about 70 percent of the population was in the middle class. The main goal had changed, for many, from upward mobility to self-fulfillment. The notion of earning the good life was less prevalent than a growing "psychology of entitlement." Emphasis shifted from "we" to "me" and lifestyles became more hedonistic, non-conforming, and oriented to the present rather than the future.

At the same time, new values focused on "naturalism;" natural products came to be preferred over synthetic ones. Greater interest in protecting the environment also became prevalent. Attempts were made to eliminate poverty and racism, change the roles of women, improve opportunities for the handicapped, and address other problems of society.

In the emerging beliefs of this open-ended society, one could have more things and more leisure, one could short-cut the traditional requirements for economic affluence. Optimism, science, and the youth culture prevailed.

LEISURE ACTIVITIES AS INTERCHANGEABLE UNITS

The same forces which drove Americans to want and expect more of everything good also caused a change in the way in which leisure was conceptualized. Increasingly, leisure was thought of not as a state of mind, tranquility, or qualities which one encountered when external constraints were minimal, but as a set of activities which one engaged in during "leisure time." Part of this transformation was no doubt in keeping with the desire of science to classify everything. Many public recreation and park agencies began to take a "cafeteria" approach to recreation programming. In such an approach, all conceivable recreation or leisure activities were offered to the public as long as they were desired. People were expected to choose leisure activities in which they wished to participate in much the same way they chose food in a cafeteria or from a menu. Just as Americans began to eat more, they also began to choose more and more activities from the menu.

Park and recreation agencies had, in their earlier stages of development, stressed participation in only certain activities which were believed to be superior to others. For example, camping was promoted but not bowling. Gradually, however, these agencies began to lose the sense of an ideal with regard to leisure. The important thing slowly became the act of participation in and of itself. Government agencies began to urge people to participate, and increased attendance at parks and recreation centers was automatically assumed to be a good thing. People were encouraged to be well-rounded in their leisure, which generally meant the development of a wide range of leisure experiences.

The concept of recreation or leisure as a set number of units of human experience also had the effect of making these units seem interchangeable. One could, from a YMCA program brochure or a questionnaire from a local recreation and park department, make a shopping list of his or her interests in participating in experiences as diverse as camping, dancing, or writing short stories. The format for these diverse experiences, however, was increasingly standardized. To the "consumer" of leisure experience, these activities became increasingly standard units of leisure. The assumption of the leisure service and also public education agencies, increasingly, was not that people sought joy, solitude, beauty, competition, a sense of their own uniqueness, fun, or other qualities, but that they sought softball, crafts, ball room dancing, drama, or stamp collecting. As these units of leisure activity became increasingly similar and interchangeable, it was natural for people to seek more and more of them and for the emphasis to shift to the fact of participation and the amount of participation. The motto of the State

University of New York: "Let each become all he or she is capable of being" was an ideal which, it was increasingly assumed, could be reached if we "let each do all he is capable of doing" during free time.

One of the first real scholars of leisure behavior in the United States, George Lundberg, recognized the problem inherent in this approach to the provision of leisure activities:

> The value of leisure-time activities, play and recreation, is usually conceded to be in the nervous release which they afford from the customary and coercive activities which the social order imposes upon us. To the extent, therefore, that the pursuits of our leisure time tend to become organized under conventional patterns determined by competitive consumption, they lose their unique and primary value as recreation and so become merely another department of activity devoted to the achievement of prestige or status. (Lundberg, et al., 1934: 136)

Park, recreation, and leisure service agencies increasingly began to attempt to use scientific management techniques and to view their mission as supplying these units of experience to the public. Unfortunately, as much research tells us, the same "unit" of leisure experience—softball, for instance, is undertaken for a wide range of motivations by different individuals and provides them with very different satisfactions. The aesthetic qualities of softball, its social meaning, physical demands, the consequences of participation, and its other aspects vary greatly from situation to situation. An activity label (e.g., softball) really disguises a wide range of life and treating it as a standard unit, like one dollar bill among many others, negates the uniqueness which accompanies any leisure experience individuals undertake. Certainly it is easy to see how this standardization mentality occurred. Softball involves a field, bases, bats, balls, teams, positions, rules, and other common elements. These common elements, however, are far overshadowed by the elements which are unique to each game. Nonetheless, leisure activities became interchangeable units or commodities, however, we began to believe there was a "standard" recreation program made up of standard activities. While automobiles were being more efficiently built this way, for leisure, the consequences were different. Standardization is not a characteristic of leisure experience.

EXISTENTIALISM AND LEISURE AS AUTHENTICATING ACT

While recreation and leisure were being standardized both by the public sector providers and by the "mass leisure" products and services of the growing commercial sector, another philosophical movement, existentialism, concerned itself with the limits of rationalism and the dilemma imposed by the very freedom for which logical positivism claimed to have answers and techniques with which to deal. Existentialism was not, however, a single philosophy.

> The refusal to belong to any school of thought, the
> repudiation of the adequacy of any body of beliefs
> whatever, and especially of systems, and a marked
> dissatisfaction with traditional philosophy as superficial,
> academic, and remote from life—that is the heart of
> existentialism. (Kaufmann, 1956: 12)

The rational side of mankind, which the logical positivist saw as being capable of infinite development, was seen by the existentialist as being only one facet of our existence. In a world in which God had little role to play, the notion of "self" was abstract and in need of further definition. That need the individual met through his or her own actions. As the philosopher Kierkegaard wrote in the middle of the 19th century, "When I behold my possibilities I experience that dread which is 'the dizziness of freedom' and my choice is made in fear and trembling" (In Kaufmann, 1956: 17). Freedom, without the comfort of theological and ethical systems, could produce terror and absurdity.

> . . . the essence of the existential protest is that rationalism
> can pervade a whole civilization, to the point where the
> individuals in the civilization do less and less thinking,
> and perhaps wind up doing none at all. It can bring this
> about by dictating the fundamental ways and routines by
> which life itself moves. Technology is one material
> incarnation of rationalism, since it derives from science;
> bureaucracy is another, since it aims at the rational control
> and ordering of social life, and the two—technology and
> bureaucracy—have come more and more to rule our lives.
> (Barrett, 1958: 269)

The structured, rational approach to recreation and leisure was seen by the existentialist as one more example of the inappropriate use of rationalism leading to meaninglessness. Consider what the social critic Paul Goodman thought of the ideas of the National Recreation Association (now the National Recreation and Park Association):

> What are the goals of the present philosophers of leisure; for instance, the National Recreation Association? And now imagine these goals achieved. There would be a hundred million adults who have cultured hobbies to occupy their spare time: some expert on the flute, some with do-it-yourself kits, some good at chess and go, some square dancing, some camping out and enjoying nature, and all playing athletic games. Leaf through the entire catalogue of the National Recreation Association, take all the items together, apply them to one hundred million adults—and there is the picture. . . . The philosophy of leadership, correspondingly, is to get people to participate—everyone must 'belong.' Now even if all these people were indeed getting deep personal satisfaction from these activities, this is a dismaying picture. It doesn't add up to anything. It isn't important. There is no ethical necessity to it, no standard. One cannot waste a hundred million people that way. (Goodman, 1954: 234-5)

Participation as a goal, done merely for pleasure, was doomed to failure, Goodman thought. Enjoyment is not a goal, but rather a feeling which accompanies important on-going activity. Pleasure is dependent upon function. No new culture could spring from such an approach to recreation.

Goodman also noted the belief that everyone must participate, everyone must belong. This belief was described, in the mid 1950s, as the "social ethic," a phrase coined by William F. Whyte (1957) and defined as:

> . . . that contemporary body of thought that makes morally legitimate the pressures of society against the individual. Its major propositions are three: a belief of the group as the source of creativity; a belief in 'belongingness' as the

ultimate need of the individual; and a belief in the
application of science to achieve the belongingness. (p. 7)

It has been suggested that workers in the recreation and leisure
service field, and perhaps in the culture, are biased toward group activity and
the desire that everyone join in. That may be because programming is
typically done for groups rather than individuals or it may reflect the social
ethic swallowed whole. In either case, existentialists found it unsatisfying.

The existential view toward much of recreation and leisure, as
provided by the public and commercial sector, was that the fundamental ways
and means of participating had been dictated to the extent that the individual
could not find, in such participation, "authenticating" activity; that is, acts
which helped the individual to discover or define who he or she was.

LEISURE AND THE SEARCH FOR THE AUTHENTIC

In a world in which technology, bureaucracy, and rising affluence
provided more opportunities for leisure but increasingly defined in advance
the ways in which those opportunities would unfold, the existential search for
the authentic was a natural consequence. The line between work and leisure
had become artificial for those who viewed the world in existential terms. If
there is no "human nature," if we must define or seek to define the self
through authenticating acts, if we must literally bring ourselves into being on
an individual basis without the comfort and guidelines of religion and ethics,
then the line between leisure and work is meaningless. All activity, whether
"work" or "leisure," can potentially contribute to a fundamental task: the task
of defining who one is.

The existential revolt against science and mass culture also produced,
according to MacCannell (1976), a framework in which to understand the rise
in tourism. Modernism, said MacCannell, was characterized by advanced
urbanization, expanded literacy, generalized healthcare, rationalized work
arrangements, geographic and economic mobility, and emergence of the
nation-state. A final, essential, condition of modernism among those who
lived in the modern world, was the belief that "authentic" life was occurring
somewhere else in the world.

Authentic life, which is what the tourist sought, only occurred in
regions which had not yet been swept into the modern world in which the tourists
resided. Thus, the tourist sought places where life was different, but the very

act of tourism insured that these regions would change to accommodate the tourist. Thus they would have to search elsewhere—nomads of the 20th century.

Many tourists, perhaps even most, seek not authenticity but merely diversion in their travels—sun, sand, sea, and sex. MacCannell, it seems, has dealt with a portion of the tourist population who is better educated and somewhat more intellectually complex than others. Nevertheless, as our society becomes more educated, tourists are turning wanderlust into the world's largest industry.

The modern condition has created a mentality which sets society in opposition both to its own past and to underdeveloped nations. Modern interest in tourist activity appears to be motivated by a collective quest to find some "overarching system," some higher authority which made the entire world a single unit.

THE SPEED UP OF LIFE—TIME DEEPENING

A number of factors accounted for the speeding up of the pace of life, both in fact and in our minds. The existential need to find the authentic, the new possibilities brought about by science and technology and the belief that "progress" was unlimited, the expanding understanding, which the mass media provided, of one's potential to participate in pleasure, the increasing mobility which the automobile and growth of commercial air travel brought about, these and other factors set the stage for "time deepening."

Time deepening occurs when the individual attempts to undertake more activity than can be accommodated with existing resources. And because activity tends to be cumulative, the more activities people undertake, the more they desire to undertake. Time deepening has three characteristic forms: (1) undertaking a given activity or behavior in less and less time, e.g., eating lunch at McDonald's in 15 minutes or less; (2) undertaking more than one activity or behavior at the same time, e.g., watching television while eating dinner; (3) undertaking an activity or behavior more precisely with regard to time, e.g., knowing within 15 minutes how long a 300-mile trip will take (Godbey, 1985: 246).

Time deepening was within the spirit of mass consumption and of capitalism's divorcing both production and consumption from need. People, particularly during the post World War II era, began to buy and consume more things. They also came to expect they would own more and more things throughout their lives. This open-ended attitude toward things, e.g., two televisions are better than one, three are better than two, began to carry over into the realm of experience. If one "unit" of leisure experience is good, two are better. Time deepening was a style of life which sought to increase the yield on time for increasing pleasure and, for many, increased self-definition.

POSTINDUSTRIAL CAPITALISM AND NEW COSTS

Daniel Bell (1973) characterized the emerging society, not so much by the absence of certain traditional forms of material scarcities such as food and shelter, but by the development of new forms of scarcity. Such new costs or scarcities included the cost of information, the cost of coordination, and the cost of time.

Information became mandatory and the rate at which individuals were bombarded with information increased daily. Every new social or political movement sought to "educate the people." Thus, consumer activists wanted to provide more and more accurate information to the consumer to insure logical choice. This movement's success, however, was predicated upon individuals digesting and processing large amounts of information, much like a computer. To buy the best tennis racquet, for instance, requires extensive data not only concerning comparative price, but also on durability; flexibility of head, throat, and shaft; weight and weight distribution; head shape; size of "sweet spot;" racquet head torque; vibration; stringing pattern; grip composition; string type; string composition; and so forth. Such an approach assures that the individual pays for the racquet not only with money, but also with time, energy, and a more complicated life. Here the consumer movement became an apology for materialism, usually not questioning the need for products, just instructing the potential buyer on how best to choose among alternatives.

Similarly, our society became characterized by new costs of coordination. A more complex society meant more interdependence; and, as our ability to interfere or do harm to each other increased (Hiroshima left little doubt that the world could be destroyed by humans), planning and regulating our society became more important and more complex. The necessity of interacting with increasing numbers of people and in a greater number of social situations involved more and faster communication and travel, and all requiring more coordination. Such coordination was not just the prerogative of elites, but necessary for everyone to minimize the possibility of killing ourselves with our own cars, chemicals, or radioactive wastes.

The need for both information and coordination helped create a third scarcity—time; the ultimate scarcity for those who wished to consume and experience at an historically unprecedented rate. Those who wished to achieve or conquer in such fashion had a problem which was, in many ways, a luxury to have: not enough time to do all the things they wanted to do.

> The desire to experience all things pleasurable, to be needed and involved in as many sets of human experience as possible is, in many respects, the ultimate greed. Two things must be said about this greed for experience. First, it sprang directly from the processes and mentality of economic capitalism, where competition for goods and the production process is divorced from need. It is natural that this progression took place. Much as the capitalist accumulates and invests money, we can see that the investment of time by individuals in diverse, pleasurable activity is a capitalist form of self-actualization: a competition with time as the scarce resource to find out who we are by literally recreating ourselves experientially.

> Capitalism also sowed the seeds of experientialism by saturating us with unneeded material objects. As the ability of our economic system continually to create needs for new material products began to find limits, these needs were transferred to leisure experiences. People are sold the experience of gambling, traveling through Europe, viewing other people's sexual activities, going down a wild river on a raft, learning tennis from a Zen Buddhist perspective, changing personal relationships through a multitude of therapies, making wine, and any other experience they will buy. What is produced is a wanderlust, not for other places but for other lives. (Godbey, 1985: 251-2)

WANDERLUST AND LEISURE AS OPPOSITES

Certainly the society which emerged at the end of the World War II had more than its share of wanderlust. The reasons cited previously—sudden economic growth, an emerging youth culture, optimism, better access to transportation, easy credit, the search for the authentic, the orientation to the present rather than the future, emphasis on self rather than others—all these factors and others produced wanderlust. Restlessness, the urge to travel, to discover and experiment with new forms of voluntary behavior, to travel, figuratively, one's own self to see what was there; these characteristics became more and more a part of the culture. The American family began to move, on the average, every five years. Much of our "leisure" behavior could be characterized as "searching" behavior, much else as escaping.

Can "leisure" be thought of as "searching?" In many conceptualizations of the term, "leisure" means "finding" rather than searching. If so, leisure and wanderlust are opposites.

Many ideas about leisure assume that to have leisure one cannot be what the poet Theodore Roethke called a "perpetual beginner." That is, one has to have some socialization into an activity and learning about it for that activity to become "intuitively worthwhile," or done as "an end in itself" or even "freely chosen" at the cost of sacrificing other activities. Human beings, in other words, must have some specialization in a behavior (as well as some freedom from external constraints of nature and society) to experience leisure. Several leisure researchers have observed that an individual may go through a continuum of increased learning or specialization with regard to a leisure activity (cf., Bryant, 1979).

The individual who simply wanders from experience to experience, like a shopper in a food store, does not have the opportunity to gain an appreciation of the activity which will make it intuitively worthwhile. There must be, in other words, repetition, learning, and growth. Even activities which we may think of as immediately pleasurable, such as eating, drinking, and sexual behavior, are actually learned. We are not born knowing how to express affection, have sexual intercourse, prepare pleasing foods, or know what foods we like. All of the behaviors involve learning and repetition for them to become leisure.

Regardless of the activity, most people have experienced and come to understand that the enjoyment of and satisfaction with engagement in an activity increases as knowledge and skill increase. Whether cooking, canoeing, golfing, writing poetry, collecting antiques, woodworking or playing bridge, all are enriched by each increment of knowledge and skill.

As this process unfolds, other alternative uses of time are more readily sacrificed and one's understanding that the activity is intuitively worthwhile is unquestioned. We develop faith in the activity and our engagement in it. We come to understand its aesthetic elements: grace in movement; harmony in music; complexity in games and sport; subtlety in taste and expression of every kind.

Perhaps familiarity breeds contempt but perhaps that is only for those predisposed to seeing darkness and shadow. For the rest, familiarity more likely breeds appreciation. Wagner's "Tristan and Isolde" is more meaningful to those who know, from the legends of King Arthur and his knights, the tragic story of Tristan and Isolde. Leonardo da Vinci's "Lady with a Stoat" is more meaningful to those who know of his years in the Sforza court in Milan. Knowledge alone produces appreciation. One need not be an accomplished musician or painter to appreciate Wagner or Leonardo. But perhaps those who have "tried their hand" have a deeper appreciation still. As Bronowski (1965) pointed out, appreciation is essentially an act of re-creation; a deep sense of appreciation envelopes us and lifts us to a higher plane where we discover that there is peace, beauty and joy in this world. And that may carry over in increased appreciation of life itself. That is leisure's promise.

THE DENIAL OF SACRIFICE

Historically, for most people voluntary choice had been a process of choosing one alternative from among many, with the understanding that the alternative choices would be sacrificed as a result of that choice. Also, most of the choices were still, in some senses, prescribed by one's culture. There were appropriate ways to use free time and, if one acted "voluntarily," they did so within the bounds of these cultural guidelines or perhaps as a reaction to them. Voluntary choice also took place within economic and technological constraints. The farm boy who voluntarily spent the evening skipping smooth rocks across a pond may have had no way to get into town for the evening, no specialized equipment to use other than the smoothest rocks he could find, and no feeling that, whatever he chose to do, there could always be more. Slowly, voluntary came to mean freely chosen or consumed but the notion of sacrificing alternatives in the free choice process was forgotten. Just as consumerism means buying more and more things, voluntary choice during free time came to be thought of as doing or experiencing more things rather than choosing one from among many.

Leisure involves sacrificing that which is potentially good for that which is potentially better. Thus, the free choice of leisure has a cost; we may do A only if we give up B. Many in the post-World War II era were increasingly unwilling to pay that cost. The combination of individual freedom of choice, voluntary action, mass consumption, and technological capitalism emphasized profit and production divorced from identified needs. These combined to change society's notion of voluntary.

People were suddenly more nearly able to avoid sacrifice, seeking instead to experience all choices, do it all, see it all, and do it and see it now.

In the 1977 Nationwide Outdoor Recreation Survey (undertaken by the U.S. Heritage Conservation and Recreation Service), respondents listed "time" more frequently than anything else as a factor limiting their participation in outdoor recreation; not money, or transportation, or crowding, or health problems, but time. This could be taken as a statement of our system's success. Imagine a former generation saying that the main limitation on their leisure was neither capital nor technology but merely enough time to use them. In *How Americans Use Time*, Robinson (1977) found that one of four American adults said they "always" felt rushed. This rush to experience, in one sense, indicated people had more freedom to do more and more chosen activities.

The lack of willingness to sacrifice one desirable activity in order to undertake another, however, suggests an inability to obtain leisure.

Leisure was often not possible because of an inability to select from among many potentially pleasing alternatives. Both the wandering of the existentialist in the perpetual search for the authentic, and the pragmatist's calculated attempts to "maximize the profit" on time, prevented making the willing sacrifice of other activities which leisure requires. Thus, while leisure and the potential for leisure increased for millions of Americans, so did wanderlust. In the lifecycle of individuals in many previous societies, "searching" was associated with adolescence and "finding" with adulthood. In the new society, one can avoid growing up by continuing to search for new forms of pleasure and meaning.

AM I HAVING A GOOD TIME?

Experience has become, for us, a crusade for self-discovery and definition. The end of our quest, self-actualization, is the Holy Grail of a secular society disillusioned with materialism and rationalism. Consequently, we have turned inward, rummaging about in the attic of ids, egos, fixations, mechanisms, and suppressed desires in search of a self, particularly, a happy one.

But there are paradoxes here, paradoxes which many philosophers have commented upon. As John Stuart Mill suggested, if you ask yourself whether or not you are happy, then you are not. As the Duc de la Rochefaucault suggested, the self can only be found in enchantment.

Can happiness be found by pursuing it directly or does it come in the course of other pursuits? Is it a gift rather than a payoff? Similarly, as most theologians ask, must you lose yourself in order to find yourself? Must you lose yourself in wonder and enchantment and celebration? Must you lose yourself in absorption in anything other than oneself?

Perhaps self-awareness is a more positive notion than self-absorption or preoccupation. Still, it does not characterize play and leisure, except as one perceives oneself as a speck in a grand panorama. As Yankelovich (1982: 239) suggested:

> By concentrating day and night on your feelings, potentials,
> needs, wants and desires, and by learning to assert them
> more freely, you do not become a freer, more spontaneous,
> more creative self: you become a narrower, more self-
> centered, more isolated one. You do not grow, you shrink.

REFERENCES

Barrett, William. 1958. *Irrational Man—A Study in Existential Philosophy.* New York: Doubleday and Company.

Bell, Daniel. 1973. "The End of Scarcity." *Saturday Review of the Society,* (May).

Bronowski, J. 1965. *Science and Human Values* (rev. ed.). New York: Harper Torchbooks.

Bryant, Hobson. 1979. *Conflict in the Great Outdoors.* Alabama: University of Alabama, Bureau of Public Administration.

de Tocqueville, Alexis. 1899. *Democracy in America, Vol. II.* (Tr. Henry Reeve). New York: Colonial Press.

Godbey, Geoffrey. 1985. "Planning for Leisure in a Pluralistic Society." In Thomas Goodale and Peter Witt, *Recreation and Leisure: Issues in an Era of Change* (2nd ed.). State College, Pennsylvania: Venture Publishing.

Goodman, Paul. 1956. *Growing Up Absurd.* New York: Vintage Books.

Heritage Conservation and Recreation Service. 1980. *National Recreation Survey.* Washington, D.C.: United States Department of the Interior.

Kaufmann, Walter. 1956. *Existentialism from Dostoevsky to Sartre.* New York: Meridian Books.

Lundberg, George et al. 1934. *Leisure—A Suburban Study.* New York: Columbia University Press.

MacCannell, Dean. 1976. *The Tourist—A New Theory of the Leisure Class.* New York: Schocken Books.

Mead, Margaret. "The Pattern of Leisure in Contemporary American Culture." In Eric Larrabee and Rolf Meyersohn (Eds.). 1958. *Mass Leisure.* Glencoe, Illinois: The Free Press.

Outdoor Recreation Resources Review Commission. 1962. *National Recreation Survey. (ORRRC Report No. 19).* Washington, D.C.: U.S. Government Printing Office.

Robinson, John. 1977. *How Americans Use Time: A Socio-Psychological Analysis of Everyday Behavior.* New York: Praeger.

Theodorson, G. A. and A.G. 1969. *Modern Dictionary of Sociology.* New York: Thomas Y. Crowell.

Whyte, William F. 1957. *The Organization Man.* Garden City, New York: Doubleday Anchor Books.

Yankelovich, D. 1982. *New Rules: Searching for Self-Fulfillment in a World Turned Upside Down.* New York: Bantam Books.

Yankelovich, Skelly and White, Inc. 1982. "The Impact of Changing Social Values on Leisure." Unpublished, (November).

Many friends, when I ask them what they like best to do, after hanging their heads and apologizing—finally get up courage to tell me that they would not want to be quoted but 'what I really enjoy most is eating'! And why not? Why so apologize?

Other friends, again after sufficient apology, tell me they like best to sit and talk—if the other person or persons do not do too much of the talking.

Again with apology I am told, 'I have to confess that I suffer from spectatoritis. I know that I ought to do things myself, but I much prefer to watch the other persons in dramatic performances, to watch other persons in athletics, to watch other persons play games.'

Not one is ashamed to confess that he likes to read; indeed, this statement is made with ill-concealed pride in oneself.

(Howard Braucher, 1950: 141)

XIII. ARE SOME ACTIVITIES BETTER THAN OTHERS?

As we have seen previously, the major question of the 20th century, next to the question of our survival, is "Given a minimum of constraints, what is worth doing?" In some senses, this question seems ridiculous, since none of us answer it in abstract, philosophical statements. We answer it by what we do or what we admire that others do. Also, we may be tempted to answer the question only by saying that "it depends." Most of us, however, spend considerable time when the constraints upon what we do are minimal and we do make decisions concerning what we think is worth doing, even if we are unable to recognize or express why we choose to do certain activities and not others. Not only do we make such judgments for ourselves, we probably make them about others. Leisure (in this chapter the free time sense dominates) is the ultimate arena for the demonstration of values since in leisure one chooses from an almost infinite array of alternatives. One invents from one's imagination or mimics what others do who serve as references.

Perhaps we may decide that the question of the worthy use of leisure is different for different people. Ralph Glasser (1970: 62) raised this issue in his book, *Leisure—Penalty or Prize?*

> What, for instance, is the test of the 'ranking' of an activity
> in the assumed hierarchy? And how do we provide for the
> differing levels of ability among people who presumably
> equally need the emotional fulfillment that 'creative leisure'

is presumed to offer, but are unequally equipped to obtain it? Is there some formula for creative fulfillment in leisure time, which is equally fitting and effective for all grades of ability, intellect, perception, spiritual capacity? And what is 'fitting' or 'effective'?

If we are unequal in a variety of ways, can judgments be made at all about the best leisure activities? Not only is this a problem but there is also the more fundamental dilemma that leisure supposedly involves the exercise of the human will and imagination. If we try to prescribe what leisure activities are most desirable for others, or ourselves, in advance, we may preclude the very choice process which is fundamental to leisure. Perhaps that is why so many people, when asked about the "worthy" use of leisure, respond by saying: "It depends."

It depends upon many things. As Kaplan (1960) pointed out, we can't intelligently determine what is good leisure without a prior conceptualization of the good life. Further, Kaplan admonished us, free choice involves the criterion of values and the danger exists that we will impose a fixed external value rather than allow the person to be active in developing his or her own value system. It might be well argued that such a fixed external value system, if imposed, would limit the leisure potential of humans. Finding what is worthwhile at an individual level during leisure may be, in effect, finding out what you think is important. If this is the case, we can answer the question asked in this chapter's title by saying that some leisure activities are better than others but each person must determine which are better for himself or herself.

IS ANY ACTIVITY ACCEPTABLE?

In spite of that, imagine leaving the question of superiority of leisure activities to the individual, and one person finds that his or her favorite use of leisure is going to the shopping mall to steal, another likes to eat three or four gallons of ice cream each day, while a third enjoys beating up strangers. Perhaps, just perhaps, we will acknowledge that one leisure activity is as good as another, but there are exceptions.

As de Grazia pointed out:

> The word leisure came into English through French from the
> Latin *licere* meaning to be allowed. Thus it has something
> that involves the idea of permission, lawfulness, and
> morality. But the word 'license,' meaning excessive or
> lawless liberty comes from the same root, reminding us
> thereby of the difficulty of hanging a social meaning onto a
> term having the sense of personal freedom. (1962: 405)

Therefore, we may be ambiguous or at least anxious to delimit our
original statement. Are some uses of free time better than others? No, but
there are some exceptions. Yes, but the limits are very broad. The basis of
such exceptions and limits, of course, is critical—and complicated. Perhaps
we might first say that any use of leisure is acceptable as long as it does not
hurt someone else. This sounds rather straight forward and simple until we
realize we might have to rule out activities in which people can and do
physically hurt each other, such as boxing, football, karate, or auto racing. In
these examples, however, we might assume that most participants, or at least
many, understand the danger in these activities but freely accept the risk. But
to what extent should that include flagrant violations of the rules, throwing
"bean balls," "killing" quarterbacks, or sending the "goons" into hockey
games? Perhaps we will choose only to exclude leisure activities from being
worthwhile if other people are likely to be injured who do not freely accept
the risk. Thus, we would rule out rape, driving while drunk or throwing rocks
at passing cars.

Do we extend this exclusion when the "others" involved are animals
instead of humans? If so, we would rule out hunting and fishing. If we do not
rule out hunting and fishing, at least that which is done for pleasure, then we
must assume that other animals are of little worth, perhaps because their
brains are less developed. There is much ambivalence in our treatment and
use of animals.

The limits we set on what causes harm to other people is also subject
to differing interpretations. If I practice playing the drums and the noise
offends others, is my playing a morally inferior use of leisure? If you are such
a good squash player that each time I play you I am likely to hurt my elbow or
knee trying to compete, should squash be thought of as an exception to
worthwhile uses of leisure?

This, of course, leads us to the second basis upon which exceptions can be made: acts harmful to oneself. If you are demonstrably hurt by what you do during your leisure, perhaps those behaviors should be considered inferior. Here again we have problems of degree but perhaps even questions about the general principle. Suppose someone wants to attempt to jump over fourteen parked cars on a motorcycle, appears to understand and accept the risk of being hurt or killed, and still wants to attempt it. Our society often allows such behavior. If our motorcyclist (1) is competent to make the decision and is fully informed of the risks and (2) will not endanger anyone else with his or her actions, we can only object if we believe our value judgements are superior to those of the motorcyclist. If we conclude that our judgment is superior, we are still faced with the decision of whether or not to try and stop the person from undertaking such behaviors. This process is a complex one. We may pass laws to prevent some forms of gambling on the assumption that people will hurt themselves (and others) economically but still allow state lotteries. Bare knuckle boxing is outlawed but not boxing with gloves, even though brain damage and death is common in boxing. We outlaw the use of some drugs such as heroin and cocaine, since many people suffer and die from their use, yet we allow others, such as alcohol, nicotine, caffeine, various tranquilizers and stimulants, which often impair health and hasten death.

A further complication to all of this is that different individuals may participate in the same leisure activity with vastly differing consequences. Many gamble occasionally, in a football pool or a small stakes poker game with little personal harm, but a person who is addicted to gambling may lose fortune, friends, and family in the process. Rock climbing, skydiving, hang gliding, whitewater canoeing and other high risk sports may be perfectly safe for those properly prepared but not for others. Should some be allowed to participate and others prohibited from it? If so, how is that to be done? It is, then, for these and other reasons, difficult to justify banning participants— and even more difficult to justify banning some activities.

To briefly illustrate other complications, one need only reflect upon what has come to be called a "litigious society" with everyone running to court to sue for damages. That, coupled with the "deep pocket" awards of thousands or millions of dollars for damages has led, in effect, to a form of censoring or banning activities which may result in injury or death. Apparatus is removed from playgrounds and diving boards from swimming pools, and programs are cancelled because of prohibitive insurance costs. Do some of these occurrences suggest that people are not responsible for their own behavior?

A second complication is censorship in its traditional form; who should be allowed to read or view what? This question preoccupies all kinds of official and unofficial groups. Depending on where one lives, audio, video and printed materials are variously banned, restricted or attached with warnings and advice. All this is included in questions about whether some uses of free time are better than others, and who decides.

OF THE ACCEPTABLE—ARE SOME BETTER?

If the exclusionary approach is concerned with ruling out some uses of free time as undesirable, the question remains, "are some of the activities that have not been excluded better than the others?" If we are to answer anything more than "it depends," some assumptions will have to be made.

Kaplan (1960), in examining the question of whether some leisure activities are better than others, made the following assertions:

> There is a need for a person to be rooted, to be wanted, to belong. This conclusion arises from scientific observation as well as folk wisdom. Wherever this need is apparent in a given case, some leisure activity is more effective than others.

> Conversely, there is a need for a person to be distinct from others, to have interests and abilities that distinguish him. For this purpose, some leisure activity is more effective than others.

> There is the possibility of combining leisure functions so that pure rest or relaxation can accompany the absorption of a Beethoven symphony. Some leisure activities, more than others, offer a wide dimension of function.

> Some leisure activities, more than others, serve additional persons of the society at the same time that they serve the participant. One club is entirely social; another combines a community project with its socializing.

> Other leisure activities, such as gambling away resources needed for one's family, have objective consequences

harmful by standards of indebtedness, mental health, or family solidarity. Still others, such as adult study classes, provide new experience but are accumulatively helpful by standards of personal satisfaction, improved skills, or knowledge of the world.

There is also the possibility of putting leisure into the creation of work of art, which, among other activities, provide expression of feelings, projections of self-knowledge, affinity with aesthetic traditions, enjoyment to other persons, and objects or works for future pleasure of the creator himself. (p. 27)

These assertions are worthwhile, yet they raise many additional questions. In regard to the need to belong, we must ask—to what? Belong to the family, a social group, school, religion, region, state, the world, the universe? Joining a motorcycle gang which fights other gangs may develop a greater sense of belonging than learning to play the flute. Is joining a motorcycle gang, therefore, a form of leisure superior to playing the flute?

In regard to activities which distinguish the individual from others, the critical issue may be how the individual is distinguished. If you use free time to vandalize 100 automobiles, it may distinguish you from others. How one is distinct or distinguished from others during leisure is critical.

While some leisure activities do appear, based on research findings, to offer a wider range of functions than others, the same activity may have markedly different functions for different people. Similarly, a wide variety of leisure behaviors may serve the same function.

George Lundberg and collaborators (1934), pioneers in the study of leisure in North America, provided these criteria for satisfying leisure.

Leisure has, in a relatively high degree, both its original incentive and its fulfillment in the individual himself rather than in coercions of the social and economic order.

Leisure must possess the capacity of being relatively permanently interesting.

Leisure should involve activities or states as different as possible from those which are consciously forced upon us by our station in life.

Finally, leisure should at least be compatible with, if not conductive to, physical, mental, and social well-being. (p. 19)

While what is found interesting varies from person to person, it would seem that many uses of leisure which fit this description have a long learning curve. That is, you can continue to discover new aspects of the activity or new challenges for many years. Similarly, it may take a long time to learn how to appreciate or do the activity. There may be, in effect, continual learning. While this would seem to give some activities, such as writing poetry or playing the violin, preference over activities such as watching television or knitting, no hard and fast judgements can be made. Leisure, remember, involves, internally compelling love and this love may provide the capacity for the activity to be permanently interesting.

It would seem to make sense for leisure activity, ideally, to be as different as possible from those activities forced upon us by our station in life. This difference, however, must be in the individual's perception of the activity rather than in the innate characteristics of the behavior. While driving a bus and sightseeing in a minivan may have some aspects in common, psychologically they may be entirely different. People who are forced to sit in front of a computer during their work may, nevertheless, take great pleasure in "playing" with their microcomputer at home.

Finally, it makes sense to say that leisure should be "compatible" with physical, mental and social well-being, but many questions remain when we try to determine what is compatible. If jogging, for example, improves your aerobic functioning but risks long-term deterioration of spine, joints, ligaments or tendons, is jogging "compatible" with physical well-being? Is a "social drink," whether alcohol, coffee, or "Coke," compatible with social well-being but incompatible with physical well-being?

JUDGING BY FUNCTION

Given the difficulties of determining whether some activities are better than others, it may be useful to examine the consequence of participation in whatever activity. Participation in recreation or free-time activities can have a number of functions. So the question becomes, "Are some functions better than others?"

Improvement. It is often assumed that leisure can or does contribute to improvement of a number of things and that it should be used for improvement. Much of the improvement associated with leisure, as we have discussed earlier, has historically been associated with self-improvement. The Athenian ideal of leisure was concerned with self-perfection, and because it was, only a handful of activities were worthy, such as music, gymnastics, poetry, political dialogue, contemplation.

Not all those who have studied leisure consider self-improvement through leisure as being, automatically, a positive thing. Glasser (1970: 150), in discussing "victims" of leisure, mentioned:

> Those who feel their free time must lead to some worthy
> purpose, be filled with constructive activity of the kind that
> leads to better work or success. Reading, for example, is a
> favorite of these people, so long as it means reading for
> some end, reading something constructive, informative, self-
> improving, educational, worthwhile. Going to lectures at
> night school, for example, is also constructive, informative,
> self-improving, educational, worthwhile.

There seems, today, to be a greater emphasis in our society on activities which are self-improving. Magazines are filled with articles concerning self-improvement, but much of such concern is in the realm of physical improvement: exercise, diet, safe sex, stress reduction or other essentially physical aspects of ourselves.

Improvement of self could also center around moral betterment, improving one's knowledge or understanding oneself. The activities which may improve us in these diverse ways are potentially infinite, would be subject to disagreement and might differ in their impact on different people. Certainly, however, we may assume that some form of physical exercise would physically improve most people, some form of reading during free time would contribute to our intellectual betterment.

Leisure may also be used to contribute to the improvement of others. Using free time to voluntarily help others would seem to be a superior form of leisure. Although not all voluntarism is successful, there is much evidence that leisure arises in activities which benefit others. In some countries, there is the belief that the individual has an obligation during free time to do things which benefit his or her community or country (assuming one can have "free-time" obligations). The French notion of social animation, for instance, assumes individuals can use free time to identify common problems and develop and carry out a plan of action to overcome them. Community organization, development, and action are traditional and essential tools of a democracy.

Our society is one in which leisure is conceptualized, to a great extent, in individual terms and as pleasure. A central moral question concerns the legitimacy of using free time for individual pleasure in a world full of needless suffering. To some extent we learn what behaviors are pleasurable and, in the future, perhaps we must promote leisure uses which are less selfish.

Freely chosen activity can also improve or harm the natural environment (we, of course, are a part of that environment). In some cases, the impact upon the natural environment has to do with the style of participation rather than the activity itself. Camping, for example, may result in a forest being polluted or burned down or it may not. Some forms of free-time behavior, however, seem inherently to do harm. Riding all-terrain vehicles in the desert almost inevitably destroys that fragile ecosystem. Many activities pollute the air and water and consume vast amounts of fossil fuels and other raw materials. It seems obvious that activities and styles of participation which have no negative impact upon the environment must be considered morally "better" than those which have negative consequences. Thus, sailing or canoeing is better than yachting. Camping in a tent is better than camping in a huge, motorized "camper." In making these judgements, we place individual desire behind collective benefit. Ultimately, we have no choice but to do so.

Pleasure. Many activities, perhaps all, are undertaken because they are pleasurable. To say an activity is pleasurable, however, tells us very little. There is first the question of what is pleasure and second the question of whether pleasure is received in the actual doing of the activity, a consequence of having done the activity, or both. More basic is the question of whether pleasure is linked to certain activities in any direct way. Pleasure may be linked to a variety of other variables.

It has been argued by Csikszentmihalyi (1975) that experience is made more pleasurable when a given activity or task is neither too difficult for the individual, which causes stress, nor too easy, which causes boredom. When the challenge of the activity and the skill level of the participant are in balance, the individual may more totally give himself or herself to the activity.

This situation, a state of "flow," is one in which the individual confines his or her attention to the activity at hand, has less consciousness of time and self, and acts with great assurance. This idea is certainly in keeping with the definition of leisure presented in Chapter I. Flow is more likely to occur under certain environmental conditions and when there are some regularities or rules which permit the individual to concentrate on doing the activity rather than figuring out what is permissible or appropriate.

The flow state, however, is not confined to certain free time or recreational activities. As Kelly (1987) stated: "In theory, at least, the context can be one of physical or mental effort or of intense interaction that results in a kind of 'social flow'" (p. 27). Flow has many of the characteristics of play and, just as Huizinga saw the spirit of play, historically, running through a broad range of human behaviors, the flow state does as well. In both flow and play, we find the elements which Sutton-Smith (1971: 93) identified in a definition of play:

> . . . a transformation of feelings, volitions, and thoughts for
> the sake of the excitements of the novel affective, cognitive
> and behavioral variations that occur. In play the ends are
> subordinated; the means justify the ends.

Another idea related to pleasure derived from experiences is that of specialization. That is, as people progress in a given leisure pursuit, they may learn more about the activity, develop more specific preferences and aesthetic appreciations, and begin to appreciate it as an end in itself. Bryan (1979) found four stages of specialization in a leisure activity. In the first stage, newcomers are interested in getting results, any results. The beginning photographer, for instance, simply wants his snapshots to turn out. In the second stage, when the activity becomes an established behavior, the participant starts to gain competence and seeks to validate that competence with a number of successes or with those providing greater challenges. The next stage is one in which specialization occurs. The person who likes to fish now specializes in flyfishing and begins to prefer to participate with others who are similarly specialized. Finally, at the extreme stage of specialization, the participant places emphasis upon doing the activity for its own sake and the qualitative aspects of the experience become central. "They sometimes center much of their lives and identities around their sports or hobbies" (Bryan 1979: 88).

Both flow and specialization theories seem to assume that there is greater enjoyment when there is greater absorption in the activity and when a set of skills and aesthetic preferences have been established to meet the challenge of the activity. Learning, in most cases, is necessary to obtain maximum pleasure from a free time, or any other, activity.

The notion that learning and absorption in the activity are sources of pleasure was elaborated upon by Smith (1985). He argued that, in biological and evolutionary terms, what distinguishes homo sapiens (man the thinker) from other animals is their ability to derive pleasure from thought. He argues, then, that those activities in which pleasure drives from thought (cortical), rather than sensations taken from the external environment (sensory), are best because they are uniquely human sources of pleasure.

> With this simple distinction we can now perceive a pattern
> in recreation activities which is more basic than existing
> classification schemes. . . . Recreational activities, or
> anything else one does for fun or pleasure, can be placed on
> a continuum from purely sensory to purely intellectual and
> thus on a spectrum of subhuman to human activity. (p. 62)

Clearly pleasure is one of the reasons why people choose and engage in activities and pleasure is one of the results or functions. But the question of whether some activities or functions are better than others implies also the question of whether some sources of pleasure are better than others. Altruists derive pleasure from activity, but (apparently) sadists do too.

Socialization. Being and interacting with other people is an important source of pleasure in many leisure activities. Cheek and Burch (1976) attributed a characteristic similarity of nonwork activity to the fact that humans rely on a small number of "significant others" and that culture, particularly in learning and internalizing the normative order, stresses effective relations within bounded groups. These affective relations are exhibited in trust and reciprocity, and also in patterned expressive activities which are leisure. This leisure, as opposed to recreation (rationalized nonwork) is resistant to modernization. In a leisure activity, then, the source of pleasure may be the interaction with people who are important to the individual. Obviously, a wide range of leisure activities could provide socialization.

In many instances, too, free time is the realm in which people seek and meet individuals they did not previously know. Whether leisure takes place with those we already know or those we are just meeting, a unique feature of free-time activity is the formation of social groups.

Identification. Writing about tennis, *Outing Magazine,* in 1881, assured feminine readers that this was far too refined a game to offer any attractions for the lower orders of society. A lady who took part would find herself "in the company of persons in whose society she is accustomed to move" (Dulles, 1964: 192). Similarly, when rollerskating was introduced in 1863, New York's social leaders hoped it would be restricted to "the educated and refined classes" (p. 193). The use of free time, as these and countless other examples indicate, implies something about the individual. Cribbage players, we believe, are different from bowlers. Backpackers are different from those in Airstream campers. It is, perhaps, natural that free-time activities are a major source of identifying who an individual is. In the modern world, as we have said elsewhere, what we choose to do, what we find worthwhile, and when we get to choose, goes to the heart of self-definition.

While activity choices are increasingly central in defining who we are, it seems highly questionable that some activities produce an identity to a greater extent than others. Each activity we choose is a clue to understanding us. Certainly, however, it may be argued that some activities, and the individual style of participation, produce a more unique identity.

Creativity. It would seem that activities differ in the extent to which they can be creatively undertaken. It is probably more difficult to creatively watch television than to creatively paint a picture. Nevertheless, a wide range of activities would seem to have the potential for creative participation. It is difficult, of course, to define just what creative participation in a leisure activity means. Physical educator Jay B. Nash (1953) described creative participation as "the maker of the model." This could mean that the person was participating in some way which was both novel or unique and appropriate within the context of the situation. The novel is not always appropriate, the appropriate not always novel; the creative is both novel and appropriate (Bishop & Jeanrenaud, 1985).

The maker of the model could incorporate a broad range of behaviors in any activity realm. In music, it could be inventing a musical instrument, developing a unique style of playing, or writing music in a new form. What ever form it took, creative participation was, to Nash, the best use of free time. Next best, in descending order of desirability, were active participation, emotional participation, killing time or escaping monotony and boredom, and activities detrimental to one's self. At the very bottom of the hierarchy are activities detrimental to society (Nash, 1953: 89). Clearly, Nash believed that some activities were better than others, the creative best of all.

Recovery or Catharsis. Many activities are assumed to be undertaken because they restore or refresh an individual from the harm done by work or other obligated activity. The institution of the vacation is an example. We need and deserve a break, it is believed, from routine. Forms of activity which supposedly have the function of restoring the individual are not always easy to define since the physical consequences or psychological responses to participating in a given activity vary from one person to another or from one occasion to the next for the same individual. One person may feel emotionally restored from an Ibsen play while another is merely depressed. A second viewing may produce a response different from the first. Even reactions to physical exercise are markedly different. One theory for this is that intense physical exercise releases endorphins in the body which produce a kind of euphoria, but this occurs in some individuals to a greater extent than others.

The recovery function of free-time activity may be necessary because of the physical and emotional harm done to individuals during work or merely because of the need for diversion. In either case, the assumption remains that work is what is of primary importance and free time, recreation and leisure are clearly secondary.

Consumption. In some sense of the word, it may be said that all activity involves consumption—of an experience. Many forms of leisure activity, however, are for the purpose of consuming some material goods such as eating, or for related aspects of consumption such as shopping. Consumerism may also be thought of as a style of participation in which large amounts of material goods are utilized in activities which could have been undertaken with less. In 1937 Keynes said, referring to consumption: "We shall be absolutely dependent for the maintenance of prosperity and civil peace on the politics of increasing consumption" (p. 48). If that is true (and many economists agree), then consumption of goods during leisure may be our moral, or at least economic, obligation. If it is undertaken as an obligation, of course, it is unlikely to be leisure. Nonetheless, shopping appears to be a freely chosen form of behavior for millions of teenagers and adults, a testimony, at least in part, to the powers of persuasion and seduction. This function of free time includes a wide variety of behaviors, some of which, such as looking for bargains, have many of the elements of a game. Shopping also involves, to some extent, the opportunity for socialization. Shopping, in effect, may be an end in itself or a means to an end. It may also be, like many experiences in our society, a combination of both.

Spiritual. Since the Golden Age of Greece, free time has served a spiritual function. Many uses of free time have a religious component in that they involve celebration, the exercise of free will, ritual, a search for the authentic, integration of all aspects in the individual, and a sense of personal well-being and self-realization. In some sense the spiritual element in leisure is associated with states of being rather than time spent at specific activities. Prayer, meditation, or contemplation, which may be thought of as spiritual activities are not so much activities as they are states of being. This spiritual state of wonder, celebration and wholeness, however, appears to be present to some degree in a wide variety of activities—or is brought on by participation in them. Campers, runners, tourists, and others, in describing their experiences, often do so in terms which sound highly spiritual.

Are Some Functions Better Than Others?

Free-time activities, according to what we have said, may serve a range of functions. To determine if some activities are better than others, therefore, we would need to demonstrate that specific activities correspond directly with specific functions and that some functions are inherently better than others. Perhaps unfortunately, neither of these steps appears to be possible. There are a number of studies, as well as the evidence of history, to show that different activities may perform similar functions or that the same leisure activity may perform a variety of functions. Going to a party, for example, may combine consumption, recovery or catharsis, socialization and other functions.

It is likewise difficult to state that one of these functions is better than another unless we know the specific situation. Maslow (1943) and others have suggested that there may be a hierarchy of human needs, from physiological needs such as hunger, to safety needs, to a need for love, for self-esteem and, finally, for self-actualization: "to become everything that one is capable of becoming" (Maslow, 1943). In examining this hierarchy of needs, it is apparent that a given activity, depending on circumstances, may meet different needs or more than one. Also, people have multiple needs, and need priorities change in different situations. Activities may function in different ways to meet these different needs. While creativity or self-actualization may be highest on the ladder of human needs or leisure functions, the coal miner may have a greater need for catharsis at the end of 10 hours in a deep mine.

The homemaker may sometimes need socialization, sometimes self-esteem. Are some functions of activities better than others? It depends.

MUST LEISURE HAVE A FUNCTION?

This discussion has dealt with a range of functions which free-time activities assumably fulfill on the premise that the function of those activities is what is important about them. Suppose that is wrong. Suppose the function is, more or less, an accidental by-product of activity and that the product of participation is—participation. The important thing about playing chess, ultimately, is playing chess. The importance of painting a picture is painting a picture. The attribution of functions to leisure is in keeping with modern social science. When such an approach is taken, it may be in some senses no longer possible to understand what leisure, as an ideal, was and is. Recreation may be understood more easily through the social science process of attributing functions since "broadly conceived, recreation is rationalized leisure; it is the routinization of enjoyment" (Cheek & Burch 1976: 25). Rationalized leisure is functional. It fulfills purposes defined in advance. It has been brought under control and made more predictable. Recreation is more dependable; the mystery has been removed.

The idea that leisure is an end in itself appears throughout this book. For many of us, it is a strange idea. We assume that phenomena do not exist without purpose. Occasionally, however, we need to ask why there are flowers; why does the otter slide; why is there music, poetry, or cicadas. As Ben Franklin asked, "Of what use is a newborn baby?" This argument has also been made for play. Huizinga, in fact, thought it was not possible to even understand play in terms outside itself, or as rational behavior so we must be more than merely rational beings, for fun is "irrational" (Huizinga 1970: 4). Play serves its own ends.

The same may be true for leisure or at least much of leisure. It may be in the realm of the instinctive or, at least, as our definition suggests, the intuitive. When leisure is thought of in this realm, it is directly related to love of some undertaking—an undertaking which is natural, instinctive, compelling, and irrational. We love to do it and that love is not, ultimately, explainable. It is not explainable because it is not rational. We know the undertaking is right; we know it is good. No longer do we need evidence because we have faith in the undertaking, in the process itself.

For those lucky enough to experience leisure in this sense, the result may have some spiritual meaning. Those who insist that leisure must always have some function will, therefore, say that the function of such leisure is spiritual. The spirituality, as Pieper argues, is a gift from God. The world in which all behavior—whether free time or not—has some known function which humans can understand and describe, is a world which has no need for God. Leisure need not have a function in a world in which God has some role. Perhaps the question of whether leisure has a function can only be answered by asking whether you believe there is some God other than ourselves.

SOME CONCLUSIONS

Whether examining activities or functions, our answer to whether or not some activities are better than others remains inconclusive. Yet some general conclusions may be drawn.

We are not capable of pre-judging, in any precise way, the value or worth of any activity vis-à-vis any other. True leisure transcends the realm of function or justification by objective criteria. The external reality and internal reality do not always correspond in any apparent way. The participant, not the observer, must be the arbiter of the worth of the activity and the outcomes, as he or she perceives them. It may look as though a person is running when, in fact, he or she is worshipping. Thus, some leisure activities may be better than others but the questions can only be answered at an individual level. The extent to which the individual has an internally compelling love for the activity may be the measure of judging. One leisure activity is better than another to the extent that an individual has come to love it.

In spite of this, it may make some sense to exclude some activities based upon the extent to which participation causes harm to the participant, to others, or to the environment. It is difficult to be precise even in this matter since we must still make individual judgements about how to determine such harm. Nonetheless, we do make such judgements and it seems evident that we must. That, in the main, is the purpose and meaning of government. How much government we have depends, in the main, on how capable we are of self-governance.

When leisure becomes license, the license may be restricted or withdrawn. We limit the seasons and the bag and catch of game hunters and sports fishermen. We prohibit bearbaiting and cock and pitbull fighting. We have laws against disturbing the peace of others and against defacing public property, whether coins in the pocket or cottonwoods or chrysanthemums in the park.

Free time, because it is free, discretionary time because it assumes discretion, tests the moral and ethical bases of judgements. That is expressed in our concern for the environment, which is really our concern for the future. That is expressed in our concern for other living things, which is really a concern for our own species—Homo sapiens. That is expressed in our concern for each other, reflecting in part at least, our concern for ourselves.

These, then, are criteria for judging the worth of the activities we choose. By these criteria, some activities can be judged to be better than others. They also help define the intuitively worthwhile and the internally compelling love that is the heart of leisure.

Limits of course. But within those limits an inexhaustible array of human, leisure possibilities.

REFERENCES

Bishop, Doyle and Jeanrenaud, Claudine. 1985. "Creative Growth through Play and its Implications for Recreation Practice." In Thomas Goodale and Peter Witt, *Recreation and Leisure: Issues in an Era of Change* (2nd ed.). State College, Pennsylvania: Venture Publishing.

Braucher, Howard. 1950. *A Treasury of Living.* New York: National Recreation Association.

Bryan, Hobson. 1979. *Conflict in the Great Outdoors.* Alabama: University of Alabama, Bureau of Public Administration.

Cheek, Neil and Burch, William. 1976. *The Social Organization of Leisure in Human Society.* New York: Harper and Row.

Csikszentmihalyi, Mihaly. 1975. *Beyond Boredom and Anxiety.* San Francisco: Jossey-Bass.

de Grazia, Sebastian. 1962. *Of Time, Work and Leisure.* New York: Twentieth Century Fund.

Dulles, Foster R. 1965. *A History of Recreation—American Learns to Play* (2nd ed.). NewYork: Appelton-Century-Crofts.

Glasser, Ralph. 1970. *Leisure—Penalty or Prize?* New York: Macmillan.

Huizinga, Johan. 1970. *Homo ludens.* London: Paladin Books.

Kaplan, Max. 1960. *Leisure in America: A Social Inquiry.* New York: John Wiley.

Kelly, John. 1987. *Freedom To Be: A New Sociology of Leisure.* New York: Macmillan.

Keynes, John M. 1937. "The Economic Consequences of A Declining Population." *Eugenics Review* (24: 1).

Lundberg, George et al. 1934. *Leisure—A Suburban Study.* New York: Columbia University Press.

Maslow, A. H. 1943. "A Theory of Human Motivation." *Psychological Review* (50:1).

Nash, Jay B. 1953. *Philosophy of Recreation and Leisure.* Dubuque, Iowa: William Brown Company.

Pieper, Josef. 1952. *Leisure: The Basis of Culture.* New York: New American Library.

Smith, Stephen L. J. 1985. "On the Biological Basis of Pleasure: Some Implications for Leisure Policy." In Thomas Goodale and Peter Witt, *Recreation and Leisure: Issues in an Era of Change* (2nd ed.). State College, Pennsylvania: Venture Publishing.

Sutton-Smith, Brian. 1971. "Children at Play." *National History Magazine Special Supplement II—Play.*

Private optimism is a public resource. Public optimism is a private facility. Both can and have and will become disasters when there is too little fit between the vision and the facts of heat, cold, up, down, fast, slow, rich, poor, old, young, living, dying. It is dangerous to offer entree to charlatans expert in illusion and big or little demagogues practiced in worthless promise. But perhaps there is a graver danger—because the consequences are almost endocrinological—in accepting that the only responsible commentators are those who by careful austerity have no remaining lust for next year's blooming forsythia, the infant upstairs, a thigh-kiss, or the pointless, joyful melees of birthdays and silver anniversaries.

When in the myth the various forces of life escaped from Pandora's box, one remained at the very bottom—hope. Atlas no longer holds up the world. The Trident is a nuclear submarine. The gods of war are lobbyists and accountants. Cupid is a February industry. Even if the gods and other such forces have fallen, or become slogans, what Pandora rescued maintains its claim on our attention, if only because where it is dark it is difficult to see.

(Lionel Tiger, 1979: 283-4)

XIV. CAN THE WORLD BE TRUSTED WITH LEISURE?

No! . . . The world cannot be trusted with leisure, or at least the freedom requisite for leisure. Perhaps you have already arrived at this conclusion. The world cannot be trusted with leisure in most of the senses, especially free time, in which we have discussed the idea so far. We wish it could be since leisure may be the arena in which human potential can be fully realized. Machines, as they come closer and closer to possessing human intelligence, would seem to be increasingly able to do the routine and dirty work of society. There is currently more than enough food grown in the world to feed us all. There is currently enough knowledge about what can be done to conserve energy, provide low-cost housing, and improve our health, that the potential for satisfying lives of leisure would seem to be a distinct possibility for most of the world's people. Let us say again, the world cannot be trusted with leisure. There is a myriad of reasons for this, some of which have to do with the characteristics of our society and others which may be related to the nature of human kind and the assumptions we make about ourselves.

THE CONTINUING DRIVE FOR MATERIAL GROWTH

Leisure in the Athenian sense, as we have said, was in direct opposition to materialism. In Plato's *Apology* of Socrates, Socrates asked his fellow citizens:

Are you not ashamed of heaping up the greatest amount
of money and honor and reputation, and caring so little
about wisdom and truth and the greatest improvement of
the soul, which you never regard or heed at all? (Socrates,
in Kaplan 1961: 23)

Our answer to him would likely be, "No, we are not ashamed; as a matter of fact, we are proud to make as much money as possible and have the most honor, or the best reputation heaped on us." There seems to be little evidence that most people today will voluntarily limit consumption of material goods that leisure required in the ancient Athenian sense of the term. (Such restraint, of course, is also suggested by Christianity but that has been conveniently ignored.) The absence of the necessity of being occupied, the essential prerequisite for leisure in the Athenian sense, simply cannot occur if one owns hundreds of possessions which must be stored, repaired, protected, insured and, even, used. Our attempt has been to make more efficient things and things with which obligated activity can be done in less time, such as a microwave oven. That strategy may produce incremental improvements in terms of obligations but still not produce the absence of the necessity of being occupied. Yankelovich, Skelly and White (1982) found our society shifting back to values which laud the tangible signs of financial success. While the same study found that leisure was an integral part of the American lifestyle, the ancient Greek ideal for self-perfection through a retreat from materialism and from the affairs of the world remains unfamiliar to us.

Certainly leisure and the drive for material goods will have to co-exist in our society in the foreseeable future (if any future is today foreseeable). This coexistence means that leisure values will blunt our desire for material success to some extent. Many people, today, will not take certain jobs which pay very well simply because the job interferes with the way they wish to live, where they wish to live, or how they wish to use their free time. For the most part, however, it would appear that free time will be shaped to accommodate financial growth and material gain. Trafton (1985: 24), in *Transitions to Leisure*, stated:

> A very large amount of the leisure afforded us today by technology is at best trivial and at worst sordid. Our opportunity to regain something of Eden is being wasted in a frenetic rush into trivial pleasures, escapism, and worse.
>
> Perhaps a constant round of trivial pleasures and stupefactions is what people want. Perhaps regression into childish play and mindlessness constitutes a natural response to civilization and its discontents. I hope not, and I think not. Our leisure industry is better at providing a quick fix than it was at providing lasting satisfaction, not to speak of happiness, and I think that people are coming to recognize this.

While we may realize this, it seems that, in the main, we continue to use leisure in the same ways. Television viewing increased during much of the seventies and seems only now to have reached a saturation point. Marijuana is the leading agricultural cash crop in California and elsewhere. Free-time activities are packaged, rationalized, and sped up to fit into a life of seeking increasing levels of material goods. We cannot trust much free time to people living this style of life because these activities are designed to be diversion, not the quest for self-perfection. When diversion becomes a central focus of our life, we become bored and decadent. Such people cannot be trusted.

BECOMING ONE WORLD

While much lip service is given to the idea that all humans are members of one world, with the same rights and needs, North Americans have lived in comparative isolation from the rest of the world. During the last few decades, improvements in mass communication media, transportation, and the increasing internationalization of our economy, have brought about greater involvement with those in other nations. These events have brought us to a greater understanding that only a handful of nations have a substantial middle class. Only a few have a democracy in most senses of the word. Only the few which have begun the process of industrialization have much leisure and among unindustrialized nations many have available time for leisure but lack educational preparation which the ancient Greeks thought necessary for its proper use. Veblen's "Leisure Class," however, is alive and well in many parts of the world. In many countries, leisure remains the domain of an economic elite which seeks to protect the existing economic and political order and to use leisure to differentiate itself from the rest of the population. You can find them in most countries, both capitalist and socialist. Will the world tolerate leisure and privilege for a few while so many others have only the false leisure of unemployment? Will the world tolerate freedom of choice in the hands of a few while many others have little choice about what they read, do, or even think? Will the world tolerate a comparative few being introduced to and educated in hundreds of skills while many cannot read, have never traveled, and are restricted to a few activities during their nonwork time which provide only temporary escape? To date, of course, the answer is "yes" to all these questions. Lives of leisure and economic privilege are lived next to lives of marginality in Brazil, the United States, and France. Lives cut off from freedom and democracy are lived in North Korea and Cuba. Perhaps this will change in the future as we find out more and more about each other through the mass media the use of computers, aerial photography, mass travel, and cultural exchange. Perhaps the increasing economic interdependence of the world will bring about a heightened imagination about the needs of those in other countries.

What roles will leisure play in such change? Leisure thought of as materialistic pleasure-seeking or self-perfecting activity may have little role to play in such change and may actually retard it. In the Athenian notion, lives of leisure for a privileged few were thought to benefit the state, and did; but leisure for those few required that others in society exist as slaves. Leisure did not and still does not fit well with the simultaneous desire for equality, materialism, and democracy, as de Grazia (1962) so cogently argued.

THE FLAWED NATURE OF HUMANS

To understand if the world can be trusted with leisure, we must examine not only the condition of the world but also the condition of our minds. Who are we from an evolutionary standpoint, and what are our prospects? Of the countless sources of ideas on this subject, the writings of Arthur Koestler may be most helpful. In *The Ghost in the Machine* (1967), Koestler undertook an exhaustive examination of the evolution of the human brain (and mind) and arrived at the following conclusions. The growth of the human brain resulted in a faulty coordination between ancient and recent brain structures, creating a pathological split between emotion and reason. The creativity and the pathology of the human mind are two sides of the same coin.

According to Koestler, the conscious and unconscious processes underlying artistic inspiration, scientific discovery, and comic inventiveness have a basic pattern in common—a coagitation or shaking together of existing and separate areas of knowledge; an undoing and reforming of the mental hierarchy. "It is the highest form of mental self-repair, of escape from the blind alleys of stagnation, over-specialization, and maladjustment" (1967: 217). The creative act is one of leaping into the dark, where one is no longer guided by logic but by an undefinable sense of beauty. Habit is the enemy of freedom, as is passion, particularly the self-assertive, hunger-rage fear-rape class of emotions. There is a polarity, Koestler asserted, between creative acts of self-transcendence and acts of self-assertion. Under conditions of stress, self-assertive tendencies may get out of control and result in aggressive behavior. Historically, however, the damage to the world brought about by individual violence for selfish motives is insignificant compared to the holocausts resulting from self-transcending devotion to collectively shared belief systems.

Such behavior is derived from primitive identification instead of mature social integration. It involves the partial surrender of personal responsibility and produces the quasi-hypnotic phenomenon of group psychology. Under such conditions, people have historically been willing to kill for God, for state, for coming social progress, for political ideology or other beliefs in which the envisioned end justified the means. People have a history of slaughtering each other to further some belief. This slaughter is something we prefer not to think about and attempt to attribute to others. Nonetheless, this phenomenon is quite intact, even in North America. European settlers in America killed off almost an entire race of people. The French and English killed each other; the Civil War produced unbelievable slaughter; America fought the insanity of Nazism; dropped the first atomic bomb on Japanese civilians; killed North Koreans; supported an invasion in Cuba; fought the North Vietnamese, dropped jellied gasoline bombs on innocent peasants; and developed the capability of destroying the world several times. We can find such a history of slaughter throughout the world. As Koestler (1967: 239) observed:

> To put it vulgarly, we are led to suspect that there is somewhere a screw loose in the human mind, and always has been. To put it into more scientific language, we ought to give serious consideration to the possibility that somewhere along the line something has gone seriously wrong with the evolution of the nervous system of *Homo sapiens*. We know that evolution can lead into a blind alley, and we also know that the evolution of the human brain was an unprecedently rapid, almost explosive process.

As a hypothesis, Koestler suggested that the delusional streak which runs through our history may be an endemic form of paranoia built into the "wiring circuits" of our brain.

If this hypothesis is correct, and there is much evidence to suggest that it is, humans cannot be trusted with themselves, much less each other. We are, as many have observed, our own worst enemies. Certainly, we cannot be trusted with leisure or with any social institution. Koestler believed that self-transcending devotion to collectively shared belief systems produced the greatest evil in the world and resulted in the most barbaric slaughter. We will return to this issue shortly.

Responding to Our Madness

If a streak of insanity runs through humans, what implications are there for leisure? We must reconsider the idea of leisure as freedom. To do so, we must reflect upon the ideas of B. F. Skinner (1971). While humans have produced a world in which they are relatively free of many threatening stimuli, such as temperature extremes or infection, we are not free from intentional aversive control of other people. Government, religion, education, and other social institutions have used aversive control to a large extent. That is, if an individual does something which those in power do not want done, a negative sanction is imposed. The inept thief, for instance, will be captured and punished. Human response to aversive control is either escape or avoidance. If these mechanisms are not possible, we may try to attack those who impose the aversive controls. Skinner discussed what he termed "the literature of freedom" which has historically encouraged people to escape from or attack those who control them aversively. "Freedom" he defined as the absence of aversive control with emphasis upon how the condition feels—a state of mind associated with doing what one wants. Freedom is viewed as a possession. One destroys the power of his or her controller in order to feel free and do what one wants. The literature of freedom makes no further recommendation except to remain eternally vigilant against others who would remove this freedom.

The feeling of freedom, Skinner stated, is an unreliable guide to action as soon as would-be controllers turn to nonaversive measures. For instance, instead of punishing someone for smoking, some inducement or reward may be given for not smoking, i.e., rewarding positive behavior rather than punishing negative. This may change behavior without making the person want to escape or attack. Wanting, said Skinner, is not a matter of feeling nor is feeling the reason a person acts. "Freedom is a matter of contingencies of reinforcement, not the feelings the contingencies generates" (1971: 37). Freedom, in other words, has to do with what happens to us or can happen to us as a result of our actions, not our emotional reaction to these consequences. The literature of freedom, Skinner claimed, has failed to rescue the happy slave. It has taken the extreme position that all control is wrong.

> Those who manipulate human beings are said to be evil men, necessarily bent on exploitation. Control is clearly the opposite of freedom, and if freedom is good, control must be bad. What is overlooked is control which does not have aversive consequences at any time. Many social practices essential to the welfare of the species involve the control of one person by another, and no one can suppress them who has any concern for human achievements. . . . The problem is to free men, not from control, but from certain kinds of control, and it can be solved only if our analysis takes all consequences into account. (1971: 38-9)

Our struggle, Skinner asserted, is not to be free but to avoid the aversive features of the environment. Defining freedom as a state of mind has forced us to define all control as bad and leaves us unprepared for the next step in our evolution, which is not to free men from control but to analyze and change the kinds of control to which they are exposed.

What are we to make of Skinner's assessment? Certainly we would have to argue that not all control is bad. A world without control is unimaginable. We willingly subject ourselves to many forms of control and believe that others are worthwhile even if we don't always willingly subject ourselves to them. We may, for example, occasionally run through red lights in a car but still believe drivers should be forced to stop at four-way intersections instead of driving through regardless of consequences. Certainly leisure in the Athenian ideal involved control, but the process of being prepared for and obtaining leisure was one in which the source of the control of an individual gradually changed from control by other people to self-control. That is, a person was prepared for leisure through education and training during a period in which other people made decisions for the individual concerning what was worth examining and knowing. Gradually, however, the individual took control of his or her own life and, being relatively free from others, took responsibility for control and improvement of the self. This process occurred at an individual level in Athenian society (at least for native-born males).

Skinner's ideas seem shaped by a society in which it is assumed all individuals should be free (unlike the Athenians who granted leisure to a distinct minority of their citizens) but the necessary education and training of each individual is often lacking. We seem not to have made up our minds, as a society, whether freedom should be granted to only a few and the rest should be trained to be good slaves, or whether we should take the extraordinary leap of faith and assume that everyone might benefit from a life of leisure and seek to prepare them to live such a life. The egalitarian streak in our society assumes everyone should have certain rights regardless of their qualifications. People may vote, for instance, without demonstrating that they know anything at all about the issues, candidates or process in which they are participating. On the other hand, the capitalist nature of our society assumes everyone should be responsible for himself or herself, regardless of the capacity for doing so. Those who fail or are not in control of their destiny cannot always depend on the state for help.

Leisure is the gradual process of gaining freedom and finding meaning through self-improvement and understanding. It is the process of moving from being, essentially, directed by others, to becoming self-directed, regulated and controlled. This process requires so much preparation of the individual by society, so much individual learning that we, as a society, are likely to continue to use Skinner's methods as a necessary shortcut since we are unwilling or unable to devote the required attention to the individual. We will be forced to use Skinner's methods because we still treat the birth of other humans beings as events that have no impact on our individual lives.

Leisure remains an elite idea because the world's population continues to increase at an exponential rate and the pathological streak which runs
through us makes it impossible for us to collectively meet the lower order
needs of all humans, such as food and shelter the starvation in Africa which
could be stopped by the very military juntas which willingly accept it for
political gain; the homeless in America who could be given shelter with the
money being used to plan wars among the stars; the Russian peasant whose
life expectancy actually declined due to a political system which denied
economic and spiritual reality.

Leisure is an elite idea and we can expect to see more of Skinner's
ideas take root in the world because we will not or cannot take the leap of
faith needed to ensure our continuation as a species. The continued existence
of humans is not assured; the greatest threat to our continued existence is our
own behavior, so we must respond and we must respond quickly. As
Buckminster Fuller (1979: 156) argued:

> Humans will live aboard our Planet Earth in the 21st century
> only if the struggle for existence has been completely
> disposed of by providing abundant life support and accom-
> modation for all humans. Only under these conditions can
> all humans function as competent local universe problem
> solvers. That is what humans were invented for. Only if
> Abraham Lincoln's 'right' has come into complete ascen-
> dancy over 'might' will humanity remain alive on board our
> planet in the 21st century.

Our Near Term Prospects

Human beings, it seems, are dangerous to themselves and the rest of
the world. The ability to use leisure may be the final test of a civilization but
the first test is ability to survive ourselves. Freedom is not the answer to all
our problems but may necessarily be a commodity which is best increased in
accordance with the ability to satisfy lower-level needs, such as food and
shelter, at some minimal level. We cannot trust the world with leisure if
leisure is presented as empty time to be filled, as the privilege of an elite few,
or as something granted by government in place of resources to meet basic
needs.

The problem here is not that individuals who use free time in unsatisfying ways will destroy the world. While the world suffers much from those

who misuse their freedom, the problem is a different one. Leisure involves the development and exercise of the individual human will and those who find little worthwhile leisure, who are bored by it, may fall prey to the phenomenon of group psychology, the surrender of self to the cult; the greater organism in which the exercise of the individual human will becomes subservient to the collective belief, which will supposedly bring meaning and identity. In such a situation, the individual no longer desires freedom and is willing to have the meaning of situations defined by some greater authority. Such people have, historically, blindly attempted to destroy much of the world when it did not conform to group beliefs and, given advancing technology, have the potential to do increasing harm.

Josef Pieper rightly pointed out that we must not confuse this problem with the problem of physical poverty. It is, rather, a problem of spiritual poverty. The individual may slowly become willing to suffer, as Pieper stated, in a vacuum. In an extreme state, such individuals, whom Pieper called the proletariat, no longer want to be freed from their world of subservience or work, and cannot understand why others may be unwilling to suffer with them.

Such people do not want leisure because they do not, at an individual level, want to confront who they are. Each of them suffers, as Pieper said, from a "despairing refusal to be oneself." Part of our definition of leisure implies the ability to act from internally compelling love and the proletariat, in Pieper's sense of the term, is not capable of doing that.

Leisure is the gradual process of gaining freedom and finding meaning through self-understanding and improvement. It is the process of moving from being, essentially, directed by others, to becoming self-directed. The proletariat becomes less dangerous when this process begins.

Can the proletariat be freed from the limited and limiting world of work? Pieper did not assume they could, since leisure involved the ability to experience spiritual celebration. He argued that ". . . the ultimate root of leisure is not susceptible to the human will. Absolute affirmation of the universe cannot, strictly speaking, be based upon a voluntary resolve" (Pieper 1952: 25). Freedom, even from work, is not enough.

Leisure cannot be achieved at all when it is sought as a means to an end, even if that end is "the salvation of Western civilization." Said another way, people cannot attain leisure just because they want to. It is a gift that resides in the realm of the spirit. Some people receive it; some don't. If Pieper is right, perhaps we must change our original claim in this chapter to say that the world might be trusted with leisure but that we cannot trust those who are not capable of leisure.

BARRIERS TO LEISURE

What are the barriers which prevent people from experiencing leisure or, more precisely, from participating in specific leisure activities? Through out this book there have been indirect discussions of barriers to leisure but, as of yet, we have not considered what barriers to leisure are and how they can be conceptualized. In a highly specific sense, there is a tendency for us to think of barriers to participation as occurring after a person desires to partici- pate in some activity. Then a barrier intervenes and the person is unable to do what he or she wants. For example, a person desired to play tennis, it rained (there were no indoor courts around) and the person was unable to play. Another example would be that a person wished to go for a walk, was afraid that they would be the victim of a crime if they went outside, and so stayed home. These examples illustrate one type of barrier and one way in which barriers intervene between what one wishes to do and what one actually does. But there are other barriers and they affect participation in other ways (Crawford & Godbey, 1987).

The first type of barrier, which may be called intrapersonal, includes psychological and spiritual attributes which influence activity preferences rather than intervening between preferences and participation. Examples of intrapersonal barriers may include stress, anxiety, depression, religious beliefs, an individual's perception of his or her skill in a specific leisure activity, and the individual's evaluations of the appropriateness of a particular activity. If you are depressed, you may not want to go to a dance; if you are anxious, you may not be interested in watching a drama. Barriers of this type are relatively unstable and are, by nature, changeable over time. If one's depression lifts, he or she may be interested in going to the dance. While some of these barriers are socially influenced, they are experienced at an individual psychological level. Thus, the despairing refusal to accept one's place in the world which Pieper alluded to may change (or it may not). Our ideas about what is appropriate for us to do during leisure may change so that we will willingly read poetry or tend the garden, or may no longer be willing to play the tuba. Look at how radically the intrapersonal barriers which impact upon the leisure of women are changing. Many women who would not, a decade ago, have thought it appropriate to participate in karate, run in a marathon, go into a cocktail lounge unescorted, drive a racing car, climb rocks, or participate in other activities traditionally restricted to men, are now convinced that such activities are appropriate for them and for other women. Look, also, at the changes in perception among the elderly as to what leisure experiences are worthwhile.

The second kind of barrier to participation, interpersonal, is the result of relationships with other people. These barriers may interact with both preferences for, and subsequent participation in, leisure activities done with other people. One may, for example, stop racing cars, even though wishing to continue doing so, because one's family dreads the danger involved. If you like to play chess but all your friends play poker, you may slowly come to prefer poker over chess. If your reference group believes work is all important, you too may find yourself with little free time. Interpersonal barriers may stem from family, friends, or other reference groups.

The last category of barriers, structural barriers, represent blocks or obstacles to participation as barriers are commonly conceptualized. These are barriers which intervene between personal preference and participation. Climate, work schedule, or availability of opportunity are examples. You may wish to relax and watch the sky but find it necessary to work all your waking hours to keep from starving. You may want to learn to sail but have no boat or suitable body of water nearby.

While appropriateness and availability may be involved in all three types of barriers, the individual's experience with an activity is the distinguishing feature in the operation of these potential barriers. At the intrapersonal level, the individual's preference for the activity has not been established; at the structural level, preference has already been established, perhaps through prior participation in the activity which was satisfying; at the interpersonal level, one's preferences may change according to the interests and attitudes of others.

It is important to remember that barriers are influences upon, not determinants of, what one does or foregoes, and it is the relative strength of barriers in relation to preferences which most likely predicts leisure behavior. At the structural level, if preference is significantly greater than perceived constraints, the leisure activity in question may be undertaken despite the presence of such barriers. For example, if you wish to play golf but there are no golf courses nearby, you may, if your desire is strong enough, travel some distance in order to play.

Responding to Barriers

How do we respond to these barriers? How can progress be made toward breaking them down? Perhaps we should first point out that our definition of leisure does not assume anything about the perfectibility of human beings. We accept that we are imperfect, perhaps even tragically flawed as Koestler believed.

Leisure, as we defined it at the outset, "is living in relative freedom from the external compulsive forces of one's culture and physical environmental so as to be able to act from internally compelling love in ways which are personally pleasing, intuitively worthwhile and provide a basis for faith."

The first part of this definition deals with living in relative freedom from "barriers" which might be thought of as interpersonal and structural. Note, however, it is "relative" freedom. As we have said elsewhere, absolute freedom is a concept which does not have much application to humans. We are constrained by time, gravity, the limits of our imagination, the needs and limits of our body, the welfare of others, and in many other ways. Such constraints are part of the human condition and we do not wish to see them removed. What we would argue for is, in effect, getting the upper hand in dealing with them; finding ways to overcome the obvious structural constraint, e.g., the child with no place to play, and the obvious interpersonal constraint, e.g., the housewife who wants to write a play but is discouraged by family and friends who think it inappropriate.

We dare to hope that a society could exist in which there were some kinds of minimum provisions made for all people which could overcome, at least, the structural barriers. To do this, of course, requires not only the provision of areas and facilities used for leisure but also a distribution of work and income such that everyone has a number of alternatives and options from which to choose. Too, interpersonal relations which encourage rather than discourage individuals' attempts to realize their potential and aspirations help overcome obstacles which are largely social in nature but also structural in the sense of social structure.

Getting the upper hand over intrapersonal barriers requires other efforts. Important among those efforts is education for leisure. As Charles K. Brightbill (1960) noted:

> When we say education for leisure, we have in mind persons developing appreciations, interests, skills, and opportunities that will enable them to use their leisure (time) in personally rewarding ways, plus understanding why this way of life is essential to their well-being and to the survival of society. It does not mean that leisure (time) needs to be regimented. (p. 93)

Developing appreciations, interests, skills, and opportunities implies a progression of socialization, learning, and provision of opportunity—a tall order for any society.

Brightbill said education for leisure:

> . . . assumes that people must be exposed early and long—in the home, in the school, and in the community—to experiences that will help them develop appreciations and skills that will help the flowering of their personalities as leisure becomes increasingly available to them. (p. 94)

There is an almost naively optimistic tone to such statements in a society in which drug use is endemic, millions of children are raising themselves, schools are a low priority, and our sense of community is fragile or nonexistent. Nonetheless, these words still ring true. There must be a progression of appreciations, then interests, then the development of skills, and then opportunities if the individual is ever to ". . . be able to act from internally compelling love in ways which are personally pleasing, intuitively worthwhile, and provide a basis for faith."

This process is a long one, and one which is often cut short when there is no development of appreciations and interests; when society, through either primary or secondary social institutions, cannot or, more likely, will not convey the magic of the world to the individual. Family, school, teachers, or friends often do not show the individual that they have come to love some activity for its own sake or let the individual know that he or she might also be capable of developing a love for the activity. In the absence of compelling examples of people enamored of life, individuals are more likely to fall into that despairing refusal to accept their place in the world. They may surrender their will to the cult; their "selves" to the group, their aspirations to the lottery corporation. Such individuals become dangerous to themselves and others. Leisure, it seems, not only presupposes some degree of freedom but, more fundamentally, that there is something worth doing if and when such freedom is realized. If there is not the development of appreciations for specific forms of activity, as well as for the world and one's life in it, freedom is hollow. If there are no interests, then there is no meaning and the loss of meaning is today the biggest barrier to leisure.

While those who have not developed appreciations and interests may be dangerous to the survival of the world, it is perhaps a greater tragedy when one has developed some leisure appreciation and interests but does not possess the resources or skills to further them. Almost all leisure activities or uses of free time require learning to be carried out in a satisfactory manner. Most also involve some minimum level of skill which must be acquired through a gradual process of learning from others, experimentation, and practice. Part of this skill may be mastering technique, such as in learning to draw, but part is also socialization. One must often learn how to behave, understand the history of the activity, and learn the folkways or customs involved before it is possible to participate in an appropriate manner.

Learning leisure skills probably takes place more frequently in the context of family or among friends than in school, church, or other secondary institutions; but schools are still critical in teaching leisure skills, as is the huge commercial sector.

BECOMING ALL WE CAN

Minimizing barriers to leisure might well make human beings less dangerous to themselves, to each other and to the rest of the world. If one can be helped to ". . . act from internally compelling love in ways which are personally pleasing, intuitively worthwhile, and provide a basis for faith," that person is more likely to feel a personal responsibility for life in the world, not because they love to suffer, but because they, through leisure, have come to think that life, and hence the world, is worthwhile. If barriers to one's leisure can somehow be minimized, people can "become all they are capable of being." The motto: "Let each become all he or she is capable of being" is the end product of leisure in the Athenian tradition—self-discovery, a striving toward self-perfection for oneself but also for the betterment and well-being of all.

What does it mean to become all you are capable of? Does it mean to experience all you can experience? Does it mean to become highly skilled and learned in a variety of free-time activities? Perhaps it means to achieve the highest possible set of ethical or moral standards in your life. All of these very different conceptualizations deal with supposedly ultimate conditions. Freedom may be thought of as the arena in which they can be achieved; freedom from unnecessary barriers, freedom to celebrate the festival.

Must leisure bring about such miraculous transformations to be worthwhile? If Koestler is right, we are probably not perfectible. If Skinner is right, the methods which lead to our perfection will be outside the realm of leisure. What, then, is the ultimate good, if any, toward which leisure can lead?

Leisure is an abstract term but, in experiencing it, one is always involved in some specific behavior which is, at least as experienced by the participant, unique. This unique experience, as it comes more and more to possess the quality of leisure, is no longer done because of some rational calculation of the costs and benefits but intuitively because the individual has grown to love the activity in question. While done for its own sake, the leisure experience comes to serve as a symbol, a sign, a clue, that the world is worthwhile and that one's life is meaningful. It is a sample of the joy that life can bring. As a consequence, the leisure experience provides a basis for faith.

Perhaps, however, if one develops some faith in the world through leisure experience, the importance of becoming all one can be is minimized. That is, if one lives in relative freedom from constraints and can act from internally compelling love, perhaps the need to act is limited. Finding a few things one loves to do for their own sake is an extraordinary accomplishment. If doing such activities produces faith, that faith may lessen the need for self-perfection.

Can the world be trusted with leisure? As we have defined leisure, the answer is yes, of course. But leisure is too often defined in other ways, most do not know what it is and, therefore, cannot be trusted with it. Leisure is not just free time, though that is a useful resource. What we choose is important. And it is not just freedom from. Aimless freedom can destroy; if it builds, it builds by chance, as if there were no human purpose. Leisure, if it be leisure, denies the absence of human purpose. So we must be trusted with leisure, for it is in leisure that human purpose is revealed.

> A man sees, as he dies,
> Death's possibilities;
> My heart sways with the world.
> I am that final thing.
> A man learning to sing.

(Theodore Roethke, 1965: 187)

REFERENCES

Brightbill, Charles K. 1960. *The Challenge of Leisure.* Englewood Cliffs, New Jersey: Prentice-Hall.

Crawford, Duane and Godbey, Geoffrey. 1987. "Reconceptualizing Barriers to Family Leisure." *Leisure Sciences* (9: 2).

de Grazia, Sebastian. 1962. *Of Time Work and Leisure.* New York: The Twentieth Century Fund.

Fuller, Buckminster. 1979. *On Education.* Amherst: University of Massachusetts Press.

Koestler, Arthur. 1967. *The Ghost in the Machine.* New York: Macmillan.

Pieper, Josef. 1952. *Leisure: The Basis of Culture.* New York: Mentor-Omega.

Roethke, Theodore. 1965. *Words for the Wind.* "The Dying Man." Bloomington, Indiana: Indiana University Press.

Skinner, B. F. 1971. *Beyond Freedom and Dignity.* New York: Bantam Books.

Socrates. 1961. *Plato's Apology. Dialogues of Plato* (399 B.C.) (Ed. J. D. Kaplan: Tr. Benjamin Jowett). New York: Washington Square Press.

Tiger, Lionel. 1979. *Optimism: The Biology of Hope.* New York: Simon and Schuster.

Trafton, Dain A. 1985. "In Praise of Three Traditional Ideas of Leisure." In B. G. Gunter, Jay Stanley, and Robert St. Clair, (Eds.). *Transitions to Leisure—Conceptual and Human Issues.* Lanham, Maryland: University Press of America.

Yankelovich, Skelly and White, Inc. 1982. "The Impact of Changing Values on Leisure." Unpublished (November).

BIBLIOGRAPHY—SELECTED AND ANNOTATED

Aristotle. *Nichomachean Ethics*, and *Politics*. (Several translations and scores of editions). *Ethics* deals with leisure in individual life and particularly with happiness as the final, desirable objective. Especially pertinent are Books I and X and chapters 11-14 in Book VII. *Politics* deals with leisure in collective, community life and discusses education of competent citizens and rationalizes the class structure of the Athenians. Especially pertinent are chapters 4-6 of Book III and chapters 1-3 and 13-17 of Book VII.

Brightbill, Charles K. 1961. *Man and Leisure*. Englewood Cliffs, New Jersey: Prentice-Hall. While the author equates leisure with time, his concern is with the quality of experience and thus life. He views recreative living as the source of happiness, including finding one's place in the universe. Warm, humanistic philosophy of leisure and re-creation for the general reader.

Cranz, Galen. 1987. *The Politics of Park Design—A History of Urban Parks in America*. Cambridge, Massachusetts: MIT Press. An historical examination of the evolution of urban parks by an architectural sociologist. Four typologies of urban parks, each representing the ideals of a distinct historic era, are defined and explained. A chronology of events is used to trace the ideology and political support that created and sustained urban parks. Cranz developed the hypothesis that urban parks sprang from ideals which changed several times but were eventually lost when the gradual bureaucratization of urban park systems led to the desire to merely maintain the existing system.

de Grazia, Sebastian. 1962. *Of Time, Work and Leisure*. New York: Twentieth Century Fund. Something of a modern classic, this book addresses leisure from the standpoint of political philosophy. The author begins with the Athenian ideal of leisure, traces the demise of the ideal and discusses the social, economic and political obstacles to leisure in contemporary western society.

de Tocqueville, Alexis. *Democracy in America* (Several translations and scores of editions). Written in the 1830s by a French observer of the American scene of that period, this is an insightful and sometimes witty character portrait of Americans and their institutions. Discusses culture, politics, materialism, restlessness and much else. Volume II is of particular interest. Very descriptive headings guide the reader to topics of interest.

Dulles, Foster R. 1965. *A History of Recreation: American Learns to Play* (2nd ed.). New York: Appleton-Century-Crofts. The author's focus is upon organized, public (but not necessarily government sponsored) free-time activity in the United States from the early 1600s to the early 1960s. From the husking bee to the Houston Astrodome, this is a delightfully illustrated anecdotal and impressionistic record of popular pastimes and amusements.

Fromm, Eric. 1941. *Escape From Freedom*. New York: Holt, Rinehart and Winston. Fromm discusses the problems people encounter when faced with individual freedom. Anxiety, insecurity and a feeling of being alone may lead to different forms of escape, including submission to authority, destructiveness and conformity. Man has found freedom from most historic forms of restraint but has not found what that freedom is for.

Godbey, Geoffrey. 1985. *Leisure in Your Life* (2nd ed.). State College, PA: Venture Publishing. Designed as an introductory text for first year students, the opening and the last two chapters are primarily philosophical. The book challenges individual readers to examine their values and the role of leisure in their own lives. Conversation and discussion between author and reader.

Goodale, Thomas and Witt, Peter (Eds.). 1985. *Recreation and Leisure: Issues in an Era of Change* (rev. ed.). State College, PA: Venture Publishing. Twenty-nine essays explore issues facing leisure service educators and providers. Essays in the first section deal with conceptual difficulties; in the second section with changing resources and services; in section three with organization and professionalization of services. Philosophical stances on central issues for the field.

Huizinga, Johan. 1955. *Homo Ludens: A Study of the Play Element in Culture.* Boston: Beacon Press. The classic study of the topic identified in the subtitle, *Homo ludens* is cultural anthropology at its best. The author cogently argued that human culture arose in the form of play but notes that the play element has virtually and perhaps inevitably disappeared from contemporary culture and society.

Kaplan, Max. 1960. *Leisure in America: A Social Inquiry.* New York: John Wiley and Sons, Inc. This is the earliest and best known of the author's writings on leisure. Here, Kaplan treated leisure as a multi-dimensional concept and related those dimensions to the major elements of the American social system, including work, family, social class, religion, secular values and more. A good reflection of the sociology of leisure circa 1960.

Kelly, John R. 1987. *Freedom To Be—A New Sociology of Leisure.* New York: Macmillan Publishing. An attempt to broaden the theoretical understanding of leisure which cuts across several theoretical models utilized in sociology. These models, which include leisure as immediate experience, existential theory, developmental theory, social identity theory, interaction theory, institutional theory, political theory, humanist theory and Kelly's synthesizing "Dialectical Theory," are presented as a spiral in which each theoretical approach leads to further metaphors where the explanation process is continually furthered but not completed. The dialectic nature of leisure, Kelly concluded, makes the propositions of logical positivism, which occur in sequence, impossible.

Kerr, Walter. 1962. *The Decline of Pleasure.* New York: Simon and Schuster. A literate, witty but nonetheless serious examination of why we find happiness so elusive. Kerr noted the importance of the appreciation of simple pleasures, the cultivation of taste, and the importance of life focused on something other than the useful, the material, and the self.

Koestler, Arthur. 1967. *The Ghost in the Machine.* London: Hutchinson Publishing Group. This sometimes unsettling book questions the name and shakes the complacency of Homo sapiens. The author argued that evolution, particularly the growth of the brain, has revealed a flaw in man which may lead to self-destruction. Apparently incapable of leisure or freedom, man may be incapable even of survival.

Larrabee, Eric and Meyersohn, Rolf (Eds). 1958. *Mass Leisure*. Glencoe, IL: The Free Press. The first anthology focused upon leisure followed on the heels of Rosenberg and White's *Mass Culture* (1957, New York: The Free Press), an interesting companion anthology. Some of the material is now of mainly historical interest but a number of essays and excerpts in *Mass Leisure* are timeless, including those of Piaget, Huizinga, Mead, Russell, and Huxley, among others.

Lewis, Oscar (Ed.). 1963. *Of Men and Machines*. New York: E.P. Dutton. An interesting collection of poems, essays, science fiction and even a melo-drama examining man's sometimes sympathetic, sometimes antagonistic relationship with machinery and technology. From Francis Bacon and Adam Smith to W. H. Auden and e e cummings, two cheers for mechanized progress but assuredly not three.

Linder, Staffan. 1970. *The Harried Leisure Class*. New York: Columbia University Press. This incisive, sometimes satirical analysis posits that time is our most precious and scarce resource. Since we take time to be a commod-ity, utility, exchange and other economic and technologic values conspire to deprive us of leisure and challenge us to rethink the purpose of progress.

Lundberg, George A., Komarovsky, Mirra and McInerny, Mary Alice. 1934. *Leisure: A Suburban Study*. New York: Columbia University Press. This study, in the classical tradition of comprehensive community studies, was conducted in Westchester County, New York during the early years of the Depression. In addition to the extensive collection of data, the authors recognized that leisure was not only of scientific interest but also of practical social concern. This is, then, as much a qualitative study as a quantitative one.

Mill, John Stuart. 1985. *On Liberty*. Harmondsworth, Middlesex, England: Penguin Books. This classic argument for individual liberty was first pub-lished in 1859. Mill believed the individual "sovereign" over his own body and mind, his or her liberty limited only to prevent harm to others. Often taken as a defence of laissez-faire government, Mill championed individual liberty so that people could rise above mediocrity, and suggested that both society and individuals would be the beneficiaries.

Nash, Jay B. 1973. *Philosophy of Recreation and Leisure*. Dubuque, Iowa: William Brown Company. This is a homespun, down-to-earth philosophy about the importance of involvement in recreative activity during one's free time. The apparent simplicity of expression belies a profound concern for leisure and statement of values about its use.

Pieper, Josef. 1963. *Leisure: The Basis of Culture.* New York: Random House. The author, a Catholic theologian and philosopher, reminds us of the link between religion and culture and the concept of leisure as celebration of the divine. In particular he rejects the scientist's notion that all knowledge stems from discursive thought and intellectual effort. Leisure, he argued, is a gift received by those open and receptive to its essentially spiritual and transcendent nature.

Plato. *The Republic.* (Several translations and scores of editions). This earliest utopia, in which few would care to live, is concerned principally with justice, which is found in harmony or balance. The most important of the dialogues, it raises such timeless questions as the role of education in citizenship and government and the relation between the individual and the collective (state). Book II includes his famous call for music and gymnastics as the core of education.

Rifkin, Jeremy. 1987. *Time Wars: The Primary Conflict in Human History.* New York: Henry Holt and Company. An interesting thesis and an interesting argument. Rifkin argues that time reckoning has evolved through four stages: biophysical (natural); calendar; clock; computer. Each step following natural time has produced great conflict and has also further alienated us from our own biophysical nature. Computer nanoseconds reckon time in ways beyond human perception and which change both social and psychological processes detrimentally. Sides are already being chosen over the new time war, and much is at stake.

Tilgher, Adriano. 1930. *Homo Faber.* New York: Harcourt, Brace and World. This brief but comprehensive book deals not with man the thinker (sapiens) or player (ludens) but man the fabricator, manufacturer or, particularly, worker. The author traces religious and sociocultural attitudes toward work, and to some extent also wealth and material accumulation, starting with the Greek and Roman civilizations before Christ and ending with the twentieth century.

Veblen, Thorstein. 1899. *The Theory of the Leisure Class.* New York: Macmillan. This classic treatise is sub-titled, "An Economic Study of Institutions." Its subject, then, is the leisure class as an economic force or phenomenon. Veblen set out to ridicule the habits of the wealthy; their "conspicuous consumption," ostentatious display, and invidious (envy and discontent) comparisons. He argued (sharp tongue-in-cheek) that pecuniary emulation of the "leisure class" (i.e., keeping up with higher classes) helped drive the economy. A delightful put-down of the rich "leisure class" of the late 1800s.

NAME, AUTHOR AND TITLE* INDEX

---

* Titles which appear in the text. For references, see reference lists at the end of each chapter and the selected, annotated Bibliography.

SUBJECT INDEX

OTHER BOOKS FROM VENTURE PUBLISHING

The A•B•Cs of Behavior Change: Skills for Working with Behavior Problems in Nursing Homes
     by Margaret D. Cohn, Michael A. Smyer and Ann L. Horgas
Activity Experiences and Programming Within Long-Term Care
     by Ted Tedrick and Elaine R. Green
The Activity Gourmet
     by Peggy Powers
Advanced Concepts for Geriatric Nursing Assistants
     by Carolyn A. McDonald
Adventure Education
     edited by John C. Miles and Simon Priest
Assessment: The Cornerstone of Activity Programs
     by Ruth Perschbacher
At-Risk Youth and Gangs—A Resource Manual for the Parks and Recreation Professional—Expanded and Updated
     by The California Park and Recreation Society
Benefits of Leisure
     edited by B. L. Driver, Perry J. Brown and George L. Peterson
Benefits of Recreation Research Update
     by Judy M. Sefton and W. Kerry Mummery
Beyond Bingo: Innovative Programs for the New Senior
     by Sal Arrigo, Jr., Ann Lewis and Hank Mattimore
The Community Tourism Industry Imperative—The Necessity, The Opportunities, Its Potential
     by Uel Blank
Dimensions of Choice: A Qualitative Approach to Recreation, Parks, and Leisure Research
     by Karla A. Henderson
Evaluating Leisure Services: Making Enlightened Decisions
     by Karla A. Henderson with M. Deborah Bialeschki
Evaluation of Therapeutic Recreation Through Quality Assurance
     edited by Bob Riley
The Evolution of Leisure: Historical and Philosophical Perspectives
     by Thomas Goodale and Geoffrey Godbey
The Game Finder—A Leader's Guide to Great Activities
     by Annette C. Moore

Great Special Events and Activities
> by Annie Morton, Angie Prosser and Sue Spangler

Inclusive Leisure Services: Responding to the Rights of People with Disabilities
> by John Dattilo

Internships in Recreation and Leisure Services: A Practical Guide for Students
> by Edward E. Seagle, Jr., Ralph W. Smith and Lola M. Dalton

Interpretation of Cultural and Natural Resources
> by Douglas M. Knudson, Ted T. Cable and Larry Beck

Introduction to Leisure Services—7th Edition
> by H. Douglas Sessoms and Karla A. Henderson

Leadership and Administration of Outdoor Pursuits, Second Edition
> by Phyllis Ford and James Blanchard

Leisure And Family Fun (LAFF)
> by Mary Atteberry-Rogers

The Leisure Diagnostic Battery: Users Manual and Sample Forms
> by Peter A. Witt and Gary Ellis

Leisure Diagnostic Battery Computer Software
> by Gary Ellis and Peter A. Witt

Leisure Education: A Manual of Activities and Resources
> by Norma J. Stumbo and Steven R. Thompson

Leisure Education II: More Activities and Resources
> by Norma J. Stumbo

Leisure Education: Program Materials for Persons with Developmental Disabilities
> by Kenneth F. Joswiak

Leisure Education Program Planning: A Systematic Approach
> by John Dattilo and William D. Murphy

Leisure in Your Life: An Exploration, Fourth Edition
> by Geoffrey Godbey

A Leisure of One's Own: A Feminist Perspective on Women's Leisure
> by Karla Henderson, M. Deborah Bialeschki, Susan M. Shaw and Valeria J. Freysinger

Leisure Services in Canada: An Introduction
> by Mark S. Searle and Russell E. Brayley

Leveraging the Benefits of Parks and Recreation: The Phoenix Project
> by The California Park and Recreation Society

Marketing for Parks, Recreation, and Leisure
> by Ellen L. O'Sullivan

Models of Change in Municipal Parks and Recreation: A Book of Innovative Case Studies
    edited by Mark E. Havitz
Outdoor Recreation Management: Theory and Application, Third Edition
    by Alan Jubenville and Ben Twight
Planning Parks for People
    by John Hultsman, Richard L. Cottrell and Wendy Zales Hultsman
Private and Commercial Recreation
    edited by Arlin Epperson
The Process of Recreation Programming Theory and Technique, Third Edition
    by Patricia Farrell and Herberta M. Lundegren
Protocols for Recreation Therapy Programs
    edited by Jill Kelland, along with the Recreation Therapy Staff at Alberta Hospital—Edmonton
Quality Management: Applications for Therapeutic Recreation
    edited by Bob Riley
Recreation and Leisure: Issues in an Era of Change, Third Edition
    edited by Thomas Goodale and Peter A. Witt
The Recreation Connection to Self-Esteem—A Resource Manual for the Park, Recreation and Community Services Professional
    by The California Park and Recreation Society
Recreation Economic Decisions: Comparing Benefits and Costs
    by Richard G. Walsh
Recreation Programming and Activities for Older Adults
    by Jerold E. Elliott and Judith A. Sorg-Elliott
Reference Manual for Writing Rehabilitation Therapy Treatment Plans
    by Penny Hogberg and Mary Johnson
Research in Therapeutic Recreation: Concepts and Methods
    edited by Marjorie J. Malkin and Christine Z. Howe
Risk Management in Therapeutic Recreation: A Component of Quality Assurance
    by Judith Voelkl
A Social History of Leisure Since 1600
    by Gary Cross
The Sociology of Leisure
    by John R. Kelly and Geoffrey Godbey
A Study Guide for National Certification in Therapeutic Recreation
    by Gerald O'Morrow and Ron Reynolds
Therapeutic Recreation: Cases and Exercises
    by Barbara C. Wilhite and M. Jean Keller

Therapeutic Recreation in the Nursing Home
    by Linda Buettner and Shelley L. Martin
Therapeutic Recreation Protocol for Treatment of Substance Addictions
    by Rozanne W. Faulkner
A Training Manual for Americans With Disabilities Act Compliance in Parks and Recreation Settings
    by Carol Stensrud
Understanding Leisure and Recreation: Mapping the Past, Charting the Future
    edited by Edgar L. Jackson and Thomas L. Burton

Venture Publishing, Inc.
1999 Cato Avenue
State College, PA 16801
Phone: (814) 234-4561
FAX: (814) 234-1651